JAZZ ME BLUES

Popular Music History
Series Editor: Alyn Shipton, journalist, broadcaster and lecturer in jazz history at the Royal Academy of Music.

This series publishes books that challenge established orthodoxies in popular music studies, examine the formation and dissolution of canons, interrogate histories of genres, focus on previously neglected forms, or engage in archaeologies of popular music.

Published

Handful of Keys: Conversations with Thirty Jazz Pianists
Alyn Shipton

The Last Miles: The Music of Miles Davis, 1980–1991
George Cole

Jazz Visions: Lennie Tristano and His Legacy
Peter Ind

Chasin' the Bird: The Life and Legacy of Charlie Parker
Brian Priestley

Out of the Long Dark: The Life of Ian Carr
Alyn Shipton

Lee Morgan: His Life, Music and Culture
Tom Perchard

Being Prez: The Life and Music of Lester Young
Dave Gelly

Lionel Richie: Hello
Sharon Davis

Mr P.C.: The Life and Music of Paul Chambers
Rob Palmer

Trad Dads, Dirty Boppers and Free Fusioneers: A History of British Jazz, 1960–1975
Duncan Heining

An Unholy Row: Jazz in Britain and its Audience, 1945–1960
Dave Gelly

Soul Unsung: Reflections on the Band in Black Popular Music
Kevin Le Gendre

Jazz Me Blues

The Autobiography of Chris Barber

Chris Barber with Alyn Shipton

SHEFFIELD UK   BRISTOL CT

Published by Equinox Publishing Ltd.

UK: Office 415, The Workstation, 15 Paternoster Row, Sheffield, S1 2BX
USA: ISD, 70 Enterprise Drive, Bristol, CT 06010

www.equinoxpub.com

First published 2014

British Library Cataloguing-in-Publication Data

A catalogue record for this book is available from the British Library.

ISBN: 978 1 84553 088 4 (hardback)

Library of Congress Cataloging-in-Publication Data

Barber, Chris, 1930-
    Jazz me blues : the autobiography of Chris Barber / Chris Barber with Alyn
Shipton.
        pages ; cm. -- (Popular music history)
    Includes bibliographical references and index.
    ISBN 978-1-84553-088-4 (hb)
    1. Barber, Chris, 1930- 2. Jazz musicians--United States--Biography. I.
Shipton, Alyn. II. Title.
    ML419.B163A3 2014
    788.9'3165092--dc23
    [B]

                                                              2013037155

Typeset by Atheus
Printed and bound by Charlesworth Press, Wakefield, West Yorkshire, UK

Contents

Acknowledgements

The authors would like to thank all the many people who have helped to get this book into print. First and foremost we are grateful to the members of Chris's family, past and present, particularly Kate Barber, Caroline Barber and Renate Elias, for their many and varied contributions to the book. We would also like to acknowledge the help and support from the team at www.chrisbarber.net, in particular Andreas Wandfluh, and (although not in the best of health) Ed Jackson. The contribution of the late Julian Purser was also important.

Wim Wigt and the office that looks after the Big Chris Barber Band provided information, photographs and support, with special thanks to Herma Lueks.

Members of the band past and present have also assisted in many ways, notably Mike Henry, Alex Revell and Dick Smith. Some of the photographs are from the collection of the late Pat Halcox, and we have also drawn on Pat's memories of the band's early American tours. We are grateful to all those who have supplied photographs and given us permission to use them, especially Terry Cryer, David Redfern and Viktor Schell. If we have inadvertently overlooked any other copyright holder, we will be happy to acknowledge this at the earliest opportunity.

For help with the recordings list we are indebted to Paul Adams at Lake Records; to the Upbeat, Timeless and Bell labels; to the late Andrew Sheehan and the Blues Legacy project; to Dave Bennett for practical help; and to Gerard Bielderman and Erik Raben for their discographical work.

Janet Joyce and Valerie Hall at Equinox have had faith in the project from the outset, and we are also grateful to Sarah Norman for her keen editorial eye.

We first met to discuss this book over lunch on July 6, 1982. It has taken us a while, but we hope the wait has been worth it!

Chris Barber
Alyn Shipton
January 2014

1 Down Home Rag

I was born on 17 April 1930 in Welwyn, a small town thirty miles north of London. My mother, Hettie, was a teacher, who later became the first and only socialist Mayor of Canterbury. My father, Donald, was a statistician and economist, and I suspect that my musical interests came from him. He had been a pupil at Christ's Hospital School, near Horsham, which was unusual in that it offered a public school education to students whose parents would not have been able to afford to send their children to a fee-paying school. Most pupils there were educated free or on very low fees, decided by a means test. In fact my father's parents earned slightly over the limit, but as they were both teachers, my father was allowed in.

There, as well as studying mathematics to a high level, which eventually got him into Trinity College, Cambridge, my father learned the violin. In due course he became leader of the school orchestra, which was conducted at the time by the future composer Constant Lambert, who was another pupil at Christ's Hospital. As a result, my father loved violin music, and so one of the sounds I most remember from my own childhood was that of his records, including the Beethoven violin concerto played by Fritz Kreisler. That recording, with Sir John Barbirolli and the London Philharmonic, was made in 1936, and I still think of it as being how the concerto should be played.

In those days, a lengthy concerto such as that was issued on a whole set of 78 rpm discs, but the Beethoven actually only occupied nine sides. So the tenth and final side was a Partita in G Minor, the Adagio movement from Bach's solo Violin Sonata no. 1. It was an earlier recording, but I loved it even more than the Beethoven, especially because of Kreisler's wonderful double stopping.

When my father went to Cambridge, he read economics and maths. His economics tutor was John Maynard Keynes, probably the world's most famous economist. My parents may well have been introduced to one another by Keynes, as they were both very involved in student politics and members of the Labour club. I know that he gave them an armchair as a wedding present, because I used to sit in it as a boy.

My mother's politics came at least in part from her father, the Rev. Dunne, who had been vicar of Laisterdyke in Bradford, and who was later Rural Dean of the Potteries, based in Newcastle-under-Lyme. His first parish in 1900 had been in Mile End. Ministering to this strongly working-class community gave him a strong sense of social justice, and he became a socialist.

My father shared this political standpoint. He won the Adam Smith Prize for Economics at Cambridge, which was given each year for the most outstanding performance in the examination or "Tripos", or – as in his case – for the best dissertation. So when he was barely out of his teens, he was already a very high level economist and he went on from Cambridge to become the secretary of Arcos, the "All-Russian Co-operative Society", a company that was set up for the Soviet Union to buy food, textiles and coal from the rest of the world, and to act as a conduit for sales of Soviet produce. In 1927, Arcos was raided by the police, on the suspicion that the company was being run as a cover for espionage. Many documents were confiscated, but as various historians have pointed out, although the police discovered that the building held the addresses of various communist organisations around the world, nothing was ever found of the UK War Office papers that were supposed to have been stolen and secreted there by Russian agents. To justify the raid, Stanley Baldwin, the Prime Minister, read telegrams to the House of Commons that had supposedly been deciphered from Russian and which appeared to endorse espionage. The end result was the collapse of Anglo-Russian relations, but up until the time of the raid, Arcos had been responsible for up to £20 million of trade a year between Britain and Soviet Russia.

As a talented economist, my father was able to find another job quite quickly. In due course, he became the secretary of the Socialist League, which was set up by Sir Stafford Cripps in the aftermath of the 1931 general election, to advocate democratic socialism. Michael Foot and Barbara Betts (later better known as the Labour cabinet minister Barbara Castle) were also leading members of that organisation and they both became friends of my father. A little later, my father moved on from the Socialist League to become the secretary of the Retail Distributors' Association (RDA), which remained his principal job thereafter.

Our family left Welwyn when I was three, to live in Primrose Hill, and then my parents built a house on a new estate in Stanmore in 1936, and we moved there, to 95 Weston Drive. After a couple of years at Burleigh Road School, I then started at King Alfred School in Golders Green, where my mother taught, and later became headmistress.

Because my parents were left wing, and particularly because my father was working with the Socialist League, they were among the few people in the country who consistently opposed the policy of appeasement towards Nazi

Germany. Stafford Cripps was advocating a united front against the forces of fascism. They could see what was coming, but they just didn't know how soon the government would wake up and do something to stop Hitler. When war eventually broke out, my mother took me, and my younger sister Audrey, to live in a cottage in the country, well away from where the bombs were expected to fall in London.

We settled in the village of Upper Welland, close to Malvern Wells in Worcestershire, near the border with Herefordshire. My father let out our house in Stanmore to a naval officer and he stayed in a flat in London, first sharing with Barbara Betts and another political colleague in Belsize Park and then moving to his own apartment in Balham. He worked extremely hard during the war, and basically wore himself out, because as well as working for the RDA, he was doing war work as a statistician for the Ministry of Supply. He devised the food rationing scheme, and immediately after the war he went on to plan the same for utility furniture. They made him a CBE for his unpaid work for the government during the war.

He was apparently offered a KBE but he turned it down because he did not believe that anybody should be called "Sir". Clement Attlee then offered him a safe seat in 1945 to be Chancellor of the Exchequer, but he also turned that down because he didn't wish to be involved in all the secrecy that went with the job. This turned out to be prescient, because the man whom Attlee appointed in his place, Hugh Dalton, had to be dismissed after not much more than a year for revealing budget secrets to the press. Yet, even without this particularly demanding job, my father nevertheless had high blood pressure, and he later suffered a stroke. At the end of the war my parents parted, and in due course my father remarried.

But in 1939, this was all in the future. When we left London, my mother taught me at home for a year, and then I went to Hanley Castle Grammar School, not far from Upton on Severn, in Worcestershire, and quite close to Upper Welland. This was because King Alfred School was still in the process of being evacuated. They were converting buildings on a farm in Hertfordshire, belonging to one of the teachers, to use as classrooms, which were not ready for us to move into. In 1941–42 my mother transferred me from Hanley Castle to Sibford School, run by Quakers in rural Oxfordshire, but I was expelled from there. It was a co-educational boarding school, which was somewhat in tune with my mother's left-wing ideas, but I was considered to be unruly. This was partly because of the Quaker ethos. On Sundays we had to walk two miles to the meeting house (a routine we called the "pig-drive"), and then sit quietly while the Elders made a lot of lengthy speeches. I found that quite hard to put up with, and I was marked down as "difficult to manage". So fortunately, when they kicked me out, I was able to go back to King Alfred School, which was finally established in its temporary home, known as Cowbridge School near Royston in Hertfordshire. There was a teacher there called Mr Morrish who let rooms in his house in the centre of Royston, so together with one or two other boys from the school I became his lodger, and lived there from 1942 until 1945. My sister Audrey was also at the school, but because she was four years younger than me, I saw very little of her during my time there.

Just three miles away to the north of Royston was the village of Bassingbourn, where what had started the war as an RAF station had been hugely extended to accommodate the B17 Flying Fortress bombers of the USAAF Eighth Air Force. The airfield had plenty of trees planted round it and the aircraft were stationed in partially wooded areas that must have been quite well camouflaged from above. One group of bombers had to be moved each day from Wimpole Park across the A14 main road to reach the runway, and then taxied back after raids to be hidden among the trees again. My friends and I used to get up before breakfast and cycle up to that point where the runway crossed the road. The rest of the perimeter was guarded by wire netting two metres high. We'd lie in the ditch on the far side of the road as the B17s came back from their night raids. Often as they came in you could see that some of them had dead front gunners. It must have been a very dangerous place to be in the nose of a B17, and as the months went by a large number of them seemed to get killed. Bassingbourn was also the airfield where Glenn Miller gave his last show and then set off the next day to fly to Paris, but he never made it.

The closest I ever came to action was one day when I was up on the hill near the school outside Royston, and below me, flying across the plain was a German V-1 bomber. This was a sort of rocket-powered drone, known as a doodlebug. It was basically a flying bomb that looked like a small aircraft with a pulse jet that went "boom, boom, boom, boom". They carried just enough fuel to get close to their targets and then they would crash and blow up. You would hear the engine stop, and we all knew that when the engine stopped you had to take cover immediately, because the V-1 would come straight down and explode. Fortunately, seeing that one fly past below me was the closest I ever came to such danger.

At the beginning of the war I had got hold of a radio. Most kids didn't have their own radios in 1939, because they were quite expensive, but I managed to find a little Bakelite set. We used to listen all the time to get news of our troops in France, and later – after Dunkirk – on the home front. I was particularly keen on the American Forces Network, the AFN, because you heard music on there that was jazz – or close to being jazz. By contrast, the BBC was a rather old-fashioned radio station. Apparently newsreaders had still been required to wear dinner jackets on the evening shift until the formation of the "Home Service" at the start of the war in 1939 and, although things were starting to relax, they still sounded very formal compared to the Americans.

On the other hand, the BBC broadcast quite a lot of music, and during the war they started *Music While You Work*, which went out in the mornings, and subsequently in the afternoons and evenings as well, to help the war work effort. This programme was designed to be relayed to the factories that were building aeroplanes and armaments, and to keep the workers cheerful, motivated and productive. But despite it being the popular music of the day in America, at the beginning of the war the BBC had no jazz programmes at all. They just did not play jazz records, although quite a few jazz records had been released in Britain before the war. However these were just not the sort of thing that the BBC would play. At least, not on purpose.

If you think about it, if they were broadcasting music, sometimes for up to sixteen hours a day, the chances were that at some point they would make a mistake and put on some music they did not intend to play. Very occasionally, the presenter might say at the end of a record, "That was so-and-so, and I think that was JAZZ!"

I remember thinking, "I like that!" Even though what I was hearing was probably something like the accordionist Eric Winstone and his little swing group playing 'Oasis', a pastiche of 'Caravan', which was the first record I ever bought. But the idea of the word "jazz" took hold. I began trying to find books where I could look up the names of musicians, and gradually I began to get the whole idea. The story of the music itself seemed interesting, and I started listening out for jazz on the AFN. In particular they had a fundraising programme called the *March of Dimes* which often featured jazz bands and singers. I occasionally sent in requests for music on V-Disc – the wartime records that were being made in the United States to bring music to the troops.

Looking back on it, before the war America had already acquired the kind of consumer society that was to arrive in Britain about forty years later. People bought things they wouldn't ever use, and sometimes they wouldn't even try to use them, just sell them on to someone else or throw them away. And a good example of that sort of consumerism was to be found in the Eighth Air Force base at Bassingbourn. Not far from the place where my friends and I used to cycle to see the Flying Fortresses was a dump where all kinds of things from the base were thrown away. Often there were things there that seemed to be brand new, and one day I came across a pile of paperback books, which were practically unread. Among them was a book entitled *Really the Blues*, by a musician called Mezz Mezzrow, and I already knew enough about jazz to know that I wanted to read it straight away.

Mezz had been quite a stalwart of the Chicago jazz scene in the 1920s, and his book told the story of jazz like it is. It set out where the music had come from, what sort of music it was – that black music was the real thing, although some white people managed it pretty well – and the whole story was there. It seemed to me that if you'd read that book you didn't need to read anything else, but the main thing was it inspired me to try and find records of the music that Mezz wrote about.

Before World War Two, what jazz and blues records there were did not sell many copies in Britain. In America during the 1920s all blues records were on what were called "Race" labels, aimed at the African American market. Many great jazz recordings were included in Race series as well, but in Britain there was no distinction. What few jazz records there were came out on major labels. So, for example, whereas Jelly Roll Morton's American records came out in the Bluebird Race series, and would probably only be stocked by stores in black neighbourhoods, in Britain they came out on HMV (His Master's Voice). This was a mainstream label, but the discs weren't widely stocked. You could only pick them up in specialist shops.

I suspect the majority of recorded jazz in England at that time was being bought by students, often medical students, who had enquiring minds and a taste for the new, the exotic or the extreme. As it happened Royston, where King Alfred School had relocated, was just fourteen miles from Cambridge, with its great university full of just such enquiring minds. It was one of the few places in the country that had a shop that kept jazz records as part of its regular stock. And, by a twist of fate, I ended up being in Cambridge regularly throughout my schooldays in Royston.

This was because I had started to learn the violin. As I mentioned, my father had played the violin when he was at school, and when I rejoined the evacuated King Alfred School at Royston he bought me a violin. Apart from cycling to the airbase, there was not a lot to do around Royston, so I thought I might as well spend some of my time practising. My lessons took place every week in Cambridge, from late 1943, with an old Frenchman, Monsieur Maurice, who was the only violin teacher in the area. So I was given the money every week for the return bus fare to Cambridge so that I could get to my lesson. It didn't take me long to work out that the amount of the fare was just about equal to the cost of one 78 rpm record, so that if I could save the fare I would be able to buy a new record every week. We didn't have a record player in the house where I was lodging – only my little Bakelite radio – but there was a wind-up portable gramophone at school on which I could hear my purchases.

So I thought to myself, why don't I go to my lessons on my bike? I could hold my violin case and the handlebars in my left hand, and then with my right hand I could grab on to the back of a delivery truck and be pulled along to Cambridge. The roads weren't very congested, traffic moved quite slowly during the war and there always seemed to be a succession of lorries or vans going to and fro between Royston and Cambridge, so it was usually quite easy to find one to tow me. Because being towed by a truck was a bit quicker than the bus, I could use the bit of free time that this gave me after my lesson to go to Miller's record store, where I'd been told there were some jazz records in stock.

The first time I went in, I asked the man behind the counter if he had any jazz records. He said, "Yes, I think so. I'm not quite sure where they are, but they're round here somewhere."

I started poking around, until he said, "Come over to the counter, I've got some catalogues here. You can use them to see what you can find."

So I looked in his catalogues and saw the lists of some of the things that were in stock. Then I managed to find them on the shelves, and started pulling them down. In fact he had quite a sizeable quantity of jazz. When the war started there had been plenty of students buying a range of music, and he hadn't reckoned on most of them being called up into the services. So although the students had gone, the records were still there. And the shop was very pleased to find someone to buy them. Which I did – at the rate of one a week.

I soon learned which British companies had issued material from the American Race labels. Parlophone was more or less equivalent to Okeh and Columbia in the States, and HMV had the rights to RCA Victor and Bluebird. On Parlophone were things like Louis Armstrong's Hot Seven, or the Bessie Smith Columbia recordings. And on HMV I found Jelly Roll Morton and Duke Ellington. I have the records still. Also in the late 1930s, the British Hot Blues Society had persuaded the English Decca label to release some authentic blues. I managed to get a Sleepy John Estes and a Cow Cow Davenport record from that series at the Cambridge shop.

Also, just at the start of the war, in 1939 or maybe just into 1940, Columbia in America began releasing what became known as albums, which were folders with about half a dozen 78s inside them. I remember there was a Louis Armstrong Hot Five one, and a Bessie Smith one. These collections became available to the British record companies, should they want to issue them, which they did. In fact Parlophone found that some Bessie Smith masters had come over to them in the 1920s that they had not issued at the time, so they pressed those and issued them simultaneously with the album, which was very good news for collectors. It might have been my interest in mathematics, but I found I was good at remembering the matrix numbers of records, and so I was quickly aware which discs had been issued before and which ones were appearing for the first time. Later on I was able to use this skill to exchange records with collectors in the States, where some of the discs pressed here in Britain during the 1940s had never been issued and were consequently quite valuable in America.

My interest in collecting records meant that when the war finished and we were able to go back to London, I had about sixty or seventy jazz and blues 78s. I'm not sure many fifteen-year-old kids had a collection like that, even of non-jazz records. It was way before the advent of the pop culture where people were buying sounds all the time.

Once I had settled back in London, I thought that there must be some jazz record shops somewhere. In due course I found out about a couple of them – just small specialist record shops, that did sell jazz. So I went to see them, got talking to them, and carried on buying records. It was the time when books about jazz records, discographies, were more or less being invented. And when these books came out, cataloguing all known recordings, *Rhythm on Record* by Hilton Schleman, and later Charles Delauney's *Hot Discography*, I bought them. Then, in 1946, Doug Dobell, whose grandfather had founded a bookshop specialising in rare editions at 77 Charing Cross Road, persuaded his family to let him convert part of the shop into a specialist jazz record store. Before long, this was the meeting place for all jazz record fans and collectors in London.

It had never occurred to me that anybody might be trying to play the music I had discovered on records, here in Britain. Obviously I knew that some jazz was being played here because by the end of the war you'd increasingly hear it on the radio. I suppose that what we heard on the BBC was a sort of modernish Dixieland, mostly played by dance bands. I was also aware that there were several amateur bands around London playing traditional jazz, and some of them even sang the blues a bit. For the most part they were just trying to enjoy themselves as best they could. The definition of an amateur jazz musician is "a jazz fan who has access to a musical instrument". They weren't trying to play the music properly, and what they were doing wasn't anything directly to do with this extraordinary music I'd found on my old records.

Then one day in 1946 I saw a leaflet on the counter in Dobell's, advertising a band playing "A varied selection of Stomps, Rags, Blues, Cakewalks and Marches". I was interested, because it seemed that here was a group trying to sound like a band would have done in the 1920s. They normally played way out in Kent, about twenty-five miles from where I lived, but the leaflet said that they would shortly be appearing at King George's Hall, a small concert hall that seated about 300, just behind the Dominion Theatre on Tottenham Court Road. It was organised by something called the Hot Club of London, and the band was called the George Webb Dixielanders. It was led by George, a pianist whom I later discovered had been working at the Vickers armaments factory during the war, and several of the band had also spent time working there.

When the day of the concert came, I went up to this place and walked in. I must have been a bit late because they'd already started playing, and as I came through the door it was like being mesmerised. I remember I walked down the aisle to my seat as they were on the stage playing 'Fidgety Feet'. The records of those days, and the machines you played them on, didn't possess enormous volume. There was really good stuff to be heard, but – particularly on the portable wind-up gramophone at school – you had to listen really hard, so that you could pick out Louis Armstrong playing in the background with King Oliver, for example.

Instead of that, in King George's Hall there was this amazing all-enveloping wall of sound coming at you. There were Owen Bryce and Reg Rigden on cornets, and Wally Fawkes on the clarinet. In retrospect, I think the only really good player on the stage was Wally. Some of the others, if you looked into what they were doing in any depth, were not really all that competent. They were nice guys and everything, and their overall sound was really impressive.

I thought, "Yes, this is it!" It must have been a bit similar to hearing King Oliver for the first time in the flesh – even though they didn't quite have the feel, shall we say.

I discovered that the place they normally played every Monday was a pub in Barnehurst, which was miles away in south east London, and by then I was living in north west London, close to Golders Green. Getting there and getting back in the same night – well, I didn't know if you could do it. One didn't do that sort of thing in those days, I don't think. I was sixteen then, I suppose, and by hook or by crook I did manage to get down there once. The band was playing even better than on the concert, and it was very good. After that I heard them quite a few times whenever they appeared in central London, until the point when Humphrey Lyttelton joined them, on trumpet, replacing the two cornets they'd previously had.

Before long, Humph got them into a resident club, which a man called Ken Lindsay and various of his friends and colleagues had started up. It was in Leicester Square, on the north side, above the Café de l'Europe, where there was a first-floor ballroom. That's where they played. It was laid out as if the people whose hall it was didn't expect people to be standing or listening on the dance floor. Their view was that if the public were there, they'd be dancing – ballroom dancing. So if you wanted to listen, you had to sit round the edge. I found a place to sit on the stage, quite near the band, because I wanted to listen and I was really quite serious about it. The thing for me was, Humph was there. Until the moment I first heard him, I didn't ever think anyone was seriously going to play the music I'd heard on records. Most of the amateur musicians around London were just playing at it. They played the music quite well, sometimes very well, but they weren't making their life's work out of it. Hearing Humph for the first time, and then many times afterwards, it struck me that this was somebody who was playing the music properly. There *was* actually a proper way to play.

You'd hear Louis Armstrong on record, with all his little phrases around the turnaround, or dropping in little syncopated things, and it all sounded exactly as it's supposed to be. You'd say to yourself, "That's how it goes!" Usually when you then heard other people playing the same piece as Louis, you'd think they weren't playing it properly. It's mainly about knowing how the timing goes. Humph – who also had a rather aristocratic manner, and was a slightly mythical character with stories of how he had carried his trumpet with him as an army officer during the wartime landing at Anzio – played really well and knew how the timing worked. Then you noticed that Wally Fawkes was playing better too, because before Humph arrived, he'd had Owen Bryce and Reg Rigden alongside him, not always playing the right notes and sometimes drifting out of time. What could he do? But now he came up against somebody who played accurately, which gave him the very things that his sort of clarinet playing needed to work from. Harry Brown, the trombone player, could hardly play at all by comparison. But I respected him because I had the band's record of 'South' on Decca, on which he plays.

As I mentioned, I would sit on the stage to be nearer the band. You couldn't watch what Humph was doing by sitting directly in front of Humph, so I sat in front of Harry Brown, so that I could watch Humph and try to learn from him. One night, Harry tapped me on the shoulder and said, "Do you want to buy a trombone?" I couldn't think of what to say. So I said, "How much is it?" He said, "Five pound ten." And I had five pounds, ten shillings in my pocket. And on the spur of the moment I couldn't think of a good reason for not buying it. So I bought it. It was a terrible trombone. He'd played that very same instrument on the record, but it was falling apart, and he intended to use the money I paid him towards buying a better one.

I began trying to play it along with records, when I got home. Having learned the violin, albeit not very seriously, but with three years or so of lessons under my belt, I was aware of scales and all the other things you have to do to practise on a musical instrument. And there is a similarity between the violin and the trombone in one major respect, which is that the notes are not found for you, as they are with the keys of a piano, for example. You have to find and create the positions for yourself. There are no frets on a violin and there are no helpful markers on a trombone slide. So I was already used to finding the next note on the fiddle by putting my fingers a quarter of an inch up the fingerboard, to create the next semitone, and so I applied a similar system to the trombone.

My mother had always appeared to me to be a music lover. She appreciated music, but as an academically minded schoolteacher, she did not share my enthusiasm for jazz. To her I was an amateur playing noisy jazz and she just didn't like the sound of it, really, and that never changed. She was a concert-goer, though she never did come to any of my concerts, even when I had an established band in later years, except once. That was for a Labour party event, a Jim Callaghan-inspired concert. In contrast, my father came to hear my band quite a few times. He got it right away, even though all the way through Cambridge and work he'd never heard any jazz. Never heard it at all. You might think how was that possible? And the answer is, he was just in with a different crowd.

Anyway, I got the trombone home and started practising. I must have been to see the Dixielanders again once or twice after I bought it, but soon after that, the group became the Humphrey Lyttelton Band. Wally Fawkes and George Webb were still with it, and also Harry Brown at first, though not for long. One time – not long before it became Humph's band – I heard the Dixielanders with Eddie Harvey on trombone, who'd come back to London on leave after he'd been called up for National Service. He played very nicely. He sounded a bit like J. C. Higginbotham then, before he adopted the no-pressure method of playing the trombone, which changed his sound to a sort of "fuff-fuff-fuff". In those early days he played good meaty stuff.

When Harry left, Keith Christie joined Humph as trombonist. I know that immediately prior to joining the Lyttelton band he'd been playing in a big band in Blackpool or Southport, because when he came down to London, my mother put him up at our house, as he had nowhere to live for a couple of weeks.

Much later, around 1960 or so, when he'd been playing with the likes of Ted Heath and John Dankworth, I saw Keith in Frith Street, walking down towards Ronnie Scott's, and he crossed the road to avoid meeting me. I don't think I was sufficiently cool for him to risk being seen with. But then, when he joined the Heath band, several of its members had called Keith an "amateur Dixielander", because that's how he sounded to them. It's all relative, I suppose. In all seriousness, Keith was a good player, and his brother Ian was a very funny man. I remember after my band had gone its separate way from Ken Colyer in 1954, Ian played clarinet with Ken for a short time. Briefly they were using a drummer who came up from Southampton. I asked Ian what he was like, and I still remember his reply: "He's the worst drummer in the Western hemisphere!" I think Ken probably had a few of those, when he got to the point where he was only hiring "believers".

Anyway, coming back to hearing Humph. It may well have been that I'd have chanced to play an instrument anyway, but Humph was what made me imagine that it was worth trying for real. It was such a lost black art – in both senses – that without hearing him I wouldn't really have thought about trying to play jazz myself.

By this time I was at St Paul's School, where I'd gone in 1946, to complete my Higher School Certificate (the equivalent of A levels). I was there for the two years until the summer of 1948. I was in the Eighth form, as they called it. I was a mathematician, and because King Alfred School hadn't got a higher maths teacher, I had to go somewhere else to do my Higher School Certificate in maths.

St Paul's was quite an interesting experience, not least the bus ride from Golders Green to Hammersmith every morning. Miss one particular bus and you'd arrive very late for school. I didn't play music there, but I do remember the journey to and fro, and that not too far away from the school was Colin Pomroy's shop at South Kensington station, which was a place where a few jazz records could be found, including reissues on his own label.

I remember vividly that on my first day at St Paul's, I turned up for assembly in the big hall and they started singing hymns. I didn't know any hymns, because King Alfred's had been a non-religious school. It was a day school in an area with several faiths, and they did not believe you could educate multi-faiths effectively. Indeed, the reason it was a fully private school was that although the State gave money to maintain some private schools, they did not do so if there was no religious instruction. So it was really quite a change to be somewhere where they sang hymns every morning.

At St Paul's I was in the same class as Stanley Sadie, who became a musicologist and the editor of *Grove's Dictionary of Music*. I think he was actually a year older than me, but he was also in the Maths Eight. We all had slightly different mathematical skills. He could remember strings of numbers, like everybody's phone number. (That's not to say I can't remember plenty of phone numbers, for example, I know that before the war mine was WORdsworth 2340.) But my skill was to add up. I can arrive at an accurate total from totting up many numbers. Doing large complex calculations in my head, I'm accurate to within two percent. It's a useful skill in business. It doesn't matter so much if you arrive at a million and one or a million and two – it's being right about the million that counts.

We were a pretty diverse collection of pupils in that maths set, because there was Stanley who came from a Jewish background, and another chap who was a steward at Mosley's fascist meetings. Another person who was at the school was Alexis Korner, whom I got to know later as a blues pioneer, and who played for a time with my first band. He was a little older than me, and I think he'd have been leaving St Paul's about the time I arrived. The disc jockey Pete Murray was there then too, but he was younger than me, so our paths didn't cross.

Normally it took two years to get your Higher School Certificate. I passed pure and applied maths after one year, and then I stayed on another year and got distinctions in more pure and applied maths, and amazingly in French and oral French. Now at that time, I had a diabolical stammer. In later life I've learned to control it – it comes on every now and again when I can't say a word – but as a teenager I had the King George VI stammer. If I got into it, I could seldom get out of it. So how I managed to do well in an oral French exam, I have no idea.

I was getting all ready to go to university then, and follow in my father's footsteps, when a chap came round from the Life Offices' Association, which was the body to which insurance companies who offer life cover belong. He said, "Why go to college for three or four years, and spend money all the time you're there with no guarantee of a job at the end of it? If you want to become an actuary, you begin working for an insurance company, you get paid, you get three afternoons a week off for study, and if you pass your exams every year, in five years' time you'll be an actuary, earning £1000 a year." That was the average actuary's salary in 1948, which was, in those days, an awful lot of money.

So after that visit, my father arranged for me to go and see one of his college friends, who was the CEO at the Prudential, to see how actuaries lived, and what they did. As a result, I tried for it, but my mind wasn't on it. It was on music. So I didn't get any further than the bottom rung of the actuarial ladder, which is a shame in some respects, but the stuff you end up having to do in that business is horrendous. Somewhere I've got some past papers from one of the exams, and, honestly, it all seems to be written in Chinese. It's full of symbols that mean nothing to me now; they just look like the sort of thing you get on science fiction television programmes, where communications come up in weird alien writing. Maths gave me up in the end.

For a while after leaving school it was okay. I had a job in the West End, at the Clerical Medical Life Assurance Society in St James's Square, right across from what later became famous as the site of the Libyan Embassy siege. If you were a mathematical student, you weren't sent to work in any part of the firm that might develop into a job in the insurance business. Instead, I was an assistant to the man in charge of personnel management. Among other tasks, I typed out the letters that went to the directors with their cheques, because I knew what they should look like; in other words, I could tell instantly if there were any obvious calculation errors.

I failed part one of the exams two years running, in 1949 and 1950. Then, after a while, they called me in one day and said, "Mr Barber, we really wanted a mathematical student, a potential actuary, but you are only a clerk. Would you mind taking your trombone somewhere else?" And I did, so that was it.

My father said, "Okay, you aren't doing maths, what about doing music?"

I said, "Well, I am doing music. I've got a band. We've just done a broadcast, we were on BBC *Jazz Club* last week."

He said, "No, I mean do it seriously. Do it properly and go to music school. I'll pay the fees."

So, in response to this, I applied to the Guildhall School of Music and Drama. When I arrived they were very keen to have me playing the trombone, and I was immediately in the first orchestra. That was because they had no other brass players in the entire school. No trumpeters, no French horn players, just one trombonist. Me. They asked me what I'd do as my second instrument, and when I said "violin", they told me they didn't really want that because they already had dozens of applications from violinists. Was there anything else I could play? So I said "double bass". This was because by that time I often used to borrow Brylo Ford's bass to do blues numbers with Alexis Korner. Brylo was from Trinidad. He had been on the London Caribbean scene for years, mainly playing with Cyril Blake. He also played four-string guitar, and he recorded as a calypso singer under the name "Iron Duke". In 1950 Brylo played bass from time to time in my band, and by borrowing his instrument I just about knew my way round it. They said, "That's fine."

I said, "I haven't got a bass."

"Don't worry, you can borrow one of ours." So I had the benefit of three years of being taught the bass by Jim Merritt, who was one of the top bassists in the world at the time, and who was perhaps best known as the principal bass with the London Philharmonic Orchestra. Strangely, I have no recollection of ever playing anything in front of him – that's because I got a half-hour's concert out of him every week. I conned him into it, and he played the bass to me, showing me things. And he had lots to tell me. During the war he'd been too old to be called up, so he'd worked with virtually all the major orchestras during those five or six years. Also the USO, the American forces' entertainment organisation, brought Broadway shows to London, which involved a full pit orchestra playing from scores. And Jim did one of those in the West End, alongside the great jazz bassist Bob Haggart. They became friends and as a result Jim could play 'Big Noise From Winnetka', Bob's solo feature, perfectly.

As an aside, I met Bob Haggart in 1981, when we were in New Orleans on the same festival programme. He was playing with a latterday version of the Bob Crosby band. My colleague Harold Pendleton was over there at the same time, meeting people and so on. There were quite a few members of the original Crosby band there including Bob Crosby himself. And somehow Harold got talking about the repertoire the Crosby band would play, and Bob mentioned 'Big Noise From Winnetka'.

Harold said, "Our Vic Pitt plays that really well."

Bob said, somewhat alarmed, "You won't do it tonight, will you?" He immediately assumed that we'd play it in our set as we often did at that time – as if we'd have dreamt of doing it in front of the man who wrote it and first played it. It was his big number!

I started a three-year course at the Guildhall in 1951, and finished just about the time when what was to become my professional band parted company from Ken Colyer.

Before I started the course, during the time when I was still at CMG (Clerical Medical Group), I was already getting known. Alex Revell, Ben Cohen and I would hire a bus for our semi-pro band and on a weekend we'd go up to play in Manchester and maybe play in Birmingham on the way back.

I was still living at home. After the war my family had come back to London, but we couldn't return to the house in Stanmore, because the naval officer who rented it off us wouldn't move out. So my mother rented a place in Hampstead Garden Suburb, which was a very nice house in a terrace designed by Sir Edwin Lutyens. The middle of the Garden Suburb was planned by Lutyens around 1906, with two churches, a Friends' Meeting House, the Henrietta Barnett School and so on. Our house was in one of the rows leading up to the central area, and my mother, sister and I lived there.

By this time, my father was living in a flat off Cromwell Road, at the back of St Paul's School. I remember driving along past the back wall of the school around that time and seeing graffiti daubed on it that read, "This Land For Homes!" There was some local resentment towards what were seen as the posh people in the school. However my father lived very close to there, before getting married to his second wife, Betty, following which the two of them eventually went to live down in Kent, near Ashford. Before he moved I saw him occasionally in London, and he came to a couple of concerts where I was playing with Ben and Alex.

His brother, my uncle Raymond, was a Lloyds Bank manager, and he was in charge of the big branch in Lower Regent Street. While I was at CMG, I went to meet him for lunch there on one occasion, and he had regency-uniformed flunkies serving the food. It was all very posh indeed, but ultimately tragic, because Ray committed suicide quite early in life, in his late forties or maybe early fifties.

Before I had a trombone, I briefly had a clarinet – an E flat one if I remember rightly – and also a cornet. So sometimes I used to try and sit in with bands. I remember once around that time being in a pub right down in the south of London, somewhere near Morden, and sitting in during the interval. I was playing clarinet and Doug Dobell was playing piano. There were very few of us in those days who were even trying to play the music. Later on, in 1953, I used the cornet to teach Ken Colyer some tunes. One of the tunes I taught him he still remembered thirty-four years later, a ragtime piece called 'Heliotrope Bouquet'. He had a great memory. He got the feeling of it, and although he very seldom played it with his band, he remembered it in every detail.

As well as trying to sit in with other bands, I also wanted to hear as much jazz as possible. I remember going to the Feldman Club at 100 Oxford Street, to hear some live music. The resident band usually featured the teenage prodigy Victor Feldman on piano and vibes. He wasn't there that night, but his brothers Robert and Monty were definitely playing. The main band I'd gone to hear that night was the drummer Joe Daniels and his Hot Shots. I remember Alan Wickham played trumpet with him; he was a lovely trumpeter. He was one of the best jazz players around in London, particularly as Joe Daniels's band played quite a lot of jazz in its dance music sets. Alan sounded a lot like Freddie Randall, only more jazzy. The Feldman Club was laid out just the way the room would be later, when it became the Humphrey Lyttelton Club, and eventually the first incarnation of the 100 Club. When you came down the steps from the street, the stage was at the far end on the left, pointing right down the room. Later it went to the other end, and nowadays it's on the side of the room, opposite the door, which is acoustically the worst possible place for it!

Once I'd got the trombone, I tried playing with one or two of the local bands. The first one I played with was Doug Whitton's, but he gently eased me out after a few weeks, because I wasn't good enough. Then I tried playing with the clarinet player Cy Laurie, but I wasn't loud enough for him. He replaced me with Bernie Newlands, who was rather large and very loud! So I reckoned if I really wanted to play in a band I'd have to organise it myself.

My first band got started because the clarinetist Alex Revell and I met during 1948 in Dobell's record shop, and in due course we became best friends. I think I ran into one or two of the other guys who formed the band there as well, meeting up with them at different times. Alex and I began it, and then a little bit later Ben Cohen came in on cornet. They were both living in roughly the same part of London, in Newbury Park. We started playing in a disused hangar on the former RAF base at Hainault, but then we began to practise at Gearies School in Redbridge, where they let us have a room. It was a short walk from Gants Hill tube station. We had Ferdie Favager on banjo,

Alex, Ben and myself. Maybe there was a piano player there as well, but I don't remember who it could have been. Ferdie had already played the banjo before meeting us. He wasn't someone who went round sitting in with other bands in order to learn, but Alex played him Johnny St Cyr's solo on 'Willie The Weeper' and he cottoned on to the style very quickly.

It was very much an amateur band to start with. Quite early in our career we entered a jazz band contest at the Empress Hall. There were dozens of bands due to appear that day, and because my name began with "B" we were actually the first one on stage, so we played before anybody had arrived to hear us. Fortunately, the house band at the event was led by the trumpeter Freddie Randall, who later became a good friend. He took pity on us and persuaded the organisers to let us play again at the end, so at least we got to be heard. I should also say that Freddie also did us a good turn in 1949 when Humphrey Lyttelton brought Sidney Bechet over to play in London. That night we were playing support to Freddie's band at Cook's Ferry Inn in Edmonton. Normally we'd have done the first set and the middle set, but that night, Freddie let us all go early, after our first few numbers, so that we could get down to the Winter Garden Theatre in central London to hear Bechet. There is a good souvenir of that event, because Bechet made some records that day with Humph's band.

In due course we tried our hand at recording ourselves, in October 1949. We went to the Modern Messages studio in the Piccadilly Arcade, where the engineer had recorded some discs for the Tempo record label. I think the best-known thing he did there was a set of 78s called "The History of Jazz" with the Mick Mulligan Band, George Melly, and the historian Rex Harris.

On our first ever recording session, we had Hugh Middleton on cornet, who had learned the instrument playing in a silver band, so he was quite a well-schooled musician. He was a friend of Alex's, and actually a very good natural jazz player on top of having been well-taught. I seem to remember he signed up to join the Navy, and so shortly after that recording he was gone, and Ben Cohen was always our regular cornet player after that. On the records, we also had Johnny Westwood on drums. I'd met him because he used to play with John Haim's band, which sometimes appeared in the Golders Green area where I lived. My most vivid memory of that band was John Haim on his motorbike, with his brother Gerry riding pillion to get to gigs, with the two parts of his sousaphone wrapped round him. I later discovered Johnny Westwood had also travelled to gigs on that bike, with a heavy wooden box of drums, stands and cymbals slung over his shoulder as he clung on to the pillion seat.

We all liked the music of the classic jazz period of the 1920s, the music of King Oliver, Louis Armstrong and Jelly Roll Morton, and Alex was quite a follower of Johnny Dodds. So the tunes we recorded were all from that period, including 'Mabel's Dream', 'Doctor Jazz', and 'Working Man Blues'. Perhaps the best piece we did was another number associated with Dodds called 'Gatemouth'. I was very keen on the playing of Honore Dutrey, the trombonist in King Oliver's band, and I remember using one of his solo breaks on 'Gatemouth', which was a contrast with the original record of the tune by Dodds's New Orleans Wanderers, where the trombonist had been Kid Ory.

Even after we had seen the inside of a studio for the first time, the band was really not much more than a few friends getting together. I don't think any of us had an ambition to play the music seriously. For a while, at the end of 1949, Alex and I played together in the re-formed version of what had been the George Webb Dixielanders, which Reg Rigden led, once Humph had formed his own group and Wally, Harry and George went off with him. Reg had teamed up again with Owen Bryce, aiming at the same two-cornet sound that the band used to have when I first heard it. I was never particularly impressed by Owen's technical advice – of which there was plenty – because when he tried to illustrate his points by playing them on the trumpet, he could seldom play them convincingly. Having said that, he clearly believed, as I did, in trying to play the music correctly in a musical sense, but he lacked Humph's sense of conviction in his playing. Alex clearly remembers that Owen would tell us off for playing minor thirds. When we protested that they were "blue notes", he would insist that they were "wrong notes". To get our own back, Alex and I used to try and work in a particularly irritating phrase from Stan Kenton's record of 'The Peanut Vendor' into all our solos. This put us in Owen's bad books, and eventually I resigned from the group. Alex was sacked a day or two later.

Nevertheless, undaunted by this, Alex, Ben and I promptly decided that our own band should have two trumpets, like the King Oliver band on which the Dixielanders were originally modelled. At first, Keith Jary joined alongside Ben as the other trumpeter. We had Ferdie on banjo, and Alexis Korner played guitar with us as well, using a Hofner electric guitar with no amplifier, which made him rather hard to hear. Roy Sturgess played piano. Somebody knew Brian Lawes, the drummer, I don't know which of us that was, but we met and hung out together a bit. We'd spend Saturday mornings in Dobell's, and before long we began playing more regularly. In November 1950, we tried our hand at recording again, at a studio in Denmark Street.

One night around that time, Alex, Ben and I were playing somewhere in Soho, and an elderly man came down to see us called Jack Glicco. We got talking to him, and discovered that he played the trombone, and he had sat in with the Original Dixieland Jazz Band in 1919 at the Hammersmith Palais, when jazz first came to London. He played a small-bore trombone, and played very much in their sort of early jazz style. I don't think any of us saw him again after about 1949, but it turns out that shortly after we met him, he published a memoir of his career as a nightclub trombonist in Soho before the war, called *Madness After Midnight*. It is a pretty lurid account of dope peddling, gangs, girls and London nightlife. He'd made his living as a hairdresser since those pre-war days, and I think he died within a year or two after he came down to see us, but he was a link back to the very start of jazz in Britain, and he proved that there'd always been a few dedicated local enthusiasts for playing jazz ever since it began.

Another musician whom we got to know from that inter-war period was the saxophonist Harry Hayes. He was a great and very erudite musician, and I remember him telling me about his first professional job in the 1920s. He played in the Savoy Orpheans, which was a dance-cum-jazz band, in which he sat next to the American bass saxophonist and vibes player Adrian Rollini. He was paid £100 per week, which was a fortune in those days. I last saw Harry at the Epsom Playhouse, when I'd just got the Big Chris Barber Band going, and we played there around the year 2000. He lived a couple of miles from the theatre, so I asked him if he'd like to come along, and even offered to send a car for him. But he refused, and although he was ninety years old at the time, he walked over to hear us. At half time I was out in the foyer signing CDs, and he came over. I said, "Hello Harry, how d'you like it?"

"Better than I expected," he replied.

In the summer of 1951, Alex, Ben, Ferdie, Brian and myself all went on holiday together to the Isle of Wight, and there was a third set of recordings made there, on which I played the bass. It was done at the Norton Grange Chalet Hotel, which was a sort of holiday camp run by the uncle of one of Alex's friends. I went on that holiday carrying a string bass and a trombone. Nowadays I'd think, "How could anyone do that?" But somehow I managed it. Brian Lawes didn't take his drum kit with him, though, so he played the washboard.

Some time after that holiday, Jeremy French joined the full band in place of Keith Jary. Later, Jeremy became very well-known as a trombonist (including a long association with Wally Fawkes) but at this point he was playing cornet. Like Keith, he played first, leaving Ben free to play the second part, rather as Armstrong had done in King Oliver's band. Around the end of 1950, Dickie Hawdon joined to replace Jeremy, and he improved the group no end. Dickie was already into all kinds of music, and he later worked with many other traditional jazz bands. But he also played modern jazz with Johnny Dankworth and ended up running the jazz course at Leeds College of Music. All credit to him because, over time, that course produced some really excellent musicians including Alan Barnes, Johnny Boston and James Evans.

The band played where we could, and in due course we started our own club, the Lincoln Gardens, in what eventually became the Ken Colyer Club, or Studio 51, in Great Newport Street, near Leicester Square in central London. We were the first jazz band ever to play there. There had been no jazz in there before, but we found out about the place and we played there on Tuesday nights and Sunday afternoons. The rest of the week it was a ballroom dancing school, run by the owner Vi Hyland. There was just one exit, so it was quite a difficult place to get out of, and it would never pass fire regulations today. But we played there for quite a while, doing something like six months of

Tuesdays altogether. In the evening on Sundays, after we'd finished playing, there began to be sessions by Kenny Graham's band, the Afro-Cubists, which he'd just formed. We used to stay and hear them, but they didn't really know who we were, apart from the fact that we played jazz as well. Their pianist, Ralph Dollimore, once told me they came to hear us before they came to work one evening, and they couldn't really work out what we were doing. We understood them all right, and I became quite friendly with Dizzy Reece who played trumpet with them from time to time.

During the period that we were playing there, John Dankworth and the Seven started playing at the club on Saturday nights, which is how I got to know John and the people in his band. And later on I met Cleo Laine when she joined them. We didn't draw huge crowds on Tuesday nights, but there were a few regulars. And away from the club, we also played things like riverboat shuffles.

As I mentioned, Alex was very keen on Johnny Dodds, and Ben Cohen aimed at the sound of Louis Armstrong during the period of the Hot Fives and Sevens, which is a difficult thing to try and get right. Ben worked hard on his music, but he had a full-time job as an electrical engineer in a radio company – Ultra, I think it was called – and so the amount of time he could spend on music was limited. But it was that sound of 1920s classic jazz that we were after.

One thing I do remember about that period when we were playing at the 51 was that we had a rehearsal or two with Ken Colyer. He had begun to make a name for himself with the Crane River Jazz Band, playing the sort of music that was associated with Bunk Johnson and George Lewis. It seemed rather absurd to us that there was this group of people over in Cranford, in Middlesex, saying that George Lewis is the only possible thing, and that everything else isn't real jazz. Whereas we were saying the Oliver Creole Band and the Armstrong Hot Fives were real jazz and nothing else counted. So we made contact with Ken. I don't think the differences between us were quite as great as our fans might have made out; after all, we liked George Lewis and they liked Johnny Dodds. So we met for a couple of rehearsals in the Hare's Foot pub in Goodge Street.

We had Dave Stevens on piano, who is now in Australia, either Ben Marshall or Ferdie on banjo, Ken Colyer and Sonny Morris from the Crane River Jazz Band on trumpets, Alex and myself. We played some tunes, and I remember it was during one of those rehearsals I taught Ken 'Working Man Blues', which he must have played hundreds of times over the years. I sat in with one of his later bands, and he played it exactly the same as that day we first did it.

Meeting up with Ken and Sonny was the first step towards saying, "We've got enough to fight against, getting jazz established, without fighting against each other". In the end, joining those two camps together was the point of the band that Monty Sunshine and I formed, and which Ken joined, but that was in the future. We didn't end up getting together with Ken at the time of those rehearsals. Ben and Dickie remained our two trumpeters.

Towards the end of the period at the 51 Club, the band did a couple of broadcasts. By that time the BBC had changed its attitude from when I was growing up, and instead of doing its best to keep jazz off the airwaves, it had *Jazz Club* once a week, at 6.30 on Saturday evenings. The programme lasted an hour, and we played on it twice. On our first appearance, we were introduced by David Jacobs, who was just beginning his career as a BBC presenter. I suppose we were comparable in style to an American band like Lu Watters, with the two-cornet front line, but as well as Oliver numbers such as 'Canal Street Blues' the broadcasts showed that we were already thinking about different sorts of tunes, such as Ellington's 'Misty Morning' or A. J. Piron's 'Mama's Gone Goodbye'. I had the Piron record, and we learned the tune from that, because it has an unusual structure with the main part in F and the verse in C minor, which you wouldn't expect. Dickie used to play one of the breaks taken by Louis Warnecke's alto sax on the trumpet.

Overall, our repertoire was based on going out and buying as many different records of classic jazz as it was possible to find. I was getting discs from the States that you could not find in Britain, because our neighbours in Golders Green were a Jewish family who had loads of relatives in New York. They were always sending letters and parcels to and fro. So I said, "If I give you the money, do you think your family would pop up to Harlem and buy such and such a record for me?" And they did. At one point I even started a small sideline in importing other kinds of rare records, by less well-known big bands, for example, and selling them.

One of the main things I was getting from Harlem for myself was blues records. RCA had restarted the Bluebird series around 1941 with a lot of performances by blues artists. I remember getting records by Tampa Red with Big Maceo from that series, and others by Tommy McLennan and Lonnie Johnson. They were all current, available discs in the States, but you could not get them at all in Britain. At one point I wanted to know who was playing on some of the records, because these later Bluebird discs did not give a full list of personnel on the label. So I wrote to RCA Victor in New York with my questions, and I got a long handwritten letter back listing all the musicians and recording details, from one of the directors of the company. I can only assume he must have been a serious blues fan, who thought it was a worthwhile thing to let some young English enthusiast know exactly which musician was playing the bass with Big Bill Broonzy and when.

I think maybe the main thing that was missing from our playing at that time was any real feeling for the blues. The first occasion I really heard blues played live was in 1951 during the Festival of Britain. The National Federation of Jazz Organisations (NFJO) had decided to try and bring some Americans in to play jazz and blues. Apart from a few rare occasions during the war when American Forces' bands had played in England, it had been almost impossible to hear any musicians from the United States playing live in the UK. This was because since the early 1930s the Ministry of Labour and the Musicians' Union had joined forces to prevent them from playing here, in order to "protect British jobs". There'd been a handful of exceptions, such as Duke Ellington touring the cabaret circuit as a pianist with a British rhythm section, plus Ray Nance, on trumpet and violin, and singer Kay Davis. But by and large it just didn't happen. Anyway the NFJO brought in the pianist Ralph Sutton and the blues singer and guitarist Lonnie Johnson, who had also played on some of Louis Armstrong's early records, such as 'Hotter Than That'. The NFJO took a chance and hired a couple of supporting bands that would fit with the visitors, in defiance of the Union ban.

Once you got to hear the real thing live it was a revelation. I remember going back and trying to adjust the tone and volume on my record player to get as close as possible to the sound that Lonnie Johnson made live. So we learned from that event, which was a good thing. The British musicians who had supported the Americans were not so lucky as they were blacklisted by the Union. One of them was a banjo payer and guitarist called Tony Donegan, who was inadvertently referred to by one of the announcers as "Lonnie Donegan" mixing him up with Lonnie Johnson. The name was to stick with him throughout his career.

As well as playing at the 51, or on occasional riverboat shuffles and broadcasts, my band was also doing proper gigs in London and elsewhere. On some of our weekends when we went up North, to play in Manchester, Leeds or Birmingham, we took a guest, such as the singer Neva Raphaello. She was quite well-known in London for singing with Humph's band, although I always thought she was rather more of a vaudeville singer like Sophie Tucker than a genuine blues singer, such as Bessie Smith or Ma Rainey. She later made some records with the Dutch Swing College. Around the same time, Humph himself did a few guest gigs with us. One I particularly remember was a festival-type occasion at Liverpool's St Georges Hall, a great big barn of a place opposite the Empire Theatre. Humph said it was like a Pre-Raphaelite railway station, though I think he was referring to the acoustics!

As well as concerts and clubs, we played for dances, such as at the Orchid Ballroom in Purley, which was a huge ballroom that catered for hundreds of people dancing. It was at a time when the proprietors were anxious to ban jiving on the dance floor, so that the regular dancers would not get kicked. But we'd get the young crowd clamouring for us to play jazz, so they could jive. I remember we'd announce things like the 'Muskrat Ramble Mambo', which we'd play as normal, but the proprietors weren't ever sure about numbers with Latin names or Latin beats, and whether the dances involved going all over the floor or not. So we got away with that, and the young dancers were happy.

After leaving the 51 Club, our band went on developing. I got Lonnie Donegan into the line-up in 1952 or thereabouts. He used to tell some story about how he'd never played the banjo until Chris Barber met him, said, "I'll teach you!" and taught him how to play. Well, bearing in mind he was playing banjo in his own band when he was blacklisted by the Union for playing in support to Lonnie Johnson and Ralph Sutton at the Royal Festival Hall in 1951, then quite clearly he was playing the banjo long before he joined me in 1952.

One thing we started doing with Lonnie almost as soon as he joined the band were the Blind Blake numbers that had Johnny Dodds on clarinet on the original recordings. These were things like 'Hot Potatoes' and 'C.C. Pill Blues', on which Lonnie sang and played either guitar or banjo. Alex took the Dodds part on clarinet, and I'd play the bass.

By that time my band had gone down to just one trumpeter, Ben Cohen, plus Alex and me, Lonnie, Brian Lawes on drums, Brian Baker on piano, who was a good solid pianist, and a variety of bass players. As I mentioned, the original piano player in that line-up was Roy Sturgess, who was excellent. He played ragtime, and beautiful boogie-woogie in the style of Big Maceo Merriweather. I'm reminded of him every time I hear Chris Stainton playing those same numbers today with Eric Clapton. Roy also used to play in our little blues group in the intervals, with Alexis Korner on guitar, and Brian Lawes and myself on bass. Alexis, who played with the band from time to time as well, went off in due course to do something more blues-orientated.

I was getting fed up with the band we had. The problem was that we did not play enough to get any better, and take ourselves on to the next stage of playing music professionally. If you only meet once or twice a week, then you're probably going to make the same mistakes again that you made last week. Even though we were all friends, we weren't from the same family, so we all got slightly different time off, different evenings when we could make a rehearsal or a gig. Sometimes we had to rehearse without the full band there. And so on gigs, the best job we could do was playing well the things we had already done. On top of that, Alex was about to get married, so he wasn't keen on a greater amount of time spent playing, and Ben had his job at Ultra, which kept him pretty busy. It was time for a change.

2 New Orleans to London

One afternoon in September 1952, I was sitting with Monty Sunshine and Lonnie Donegan in the Rex Restaurant in Old Compton Street. Run by a Greek Cypriot couple, Solomon and Angela, it was a place where jazz musicians often used to hang out during the day. They let us store instruments in their cellar, and on one occasion they lent us the money to get to a job in Birmingham. We paid them back on our return the following day.

By that stage, Monty was leading what was left of the Crane River Jazz Band, because Ken Colyer had rejoined the Merchant Navy and set off for America. The Cranes played once a week. Lonnie was playing with me, but he was also leading his own amateur band as well, so he actually had two gigs a week. As it happened, the three of us had plenty of free time. I was still studying at the Guildhall. Monty had finished his National Service in the RAF, so he had gone back to Camberwell College of Art to complete his course. Lonnie was coming to the end of his army service and was stationed in London. So getting together in the afternoons to rehearse was not likely to be a problem.

After quite a lot of discussion, we came to the point where we said, "Let's form a band that plays full-time and does nothing else." Someone asked, "How are we going to have enough money to live on?" We were all living at home anyway, and we could keep on doing that, so we decided to take the risk. What Monty and I wanted to do, and it was a step away from the classic 1920s jazz I'd learned from records, or from the bigger front line in which Monty played with the Cranes, was to develop the ability to play the loose, interweaving, freely improvised three-piece front line of trumpet, clarinet and trombone, that was the key to the New Orleans sound in its basic form. Then we had to find the other musicians.

The bass player in Lonnie's amateur band was Jim Bray. He had a day job as a scientist working for Shell, researching flame-thrower fuel, in an atmosphere of secrecy such that two policemen marched him to the company safe every night to deposit his notebooks. Anxious to escape that setup, he was very keen to play more, so when we asked him, he said, "I'm for it!" Ron Bowden was playing drums in the rump of the Crane River Jazz Band with Monty, had no other job, and was living at home on his gig money of around two pounds a week, so he was up for it too. As a result, we started as a quintet, although to get that three-piece front-line sound, we still needed to find a suitable trumpeter. In the end we found Pat Halcox, who was playing once a week in another amateur group called the Albemarle Jazz Band.

Pat joined in October and almost immediately we began to feel that we had got something real and individual. Another friend, an accountant, jazz fan and one-time drummer for the Boy's Brigade, was Harold Pendleton, whom I had met in the record department at Foyles. He had started a club at 44 Gerrard Street in Soho. It was a few doors away from what was to become Ronnie Scott's "Old Place", and Harold called it the Club Creole. At the end of 1952, believing that we were ready to be heard, we played two consecutive Friday evenings there. It went down very well with the audiences. One member of those crowds who heard us, Dick Smith, still tells me how outstanding the band seemed at the time. (He eventually learned to play the bass and subsequently joined Ken Colyer. Then in 1956, he became a member of my band, staying until 1965.)

After this success at the Club Creole, we were all set to turn professional, which we agreed to do at Easter in 1953, and we had a tour of Denmark organised to help us on our way. This came about because the previous summer I'd met Karl Emil Knudsen, a very dedicated Danish enthusiast who promoted and recorded jazz all his life. We met either in Dobell's or at Foyles bookshop, and he invited me over to Copenhagen to stay for a few days with himself and various friends in September 1952. They also arranged for me to play as a guest with a local band, the Ramblers – not the best band I ever played with – but it helped defray expenses. Karl ended up recording four numbers that I played with them.

When I told him about the plans that Lonnie, Monty and I had, Karl liked what he heard about our new band. He suggested we spend some time over there getting our sound and repertoire together. We could stay as guests with the various families who were part of his local network of jazz fans, and maybe play a different club every night for about three weeks. We could get rail passes and travel everywhere quite inexpensively by train. So we accepted his invitation and carried on practising as much as possible, rehearsing twice a week.

Then, in January 1953, Pat felt obliged to decline our invitation. He was working at Glaxo laboratories as a chemist, and he was given a day off a week to study for his professional qualifications, for which he was to sit the exam the following summer. He came to me and said, "Look, Chris, I'm terribly sorry, but my parents are holding me to a promise I made that I would finish doing my studies. We're not a particularly well-off family, and they've kept me since I left school, and all through the time I've been doing my studies as a chemist and working as an apprentice. I promised them that I'd follow it through until I'd got my qualification, rather than giving it all up, taking a dangerous step and becoming a musician. So I can't turn professional with you."

This dumbfounded us somewhat. To say the least it left us with quite a problem, because having relied on Pat, our Danish trip was all booked to start on 30 March, and suddenly we had no trumpeter. Now, I mentioned earlier that Ken Colyer had left the Crane River Jazz Band to rejoin the Merchant Navy and work his passage to America. He had been a crewmember on a shipping line that plied between London and Mobile, Alabama, and in November 1952 he jumped ship in Mobile and made his way to New Orleans. We knew all about this because Ken's brother Bill, who worked in the International Bookshop on Charing Cross Road, not far from Dobell's, had been publishing Ken's letters from New Orleans in the *Melody Maker* each week. It all went a bit quiet in January, and then in mid-February, *Melody Maker* published an article saying that Ken had been in jail for thirty-eight days for over-staying his visitor's permit. In those days, merchant seamen didn't have passports, they had identity cards, and when they came into port they were issued with a permit to stay ashore for a limited time until they rejoined their ship or signed on with another one. Ken was given twenty-nine days, which ran out on Christmas Eve. Consequently, he had been arrested under the McCarran-Walters Act and sentenced to deportation.

So we knew that he was about to be sent home. And we also knew that he had spent late November and almost all of December sitting in with many of the bands in New Orleans who played the very music that we wanted to play. So we decided to ask him if he would join us and become the band's trumpeter. Monty knew him well from playing alongside him in the Crane River Jazz Band, so he wrote a long letter to Ken, explaining the situation and asking him if he would be prepared to join us, and come to Denmark. I wrote to him, too, saying that although we were a co-operative group, we also felt that because Ken had been to New Orleans, and none of the other serious jazz and blues musicians in Britain had ever seen New Orleans, much less been there, we should call the band Ken Colyer's Jazzmen.

Ken sent a message to let us know that he agreed with the proposal, and I went down to Southampton with his brother Bill to meet him off the *USS United States*. It was ironic that if you were deported from anywhere they sent you home more or less first class. During his time in the Merchant Navy and then afterwards in the Parish prison in New Orleans, Ken had written the song 'Goin' Home', which he'd finished off on the voyage back to Britain. It said that as far as he was concerned, his home was in New Orleans. He felt more at home there than he did in England, and the music he loved was there, everything he wanted to do was there, but he was being sent "home" to England. His song has the line, "If home is where the heart is, then my home's in New Orleans". I did say to him that after he'd got away and been sent back to Britain, the police might not have been too friendly towards all the black musicians with whom he'd played, and who had actually broken the law to do so. At the time, Louisiana state law forbade black and white musicians from appearing in public on the same stage. He hadn't thought of that.

When he got back, we organised a series of rehearsals at a pub on York Way, behind King's Cross station. A friend of Lonnie's, Johnny Chown, a photographer who also played trumpet a little, came along and there are some pictures he took of the sessions, even including Ken clowning around with his trumpet. The music was great, because Ken was the best three-piece front-line lead I've ever played with, and that includes Sidney De Paris, Doc Cheatham and Percy Humphrey. It was fabulous, terrific. Ken was a very genuine musician, he loved the blues and he loved jazz, but above all he understood the feeling of the music very well. On the other hand, he was a most inarticulate man. To say he didn't have the gift of the gab is understating it. But when we began, we were raring to go, in terms of the music.

The *Melody Maker* announced the formation of the band, and that we "would not be heard publicly in England" until we came back from Denmark. We set off for the tour, and fortunately Ken didn't take offence when we were welcomed to the first town at which we were to play in the country by a banner that read: "Chris Barber's Crane River Jazz Band". Karl Emil Knudsen had taken time off from his job with the Danish telephone company, and he was there for all our gigs. He arranged a couple of sessions at the Gentofte Hotel near Copenhagen. We played in the ballroom there, which had a rather live, echoey sound, a bit like the recordings that Bill Russell had made in New Orleans of George Lewis playing at the Artesian Hall. We knew full well – indeed we hoped – that Karl would try and make some recordings of us to sell, and in the event he founded his company Storyyville Records with the 78s that Chris Albertson recorded of us on that tour. The first disc we ever made was 'Tiger Rag' done at a place called Lorry's 7-89-13 Club, where Chris was testing his recording equipment. We took some of the records he made at the Gentofte Hotel home with us and succeeded in fooling one well-known critic that these recordings featured George Lewis, Jim Robinson and so on! (He didn't forgive us!) We didn't get paid – any of us – for those records, but when Karl Emil Knudsen eventually put them out, together with some that the same band recorded a year later under my leadership with Pat Halcox on trumpet, they became the foundation of the New Orleans revival throughout Europe, and that benefited us all a lot more than a small recording fee would have done at the time.

Playing every night in Denmark, the band got better and better. It started to sound like a proper working group. We also introduced skiffle sessions into our concerts. I had been doing blues sessions with my previous band, first when Alexis Korner sang a short blues set between band numbers, backed by our pianist and me on the bass, and then with Lonnie. We wanted to do some of the best of the classic blues sung by the likes of Bessie Smith, and also blues with a more urban/country feel, like Muddy Waters was doing on the South Side of Chicago. We felt it was part of what you had to do, that without the blues you couldn't possibly understand New Orleans jazz. The two things went hand-in-hand. The only real difference between blues and New Orleans jazz is the instruments it's played on. It's mostly the same music, but played on guitars, not trombones.

Lonnie Donegan loved singing. We listened to Leadbelly records, such as the 1931 'Leaving Blues' on the Perfect label, and before Ken came back to England, we'd done some of those songs together. I played the bass and Lonnie played the guitar, and sang. He did Leadbelly's songs very well. Indeed later on when Sonny Terry and Brownie McGhee toured with my band in 1958, we had a party at my house and I put on our record with Lonnie singing 'Leaving Blues'. I said to Sonny, "Who's that?"

He said, "That's Lead."

Well if he didn't know that it was just Lonnie and me, who would? I thought, "We're doing something right!" From almost the moment we started, Lonnie sang a lot of material in those blues sessions that he later turned into hit records, such as 'Rock Island Line'. And as time went on we found a name for the blues session segments of our concerts. I had a 1929 Paramount record called 'Hometown Skiffle', which was a promotional record. Basically it was a rather poor dub of some of their new 1929 releases, including a fake party atmosphere, by the likes of Blind Blake or whoever. I'd also been reading the magazine *Jazz Information*, which had been running articles about the pianist Dan Burley. It described the music he was playing as "skiffle music", which basically meant rent party or hometown blues. So consequently we called our music "skiffle". It wasn't something we saved for the intermission; it was actually part of the show. After we'd done a few rip-roaring fast New Orleans jazz numbers, we'd reckon it was time for some blues, so we did some skiffle. It got so popular that we'd end the first half of each concert with about five skiffle tunes. We'd say, "Shall we do the skiffle now?"

On that Danish tour, Lonnie did most of the singing, but with him on the banjo, Ken on his left-handed guitar, and me on the bass, we'd do a skiffle set every night, and there is a record of Lonnie and Ken singing together on the old song 'Midnight Special'.

We got back to London slightly earlier than planned, because Bert and Stan Wilcox, two brothers who had turned from shopkeepers into jazz promoters, had just signed the lease for the crypt of a church in Bryanston Street near Marble Arch. The Church of the Annunciation – or at any rate, its crypt – was to be the new home of their London Jazz Club, which had previously held its sessions at 100 Oxford Street. They got in touch with us in Denmark to urge us home as soon as possible so we could open at the new club at once, in order that they didn't lose money on the lease. The record shop owner and occasional critic Jim Asman came down on our first night and said in print afterwards: "This was the nearest thing we had heard to genuine New Orleans music."

Maybe one reason for that was the breadth of the music we played, because in that band with Ken we were taking our repertoire from all over the place. Whereas my previous band had largely drawn its material from 1920s discs by Oliver and Armstrong, we looked a bit wider. For example, 'Isle of Capri' was a tune Ken had learned from the 1935 record by the New Orleans trumpeter Wingy Manone, where he sings "Oh Capri on the Isle, Oh Capri dressed in style . . ." It played itself, almost, I can't think of any other way of playing it. We had pieces from the Ellington band, early classics such as Freddie Keppard's 'Stockyard Strut', and we also did contemporary pop tunes like the theme from John Huston's 1952 film *Moulin Rouge*, which was currently well-known through recordings by Percy Faith and Mantovani.

I think the most unlikely piece we played was Gerry Mulligan's 'Bernie's Tune'. Ken slightly simplified the melodic line, but it sounded okay. And we played one or two other numbers in that sort of vein, without any fuss. I don't really think anyone noticed that they weren't traditional jazz numbers.

We played every week at Bryanston Street, and then we added George Webb's club in Woolwich, and soon afterwards, Wood Green Jazz Club. I'd played at Wood Green before with my original band. We hadn't been there often, but we did work there a few times, during the period when Dickie Hawdon was with us and we had the two trumpets. But now it became regular, every week. And we also started playing at Southall with Ken. Promoters liked us because we always turned up promptly and we had a strong following. One thing Ken was absolutely adamant about was that we should always be there on time and with no messing about on stage. When it was time to play a number, you played that number.

So we had these four clubs, and when the church decided they didn't want jazz any more in their crypt, we left there and went back to the 100 Club, where we played every Monday night instead. We had not been there long when Harold Pendleton started up a club in Greek Street. He called it the Latin Quarter, and it was at the back of the building that has Foyles in the front of it on the Charing Cross Road. That became our Friday night job. So within a few months of forming the band with Ken, we played there on a Friday, Wood Green on Saturday, Woolwich on Sunday, the 100 Club on Monday, and Southall on Wednesday. Tuesday filled up too, with a club at Bellingham, down in south-east London near Catford. These clubs were invariably full. Other clubs started up and then failed, but throughout most of our time with Ken we had those six regular gigs every week. They paid good money, and we probably came away from each of them with somewhere between thirty and forty pounds, which was quite respectable in those days. It was certainly enough that, being a collective, each member of the band was able to draw thirty quid a week. We were not running into debt, so those six jobs more than covered what we paid ourselves.

One of my friends, whom I knew through the community of people who collected rare and unusual records, was Hugh Mendl. I think I first met him around 1946, and we'd stayed in touch over the years. By this time he was working for Decca Records. He came down to hear the band with Ken very early on in our London career, and he was extremely impressed. I told him we'd really like to record, and so he went and talked to his head office, and they agreed to let the band make a ten-inch LP. At this point I sent Hugh off in the direction of Bill Colyer, Ken's brother, who had appointed himself the band's manager on behalf of Ken.

In fact Bill had flexed his "managerial muscles" before we left for Denmark because on the eve of departure the new band had been offered a broadcast on the BBC's *World of Jazz* series, presented by Denis Preston, who later became the producer of several of our records. Lonnie had been taken ill, and had to be replaced by Len Page from the Crane River Jazz Band, and then Bill refused to allow Ken to play. The idea was that this would "save" Ken for our first public concert in the UK in May, and so, ironically, Pat Halcox played on the "Colyer" band's first broadcast.

Anyhow, Bill agreed to Decca's proposal and consequently we recorded the first LP by Ken Colyer's Jazzmen on 2 September 1953. It was called *New Orleans to London*, and Monty, who used his Camberwell training to draw excellent cartoons, did a cover design that featured a sort of stevedore character playing a clarinet to a British gent in top hat and tails who was playing the trumpet. We did the recording for a flat fee of about £12 per man because in those days nobody got royalties from the major labels, apart from composers and lyricists, whose rights are protected everywhere. The only artists who were offered royalties were those who needed some kind of financial inducement to record, and which the labels were desperate to have. That did not – at the time – apply to us! However the album did do us a lot of good because we got to be quite widely heard. And we were helped by some very positive reviews, Jim Asman, for example, saying, "The band is well on form . . . claiming a life and style of its own."

Each of the tracks has got something to say. For example, we did a piece called 'Too Busy'. That was a tune we'd learned out of my collection of old jazz records, from the 1920s, but the people who liked jazz of that era said, "It doesn't sound like 1920s jazz." Which was the point: it was 1953 and we were trying to play it like New Orleans jazz of 1953. We weren't dismissing the Hot Five or the Hot Seven, just because we happened to like Bunk Johnson and George Lewis, but we were trying for a more contemporary New Orleans sound that you could apply to ragtime, such as 'Harlem Rag' or 'Cataract Rag', just as effectively as we could apply it to 1920s jazz or to a piece like Ken's own 'Goin' Home'.

The tragedy is that the band was short-lived. It had so much going for it; Ken's excellent lead playing, and our rhythm section, in that style, was so good I have not heard a better one yet. Every time I hear one of the records we made, I could cry because it was so quickly thrown away, but that's what happened, largely as a result of the actions of Ken's brother, Bill.

There were tensions in the band. Mainly, I think, there was tension between Ken and Lonnie. It wasn't difficult to find Lonnie annoying, because he was a dedicated cheeky chappie. Lonnie was always ready with the smart remark, and Ken could never come back at him quickly with a riposte. Meanwhile I spent almost all the time we were with Ken trying to get help from him, on behalf of everyone in the band, so that we could play the music better. He knew an awful lot about New Orleans music, but he seemed totally unable to communicate that knowledge to anyone else. Rather than trying to explain what he expected of us, if we weren't doing what he thought we should be, he just got abusive, or said next to nothing, bottling it all up inside.

Instead of Ken talking directly to us, his brother talked on his behalf. Bill Colyer was something of a control freak, and although he didn't play an instrument himself, apart from occasionally joining in on the washboard during our skiffle sessions, he was always around. On one particular Monday night, 17 May 1954, we were playing at 100 Oxford Street. Because this was in the days before the club had a drinks licence, we had gone to the Blue Posts pub during the interval, in Eastcastle Street, round the corner at the back of the club. Bill and Ken came over to me and Monty, and Bill said, "Listen, Ken's been thinking about the band and he's going to fire the rhythm section."

I said, "He can't. And what's wrong with them anyway?"

He said, "Jim Bray doesn't swing, and Ron Bowden's too modern. And he hates Lonnie's guts. You and Monty are catching on quite well, you can stay."

I thought about how I'd taught Ken several of the tunes we played, because he couldn't work them out for himself, and said to myself, "Thanks very much!" But what I said to Bill was, "No, our rhythm section is great. You can hear it on our recordings of the band. We'll never find another one as good as that."

Anyway Bill was intransigent, but it was a co-operative band to start with, and the five of us had invited Ken to join it. Bill and Ken were trying to abrogate the whole basis of the partnership. So in the end we said, "Look, there are five of us, and one of Ken, and he's out. Two weeks' notice."

There was a payphone in the corner of the Blue Posts over by the bar, so I went straight over and telephoned Pat Halcox. I explained the situation, and said "Ken's going and we're going to carry on, so what about it?"

Pat said, "Thank God for that! When can I start?"

I said, "Two weeks' time!"

And the boys said, "Chris, you'd better be the leader. You seem to have some understanding of what you've got to do." So I was to lead the band, and that was it. Pat convinced his parents that he would do all right and make a decent living, because he could see that we already were, and on 31 May 1954, Chris Barber's Jazz Band was born, with a session at 100 Oxford Street.

Harold Pendleton, who gave us our first performance chance and by this time was promoting many concerts round London, had been in the Blue Posts during my altercation with Bill and Ken. Just before it, he had witnessed a row between Lonnie and Ken, and he was very supportive of our new band. He immediately booked us back in as the resident band at the "London Jazz Centre", which was what he now called his Latin Quarter club in Greek Street, and he also did great work in helping to persuade the other clubs to book us. In addition, I immediately went round to all those other five clubs where we had been working and told them what had happened, and that I was now leading the band. I said it was the band they knew, but with Pat on trumpet, and they all said, "Yes, please come". Meanwhile Bill Colyer dashed off to Decca and persuaded them to give him the contract for the follow-up album to *New Orleans To London*. This eventually led to Ken's album *Back To The Delta*. When Decca found out what they'd got instead of the previous Colyer line-up, they rushed round to see me, and offered my band the chance to record for them. We went back to the studios on 13 July, just six weeks after the band began.

Harold Pendleton was about to start promoting the "First Festival of British Jazz" which was to take place at the Royal Festival Hall on Saturday 30 October 1954, and he offered us top billing. It was also to be recorded by Decca, which would mean that we would have two albums' worth of material done by the end of 1954. Before that, we had a second tour of Denmark lined up by Karl Emil Knudsen, which again involved us recording for Storyville.

In all my bandleading career, I've hardly ever been ill. But just a couple of days after the 100 Club debut of the band in May, I went down with a sore throat. It was the worst I have ever had in my life, and so round about Thursday 3 June, I went to the local Accident and Emergency clinic at St George's Hospital near Marble Arch. They took a swab and did some tests. As I waited for some results or information, I thought I should get back to work, and said so.

They said, "Absolutely not!" And one of the nurses showed me a blood test with abnormal white corpuscles.

"Obviously glandular fever," they said, "and so you're staying in!" They fed me on crushed aspirin in water (and that was all), which tasted disgusting. Luckily they found I was not allergic to Penicillin jabs, so that was what I got as well. About the Thursday following I saw a different pattern of white corpuscles on a blood test, so I walked out, and had no long-term ill effects. The same disease that was to seriously damage Seb Coe's career as an athlete at Athens in 1982 fortunately failed to damage mine almost before it had started!

However, something happened during my spell in hospital that was to change the course of the band. Obviously I had to miss our regular Friday gig at the London Jazz Centre in Greek Street on 4 June, because I'd only been admitted to hospital the day before. As it turned out that was the day that a young Irish singer came looking for us in London. Her name was Ottilie Patterson. She was half Latvian and half Irish, and she loved the blues. She sang and played the piano, with a particular fondness for boogie woogie. She had grown up in Northern Ireland, and while she was at college training to be an art teacher she had met a guy there who was a serious jazz enthusiast, and who had played jazz and blues records to her and the other students. She had heard the one and only album we made with Ken Colyer, and she thought to herself, "That sounds good, I must go to London and find them." At the end of her summer term, she did exactly that, but of course we had just split up with Ken.

The day that Ottilie showed up in London looking for us she didn't know where we'd be playing, but she did know about the 100 Club in Oxford Street, where it turned out that the Humphrey Lyttelton band was working that night. She went down there and tried (in vain, naturally) to convince Humph to let her sit in. Knowing how diplomatic Humph could be in such situations, I think he saw a way out in the form of the singer Beryl Bryden, who was there in the audience. He suggested to Ottilie that Beryl would know where she could go to sit in. So a little later that evening, Beryl showed her the Greek Street place, where she found my band playing without me. They did not allow anyone they did not know to sit in either, but at the end of the evening as they began packing up instruments, the pianist Johnny Parker, who had been playing with them for part of the evening in my absence, carried on doing a little solo after the session. So Ottilie got up on the stage and asked him to play 'Careless Love'. He agreed, started the tune, and then she began singing. Just like a scene from the movies, the band heard her, stopped packing up and joined in! I guess the next time she showed up might well have been Monday 7 June when I was still at St George's, but I know for sure that she reappeared when I was back in the line-up on Friday the 11th.

She was very, very good, and we offered her the chance to sing with us regularly, which she did for the next few weeks over the summer. But at the end of her vacation, she had to go back to Northern Ireland because one of the conditions of her government grant for the tuition fees to study art was that she'd teach for a couple of years after qualifying, so that the money invested in her training would not be wasted. So we thought that would be it, and apart from the odd gig in the holidays she would be back in Belfast and unable to sing with us again.

Just before Ottilie went back to Ulster, in August 1954, I got married to Naida Laine. She was a dancer whom I'd first met in 1949, around the time she was working with the West Indian bandleader Boscoe Holder, but we'd lost track of each other for a while. Then we met up again in 1953 while Ken Colyer was playing with the band. At that time, Naida was appearing in a show called *Hot From Harlem*, which I first saw at the Metropolitan in Edgware Road, and then I went to see it again after it transferred to Collins' Music Hall in Islington. The pay sheets from the show's time there survive, including the details of what everyone was earning. That list is also a reminder that one of the main acts in the revue was Shirley Bassey. The show also had an excellent Fats Waller-style pianist and singer called Bertie Jarrett. Looking back on it, I think Naida was probably keen to see her name up in lights before I achieved comparable success in my own bandleading career.

The report of our wedding in *Jet* magazine rather inaccurately described me as the "white bandleader . . . who heads the Ken Collyer Orchestra". The same report, by a freelance called Billy Kaye, described the reception as taking place at my mother's "swank home", whereas in reality it took place in my bedsit in Bayswater, which then became our home. The guests were the members of the band, plus Beryl Bryden. Naida's father was Ghanaian, and there was some press interest in the fact that my wife was black. Indeed, Naida said to one of the reporters who covered the wedding: "We coloured people sometimes carry a chip about prejudice, when there's no cause. You've all taken me to your hearts as easily as though I'd just come back sunburnt from a vacation!"

Meanwhile, when Ottilie arrived back in Northern Ireland, she found there was no full-time job for her. So after a period of part-time work she just quit, came back to London and joined us. She formally became a member of the band on 1 January 1955. Within a very short time I had fallen for her, and my marriage to Naida came to an end. Although we split up quickly, our divorce did not come through until 1959, and so I was not free to marry Ottilie until 1960. We lived for a while in Bayswater; in fact Ottilie had a flat in the same street where Naida and I had lived; and then in Maida Vale. There we had a flat in a building that belonged to the family trust of Desmond Kayton. He was a partner with Harold Pendleton and me in a small printing company in the City, and later he got involved with the Marquee Club. Eventually, after we were married, Ottilie and I bought a house in Hampstead Garden Suburb in 1962.

My sister Audrey got married around the time I first met Ottilie. She married a man a little older than me, who had also been at King Alfred School, but unfortunately it didn't last very long and they separated. She ended up getting into the music business and worked for many years with Derek Block, who was an agent-cum-promoter, who did tours for people including the Everly Brothers. She worked for him for over twenty years, and subsequently remarried. Her second husband, Godfrey, was a very nice and humorous fellow. In later life, she worked for our management office for several years, looking after the British end of the business for our Dutch agent Wim Wigt.

Ottilie joined the band at the beginning of 1955, and we had our first trip to Ireland soon afterwards. By the time we went, Jim Bray had just left the band. In fact, he went to join Humphrey Lyttelton and did a straight swap with Mickey Ashman (who had played with my previous band). Mickey left Humph to join me. In retrospect Humph and I must have been like two football managers, trying to arrange a player transfer without letting on to the other!

Our tour was to take in Ireland in general, although initially we played in Northern Ireland. It was lovely to get over there and see it. My mother's family came originally from County Monaghan, but they left during the famine in 1848. The family was part of a Protestant minority, and the area they lived in was called Tydavnet, which in the early nineteenth century had two large Presbyterian churches. They would both be full every week. Now there's just one church.

Bringing the band to Ireland for the first time was very interesting. The audiences were marvellous. They were a bit wild at times, and they'd drink a lot. I was met off the boat by Gerry McQueen, who was a well-established 78 rpm disc collector. He was not exactly Ireland's Brian Rust, but certainly getting on that way. He was very knowledgeable, and had a big collection of records. He specialised in getting youngsters to come and hear the records, and then giving them blindfold tests on what they'd heard. So through him a lot of people really learned about what they were hearing. Consequently, Gerry was a very important person for jazz in Northern Ireland.

He arrived at the port on a motorbike, so I rode pillion on his Norton all the way to his house. It was raining, and we had to ride over tramlines. So it made for a very memorable arrival, although there was no question of falling off, because Gerry was a very good rider. He had rebuilt the Norton himself, in the house. His mother, who was very old, didn't seem to mind too much.

After we played a few concerts around the North, we went on to do some dates in Southern Ireland. We were booked by Phil Solomon, who was known at the time as Phil Raymond. He later had a major interest in the pirate station Radio Caroline when it was starting out, but he began life as an agent and promoter. His first big success was with the Bachelors, whom he effectively owned. Through his father, who was a major shareholder in the company, the Solomon family had the distributorship for Decca records in the whole of Ireland. There were two sons – Mervyn had a record shop in Belfast, whereas Phil was the entrepreneur. His catchphrase was, "You can't fiddle me, I'm the biggest fiddler in Ireland."

In 1955 the South was very different from anything we'd experienced. Now it's more like a northern European country, and that's not just because of the currency, it's very European in many other ways, too. But it was quite different then. Despite what was to happen later, there was no real violence going on in 1955. There was certainly a lot of very strong thought, but it was not translated into action at that point, so we happily went down there. The music scene in Eire at that time was characterised by giant dance halls, which looked like airship hangars, right out in the country. People would cycle thirty miles to go to a dance. These halls were where the showbands played, and Phil Raymond was putting on showbands all the time. The trick was to hire a cheap Ceilidh band in Glasgow, take it to Ireland, pay them thirty pounds a night and earn five hundred.

The biggest venue we played, right in the middle of Ireland, was a place called Rosscommon. Ottilie, being a Northerner, had been to the South, but interestingly in those days, Southerners almost never came to the North. They knew it was there, but the majority of them didn't know much about it. Meanwhile plenty of Northerners used to go on holiday to the South. They liked it, because it was interesting and different.

The one thing – from a concert point of view – that was most different was that at the end of a show we had to play the Irish national anthem. When we arrived, we didn't even know there was one, and nor did Ottilie, despite her previous visits. On our first concert, there was a house band who went on before us, and they kindly wrote it out for us. It's called 'A Soldier's Song'. By the end of the gig, some of our band had partaken quite liberally of the refreshments on offer, and were pretty drunk. I think Pat – who was not in a great state – and myself and Mickey Ashman played it. All we had written out was the tune, which is very long. We dutifully played all the way through it, and the audience applauded. After we'd done this, a member of the local band tipped us off that what all the Irish bands do is just play the final four bars! But I suppose by playing the entire thing we earned some sort of acceptance. After that, wherever we played, we knew what to do.

Some of the showbands were very good musicians. One of them was just as effective a Dixieland band as Harry Gold's Pieces of Eight was in London at the time, playing that repertoire, and plenty of dance band stuff too, but playing it all very well. This was the band called the Clipper Carltons, and it was so popular that if someone put on a dance and nobody came, they'd just say "Oh, the Clipper Carltons are playing up the road." These big showbands always did enormously good business. With indigenous Irish music being so strong, and such a live tradition, jazz had never taken hold in the South of Ireland. It had also been frowned on by the authorities in the 1920s and 1930s. Consequently, people just weren't aware of jazz outside Dublin. In the city, which had a couple of jazz clubs, there were some quite good musicians, such as the Ó Lochlainn brothers, Ruan and Dara, but they were very much the exception.

When we returned to the North, we met Ottilie's parents. They were very nice people, both born in the 1890s. Ottilie's father had been an army driver, known during his service career as "Mad Paddy", even though technically speaking the term "Paddy" was usually applied to people from the Southern part of the country. In World War One he had been in Gallipoli and had seen action on the Eastern front. He met Ottilie's mother in Odessa, in what was then South Russia but is now the Ukraine, because he was in the British Expeditionary Force that stayed behind after the end of the First World War to fight the Bolsheviks. These troops actually met with quite a bit of success and were doing well at the time Ottilie's parents met. But ultimately the effort came to very little because President Wilson decided the United States should avoid the conflict. This was perhaps not great news for the White Russians and the Cossacks.

However, although Ottilie's parents met in Odessa, her mother Julie actually came from Latvia on the Baltic. She had trained as a nurse and her first job away from home was in St Petersburg – which became Leningrad. She was working in a hospital there in 1917 and she told me how she remembered walking through the streets there during the October Revolution. I found this incredible, to meet someone who had actually experienced that. I talked to her about it for a long time. Her first comment was that prior to the revolution it was indeed true that the people had been treated very badly by the Tsarist regime, but "they shouldn't have killed all those lovely children", by which she meant all of Tsar Nicholas II's family. She seemed very sympathetic to them.

I asked her if it had been dangerous in Leningrad, and she said, "Yes, there were snipers on top of all the buildings. The city had big wide streets, but during the revolution, when you were going out to work, or trying to buy food, you had to walk close to one side of the street, hugging the walls, because then only the snipers on the other side could see you, and you increased your chances of survival by fifty percent, because the ones on your own side could not see straight down."

She decided she had to leave. Why she chose to go down to the south of Russia, I don't know, but that's where she went, rather like the plot of *Doctor Zhivago*. When she arrived at Odessa, she got a job working for a Belorussian family, in fact for the wife of an officer in the White Russian army. He was fighting against the Bolsheviks. While Julie was working there, she met Joe Patterson. The British Army was fighting on the same side as her employer and Joe was a bright young bloke, up for anything. I think he "borrowed" blankets and other things from the army stores and gave them to her. This was very helpful because as that war went on, she and her family had nothing at all. When they met, she spoke nothing but Russian and Latvian and he spoke only English, with a strong Northern Irish accent. But somehow they got on. I asked her how they'd ended up getting married and she said, "He was very kind to me." Their wedding was in Constantinople and then they came back to Northern Ireland.

In due course she picked up English, or at any rate Latvian English. It may be because Latvian, or Lettish, is a totally phonetic language, but it isn't particularly compatible with English. At one point, Ottilie tried to learn Latvian, and I'd ask her mother, "How do you spell that?" And she'd say, "I don't know!" Latvians don't really have to learn to spell because the language is based on consistent sounds, and that's it. There are no exceptions in Latvian, and for this reason Ottilie's mother found English odd. Words that seemed to her not to fit phonetic patterns would get changed or confused with one another, and one malapropism I remember was that "Delphiniums" became "Philadelphians". She'd often get muddled like that.

Ottilie started singing in church when she was young, but her first real musical talent was as a pianist. She studied the piano as a child, and in her teens she was in Carroll Levis's "Discoveries" talent contest, playing 'Boogie Woogie Bugle Boy of Company B'. It took place in a theatre somewhere in Northern Ireland and she won her heat. In fact she was a very, very good pianist. I remember when the band first played in Vienna, we worked for the Viennese Musical Youth Guild in the Konzerthaus, which is a lovely place. The concert went really well, but the thing I most remember is that in the dressing room which Ottilie and I shared, there was a Steinway. So she sat down at this piano because sometimes before a concert she would play Chopin to herself to relax and focus her mind. Then and there, the promoter offered her a concert playing Chopin. She didn't take up the offer because we had a busy work schedule with the band and she was also too nervous to play classical piano music in public. She didn't believe she was good enough, which was, I suppose, rather typical of her. I wasn't going to make a fuss about that – I put my encouragement into her singing – but the man was quite serious about it. She played with great feeling, and the art of Chopin is about balancing the technical demands of the music with the feeling it contains. Of course, her great talent as a blues singer was to convey the deep feeling of the music.

Her parents, Joseph and Julie, lived in Newtownards by the time we made our visit to them in 1955. Ottilie had been born in the town of Comber, which is about ten miles or so from there. During the time they lived there, the then Prime Minister of Northern Ireland, John Millar Andrews, also lived in the town and Joe had been his chauffeur. The Prime Minister's brother Thomas Andrews was perhaps more famous, as he was known as "the man who made the *Titanic*", having been managing director of the Harland and Wolff shipyard that built her. He went down with the ship. Across the street from the Pattersons' former house stood the Andrews Memorial Hall, because John Millar Andrews had been a great patron of the local Congregational church, and built this meeting house.

The Pattersons' house in Newtownards was on the route of the Tourist Trophy Race, the Ulster TT, that ran in Northern Ireland until World War Two. I thought it must have been pretty dangerous, having the route going right past the house like that, as the cars were always flying off the road into ditches and so on. Ironically, Joe Patterson himself had become a professional driver without ever really learning to drive. When he joined up, he told the army he could drive, and I suppose cars were so primitive then that it wasn't too difficult, but he got his job as an army driver without ever having driven a car, and he got away with it.

In the sixties they lived with us for a while in Hampstead Garden Suburb, and I remember that although Joe was a staunch Northern Irish Protestant, he used to go off once a week to an Irish pub in Camden Town, where he would drink with all the IRA supporters. He did this quite happily because they were all happy being Irish together, except when the subjects of politics or religion came up.

Overall, I think we played in Ireland several times for Phil Raymond. He was the only person who bothered to arrange tours for British bands. We played a lot in Belfast, and we were very successful there. But then we were becoming very successful everywhere.

It got to the point in 1955 when it seemed as if we couldn't do any wrong. I suppose deep down we were too aware of the realities of the business entirely to believe this, but that year and for some years afterwards, you didn't ask yourself, "Is there a good crowd here?" Because there always was. Everywhere. It's a dangerous thing in a way because you do get accustomed to it. In 1954, every jazz club we played in, you couldn't get in after seven o'clock because it'd be full. Then we started doing concerts and they were full. For a while we couldn't help believing that they'd always be full.

I think this was at least partly due to the radio. We had our own series, but we appeared on lots of general programmes as well, such as *Band Parade*, and *Trad Tavern*, so we were being heard an awful lot. There was the opportunity for it then. I suppose we were in some respects the pop music of the day – although that's not exactly true because it was also the era of Tommy Steele and similar popular singers. But we were certainly a major part of the pop music of the time. If there was a problem, it was that all the shows on which we appeared were on the Light Programme – what is now BBC Radio 2 – and we were playing music that would have gone down very well with the Home Service (Radio 4) audience. But they didn't have us on the Home Service at all. By the beginning of the 1960s, Radio 2 would usually book Kenny Ball and not us. By then I think there was a misconception that we were too serious. I mean we were serious about playing, but what we played, and how we played it, wasn't serious at all.

For most of our radio shows in the fifties we just played our regular concert repertoire. Maybe we'd switch round and play a different New Orleans march or rag, but fundamentally we did the music that we were playing on the road. If there's only six tunes or so in a broadcast, that's never a particular problem. But we did have a problem with the more general shows, when we'd just do one or two numbers, which was that the producers or presenters would always ask for the same tunes. They'd always want 'When The Saints Go Marching In', and I'd usually say "No". I think I got a reputation for being very uncooperative, because I wanted them to broadcast the music that we wanted to play and with which we were being successful. But many of the producers didn't take me seriously, apart from Jimmy Grant, who produced a lot of the specialist jazz programmes. He had perfect pitch below middle C, so he was always acutely aware if the bass was not properly in tune, and he cared about making the music sound right. He was the producer of *Jazz Club*, which usually had two bands on in a one-hour slot. The idea was that the show would be half modern jazz and half Dixieland or traditional jazz.

I said I wouldn't do it. I wanted the whole hour, and that's when we started introducing guest artists, because it gave us the whole broadcast. I thought this was better for us as a band, because we got the full hour of exposure and we weren't competing with something very different stylistically. It occasionally gave us the chance to do something really different, like the time we put together a New Orleans brass band, which involved Barry Martyn and members of his group teaming up with us.

Thinking about the 1950s and the kind of business we were doing, it's clear to me now that we were in a fantastic situation then. In due course, we were offered the maximum size of halls to play in. We needed bigger ones, but there weren't any at the time. We needed football stadiums, which is what they do now, of course, but in those days there weren't suitable sound systems. At least, not for live music. Recordings were easier, and our record of 'When The Saints Go Marching In', with Ottilie singing, was played every week for several years before every match at Anfield. They had stadium sound equipment for such things and for commentary, but not suitable microphones and stage amplification for live music. They probably could have done it, but nobody had thought of it. If Simon Cowell had been around at that time, he'd have insisted on it, somebody would have done it, and it would have worked! And we'd all have become stupidly rich!

Between 1995 and 2000 I did a lot of gigs as a guest with Van Morrison. He's an old friend, his love of the music is totally genuine, and he has a great understanding and knowledge of it as well. In some ways he was rather like Lonnie. Lonnie knew everything about the folk music and blues that he was singing, but he was a bit difficult to deal with because of his own particular attitude to what he had to do. Van's a bit like that. He knows what he wants to do, and he goes out and does it. I'd go along and join in.

My sight-reading is pretty poor for jazz timing because, traditionally, it's written down as if it wasn't jazz. So you look at something that's written down straight, and know that you aren't supposed to play it as it's written down at all. Owing to my classical training, I can't do that. It's hell.

Van's band had been together for a long time. One or two well-known people such as Georgie Fame were in it and out of it again briefly, but when I was guesting he had Matt Holland on trumpet and Martin Winning on sax. They were both very good, but then trumpets and saxophones read C and play B flat – all their parts are transposed – whereas a trombone reads and plays C, with no transposing. So even if you can handle the timing, you can't read their parts over their shoulders, because you'd be in the wrong key. Van had never had a regular trombone player, so there wasn't any trombone music at all. Consequently I just used to make something up. I'd get the odd solo, and the audience always liked it.

Van likes to talk about older blues and jazz and so forth, and as nobody in his band was particularly interested in that, he and I would sit and chat for a long time after gigs. He enjoyed that very much, and I did too. I reckoned after doing quite a few concerts with him that, in the field he was in, Van had one of the hardest working and most successful bands I'd ever seen. It was a bit like us in the fifties. Wherever we played it was always sold out, sometimes with just three weeks' notice or so.

On one occasion in the late 1990s with Van we played Newcastle City Hall. It's a 3,000-seater old-fashioned town hall, with wooden seats, and we played there over two consecutive nights. Both evenings were sold out and we had a good audience. So I said to Van, "Do you do that every year?"

He said, "Oh I can't do that again, I'll have to wait two or three years."

And I thought, "Hmmm." Because in 1955 alone we had played that same hall five times, all sold out. That is a measure of how absurdly popular the band was. I think the audience we were getting was made up of the kind of people who go to festivals now. They like to think they're going to something quite modern that's not classical music, but at the same time they're not jazz fans as such. Of course in addition to those general listeners, plenty of the audience *was* made up of jazz fans, because a lot of people at the time were listening to jazz. Compared to my own schooldays, by that time in England it seemed that every properly established school had some sort of jazz band in it.

So that's how it was: we were immensely popular and the audiences kept coming. And that lasted until 1961. I think our best achievement was the Liverpool Empire, which – like Newcastle – is a 3,000 seater. We played there on the first Sunday of the New Year for the promoter Lewis Buckley three or four years in succession. The last time was the beginning of January 1961. They didn't do it again the following year – or maybe it was very poorly sold, but I remember 1961 as being the last.

I'm not quite sure of all the reasons why the audience fell away, though Liverpool was a special case because the club scene there with all the beat groups was particularly active. Though even that's not the whole story. The traditional statement you read in the rock and pop media is that the Cavern was a beat club. But it wasn't. It was a jazz club. The main bands were always jazz bands, until that turning point in 1960–61. The Merseysippis, Mick Mulligan, Acker Bilk, they all played there. We could have played there, but we did concerts and we didn't need to. We just didn't play clubs in Liverpool – well, we might have played the Iron Door once, but a lot later. Each time we went there we played in larger and larger theatres until we ended up in the Empire, and we didn't play any other concerts during the rest of the year in Liverpool itself apart from that annual New Year's date at the Empire.

But if we had played at the Cavern, because we were a nationally known jazz band, we'd have been top of the bill, as for example Terry Lightfoot, Acker Bilk, The Saints Jazz Band or the Merseysippis usually were, while the interval bands were – increasingly – the groups: the Beatles, the Mersey Beats and so on. Some, or more accurately, most, of the trad bands did not like the beat groups. They saw them, maybe, as rivals for the money, or thought that they didn't play "proper" music. But most of the jazz bands that played at the Cavern didn't know much about blues, or cared much for it. So they always tended to be very sniffy towards the local rock and roll people.

My band was different, not least because we didn't play there ourselves. In fact after we'd done a concert somewhere in the general area we'd go down there because usually Terry Lightfoot or one of the other bands we knew would be on. We'd go to the bar, where John Lennon, Paul McCartney and the others would be standing. We'd buy drinks for one another, have a chat and were generally friendly. I remember when I finally really met John Lennon for the first time outside a nightclub bar, Ottilie and I were living in Maida Vale, and I went round to see Paul McCartney.

Paul had bought a house in St John's Wood, about 100 yards from Lord's. But the house he bought had previously belonged to Ottilie's doctor. So I'd been there many times before he bought it, and on this occasion when we dropped in to see Paul, John was there. Now most times I had been anywhere near John before that, he was rude. Not to me in particular – he was rude to everybody. He was just not a person who went out of his way to be friendly. But this time he was friendly immediately. He'd just teamed up with Yoko Ono. So in my book that's one large plus point for Yoko. She has been given a bad reputation by some sections of the press, but I think they made no effort to like her or understand her. She really was nice. And she helped him to be nice.

So I said to him, "John, why is it you've said in so many places that your fans don't like jazz?"

And he said, "Oh, that didn't mean you! They didn't mean your band."

So I said, "Well could you tell some of your journalist friends to say that?" Because everywhere we went at that time it was "Oh, the Beatles don't like jazz . . ." So their fans decided they didn't like jazz, whereas, actually, the Beatles couldn't care a damn. Paul McCartney, in fact, has a dance band heritage, George didn't dislike anything, and Ringo didn't care. John was the serious one.

Nevertheless, I'm sure that in the early days at the Cavern, when they couldn't play more than two or three chords, they were getting sneered at by the jazz musicians who played there. But we were not like those other jazz musicians. Once Ottilie was singing with us full time from January 1955, we became very different from other traditional bands because we started to play the blues regularly. Accompanying a singer is something that all too many jazz musicians are terrible at. Most of them don't think it's very important, and don't listen to them sympathetically. But we did, because having found somebody to sing the blues properly, we learned how to play it.

3 Really the Blues

When it came to learning the blues, we were extremely lucky. Not long after we met Ottilie, but before she came to join us permanently, we had our first opportunity to play with a genuine American bluesman, Big Bill Broonzy. We did several concerts with him over a three-week period in July 1954. Our London appearances with Bill included a set at 100 Oxford Street and also one out at George Webb's club in Woolwich.

Big Bill had been brought to Europe some time before by Yanick Bruynoghe and some other Belgian jazz fans, who had contacted him in America. They flew him over to Europe and the first time I saw him, he was here in England playing in a big concert hall with Mahalia Jackson, the pianist Mildred Falls, and an English jazz band, which opened the show. I went along and I could see that Big Bill was really quite upset. He thought it was rather naughty to put him on the same bill as the wonderful sanctified gospel singer Mahalia Jackson. He actually believed it was insulting to her and that he shouldn't have been included on the programme with her. He was so worried that I remember he said, "I hadn't better say anything too risqué."

The unusual thing about this concern was that actually Bill sang a few spirituals while doing his normal performances, quite a lot of them, in fact. Traditionally speaking, in America, a blues show wasn't the place to sing spirituals. And the blues were not allowed in church. It was profane music. To me, blues or spirituals, you can't say what's more important, one or the other.

When he got together with us, Bill loved playing with the band. But one of my main memories is of him playing on his own. He seemed to enjoy himself most when he stood out front with his guitar, just singing and playing solo. He might sing 'I'm Looking Over a Four Leaf Clover' or 'Won't You Please Come Home Bill Bailey'. He loved singing 'When Did You Leave Heaven?' and other ballads. We asked him, "What do you want to do?" And he named all those tunes. He was in the spotlight for forty minutes and during that time he would do a blues or two. He'd also sing some pop tunes, but he generally did those with the full band, because in the 1940s he'd made records for Columbia with horns, saxes and so on. He was used to having horns around, and he really liked having the band playing with him.

One thing we'd kept going when we split from Ken Colyer was the idea of playing several skiffle tunes in an evening. Lonnie had a friend who played guitar called Dickie Bishop. He called himself "Cisco" Bishop after Woody Guthrie's colleague Cisco Houston, and he joined us for the skiffle sets. This was another way we accompanied Big Bill, with Lonnie and Dickie on guitars, myself on bass and Ron on drums. It was an absolutely wonderful sound. It's a shame I couldn't persuade our record company to record Bill with this backing. Denis Preston, our record producer, about whom more later, insisted on recording Big Bill with Kenny Graham, Phil Seamen, and other musicians who really couldn't play that type of music at all. I think we could have had hit after hit with Bill singing with the skiffle group, and if that had happened he might well have made enough money to deal with his cancer more effectively. "Big Bill needs proper musicians," Denis told me. But the end results didn't really relate to jazz or blues, indeed they were rather soulless, because there was no feeling in those records for Bill's kind of music.

We benefited enormously from the experience of working with Big Bill. Following that first tour in 1954, we played with him again in '56, when he returned with Brother John Sellers, the former gospel singer who had begun to add blues to his repertoire around that time. We wanted a chance to work with real blues people, people whose music this was. They can teach you without really trying because they play things *right*, the way it's supposed to be done. If you play things wrongly, it sticks out like a sore thumb. You can feel it immediately. On those tours we played somewhere in the country almost every day. In 1956 when Big Bill came back with John Sellers, we did twenty concerts in three weeks. We travelled a lot, but as we've done more or less throughout the entire life of the band, we got in our various cars and set off, taking our guest musicians with us in one of the cars.

By 1956, we almost always drove by car to every gig, in the UK or in Europe, and have carried on doing so since. It was convenient, and, strange to say, it is cheaper than any other way of travelling. You might think it better to do it all in one bus, but buses do about three miles to the gallon. My band, across two or three vehicles together, was collectively doing better than five miles to the gallon. And we hadn't all got to leave together at the same time.

With Ken, and in the very first days of my band, we travelled together in whatever ancient car Jim Bray was driving, until we decided on a bandwagon. But we soon gave up on that after owning a Bedford Dormobile, which we bought a short while after we split from Ken. I suppose we might have had it for around a year at most. It was a sort of small bus with fold-down seats all the way round, because those "temporary" seats meant you avoided purchase tax, and saved a lot on the price of the vehicle. After that we briefly had one of the early Transit vans. But when we got rid of that, I decided we'd travel in separate cars, and we bought two Peugeot 403 estates. It worked so well that we've never looked back, and it can be quite an enjoyable way to get about.

I remember at the time of the Suez crisis in 1956 we did make an exception, because petrol was in such short supply. We rented a Volkswagen bus, because when you rented a vehicle it came with a full tank of petrol. But that was pretty much the only exception. Even then we soon went back to the cars when one of our fans – a police officer in the West End who used to come to the 100 Club – somehow got us some petrol coupons. Where did he get them? I didn't ask!

By the late 1950s our two estate cars carried the registration numbers CB20 and CB21, and they were regularly driven by Dick Smith, who was by then our bassist, and Pat Halcox. I had CB23 on my Lotus Elite which I drove the rest of the time. In those days you got a personalised number from a local vehicle registration office. If the original number had been returned and was out of use because the original car had been scrapped, you did not have to pay a transfer fee, only the cost of the clerical search to establish that the number was available. I think each of these numbers, which came from Blackpool, cost around five pounds for the search. When I eventually sold them, they fetched well into the thousands.

We got on really well with Big Bill, although there was one unpleasant incident in Nottingham, after we'd played a very nice gig in the local jazz club there. It was a huge hall that held somewhere close to a thousand people and the club ran every Thursday. In those days, driving back to London from Nottingham after a gig was not really practical because the motorway network was still in its infancy. So we would stay in a hotel after the concert. We went to our usual hotel after playing and the night porter said, "We don't have black people here." So we just turned round and walked out – all of us. We eventually found another hotel, and we asked the clerk, "Do you rent rooms to coloured people?" He said, "We rent rooms to people with money. Do you have money?"

I said, "Yes."

"Then you can have the rooms," he said.

Bill took it in his stride. With his lifetime of experience, he could spot a redneck at thirty paces. He was a lovely man, no question about it. And after the very positive experience of playing regularly with him, we wanted to have the opportunity to play with more American blues artists. And the band's success was beginning to make this a real possibility.

After our tour with Bill, on the back of our second Decca record, the return to Denmark and the exposure we got at the Royal Festival Hall and other concerts, the band began to do really well. We also appeared in a short film in 1955 called *Momma Don't Allow*. Within a year of me taking over the leadership, the British press, always keen to display its genius for stupid nicknames, had come up with "trad" as an abbreviation for traditional jazz. During that first year, we became the biggest live attraction in show business in Britain. The first two years that we were going, none of the other players in popular music really noticed what was happening. You would think that someone might try and copy our band, but no, it took two years for anyone to do that really successfully. So we had the scene to ourselves for those two years. Part of our success was because by then there was a strong network of jazz clubs across the country and if you were prepared to travel there were plenty of places to play. We also played the blues clubs. We gradually established ourselves without realising it and before long we were filling every large concert hall in the country.

One big difference between Britain and America, and possibly part of the reason why traditional jazz became so popular, was because of the licensing laws. Although it was illegal in the UK to sell alcoholic drinks to people under eighteen, it was quite legal for sixteen year olds to be on licensed premises so long as they did not drink. So if people decided to have a jazz club somewhere, in the function room or dance hall attached to a pub, kids over sixteen could be there. They had somewhere to go. As a result, traditional jazz struck a chord with the British public. By contrast, in the USA, at that time nobody under twenty-one could even enter a place where drink was sold.

Another reason for our success was a change in record company. Although we did our first LP for Decca and then the company recorded two of our concerts at the Royal Festival Hall, we were never under contract to them on anything other than a record-by-record basis. My friend Hugh Mendl, who had become an in-house producer, was still keen to record us, but his boss, Frank Lee, was only prepared to offer a flat fee of £35 per record for the whole band. When Hugh protested that I might not agree to that, Sir Edward Lewis, the chairman of Decca, said, "Give the boy a radiogram!" Hugh told him that as a well-established record collector in my own right, I might well already have one! Because of this attitude, I decided to walk away from Decca.

I had stayed in touch with Denis Preston, who had presented the first BBC broadcast we did with the Colyer band. By this time, he was working with Lyn Dutton who had become our agent. Denis was already an established independent record producer, and he was a pioneer of the way records are produced now, with a production firm handling everything, and then selling a finished product to the record company. In those days that was highly unusual, because most firms employed in-house producers. Denis called his business "Record Supervision". He had produced the last English records of George Shearing, when George came back briefly to Britain in the late 1940s before he settled full time in America. Denis had also recorded and promoted the hit record 'Cricket, Lovely Cricket', a calypso-style song by Lord Beginner about Messrs. Ramadhin and Valentine, the stars of the West Indian team, who beat England in a home test in 1950. Another of his West Indian record successes was 'Don't Touch Me Tomato' by Marie Bryant.

Denis was sure we were going to make money, and so I signed a contract with him to produce our records. This was good timing because Denis had got word that Pye radio were going to diversify, and buy a small record company called Nixa. So he did a deal with Pye and set up a series called "Jazz Today" on the Nixa imprint. We did a couple more recordings for Decca with Ottilie, of Bessie Smith songs, and after that we recorded exclusively for Pye. That's not to say that our Decca records did not continue to sell well, but the company was very slow to issue and promote them. Our July 1954 album was not released until the end of the year. And then, as a result of dealer requests for a track from the album to be put out on its own, Lonnie's skiffle version of 'Rock Island Line', which we had also recorded that July, with 'John Henry' on the other side, was finally released as a single by Decca almost a year later in 1955. It earned a gold disc, and it also made the top ten in America. The only positive thing about that long delay is that we probably sold a lot more copies of the album than we would otherwise have done because people wanted to hear 'Rock Island Line' before the single became available. We had only been paid a session fee for the record, but the high volume of sales immeasurably helped the band.

It did have one unintended consequence, which was that it created enormous demand for Lonnie. We shared the same agent, Lyn Dutton, and he discovered very rapidly that people wanted to start booking Lonnie on his own for variety shows. Because Lonnie had been very involved in the band and in playing New Orleans jazz, I perhaps didn't realise at the time just how caught up in the world of vaudeville he was. From what he told me later, out of everything he did in his career, the recordings he made with Max Miller were the ones he was most proud of. They were full of lines like "Hello Max, d'you know, last night I had a nightmare?" And Max would reply, "I know, I saw you with her!"

Lonnie was very good at doing these comic set-piece gags on stage. He began to feel that although his records were commercially very successful, in our concerts he only got a small amount of time to sing his skiffle songs, and the rest of the evening he was playing in the band. I remember trying to persuade him that skiffle was a fad, and (prophetically as it turned out, given our later success with 'Petite Fleur' and Acker Bilk's 'Stranger on the Shore') I suggested that the next big thing in five years' time might be clarinet solos. But he was not to be moved, and decided to leave the band and try his hand at going solo and playing variety shows. He officially left in February 1956, but I think the last gig he actually played with us as a member of the band was in March 1956 at the Dudley Hippodrome, where the management had insisted months beforehand when they signed their contract with us that he would appear.

There was really no way that Lonnie would have stayed on much longer than he did as a member of the band; it was already obvious before he quit that he had become a big name and was going to become an even bigger name. Before he left, we had tended to do a group of skiffle numbers at the end of the first half, and Ottilie's songs would be scattered throughout the rest of the programme. She didn't really start doing a dedicated blues set of two or three numbers on her own until after Lonnie had gone. Yet, from the moment she joined, she had always sung the final part of each concert, ending with 'When The Saints Go Marching In' or something similar. In fact by 1957 or '58 we'd changed the ending of our shows to 'I've Got My Mojo Working', or another Muddy Waters number written by Willie Dixon called 'Don't Go No Further'. Otherwise known as 'Come On Home To Me', that song was a very nice piece of poetic writing, and ideal for Ottilie to sing. Willie Dixon wrote good songs that made lots of sense. We arrived at that repertoire a long time before most of the blues revival groups.

We didn't give up on the skiffle just because Lonnie had left the band. Early in 1956, an American bloke walked into the 100 Club who looked a bit like Lonnie, even wearing similar clothes to those Lonnie had been wearing when he left, and he was carrying a guitar. His name was Johnny Duncan. He'd come to Britain from Tennessee, and had arrived in Europe while doing his military service. He'd married an English girl and they were living in East Anglia, near where he'd been stationed. He was a bluegrass player, and a fine guitarist, with a few tricks as well. He could play a big, deep, white top Martin guitar behind the back of his head! He was really a hillbilly player, but we thought we'd better try him in the skiffle group, and once we had heard how good he was we took him on. I met him on a Monday night at the 100 Club, as I said, and he turned up two days later at the White Hart in Southall where we were playing. So really he just slid seamlessly into Lonnie's place. The skiffle group became him, Dickie, me and Ron, and with that line-up we had a series on Radio Luxembourg called *Chris Barber's Skiffle Group* in 1956. Johnny and Dickie shared the singing. As well as his trick of holding the instrument behind his head, Johnny actually played guitar very nicely and he recorded a couple of sides with Ottilie on the piano and me on the bass, during a Royal Festival Hall concert that same year.

Before that, Dickie Bishop had taken over the banjo job in the band when Lonnie left (despite the fact he hated the instrument). After all, he knew all the numbers because he'd been sitting there right through our sets for years, waiting to do his skiffle pieces. He walked out towards the end of 1956. We were playing in Staveley in Derbyshire, a mining village, and it was the first time I'd ever seen an actual fight in a dance hall as two groups of men took each other on. The promoter came over and said, "Who ordered this dance?" meaning "Why aren't you playing a quickstep?" That would have been lively and stopped the altercation, but we were doing a slow number and tempers flared. Next morning we were on Chesterfield station, waiting for our train to Manchester for the gig that night, and Dickie went the other way, back to London. There was a phone box on the platform, so I ran over before our train arrived and called Eddie Smith. He said "Okay!", hopped on a train up north, and joined the band that night at the Free Trade Hall. I'd met Eddie around various places in London, he'd played with Mike Daniels, and he was into most of the things that we liked musically. So I knew he'd fit well into the band.

Dickie, by the way, had his moment of fame in 1999 when a song he wrote with Bob Watson for the Vipers skiffle group just after he left us, 'No Other Baby', was recorded by Paul McCartney on his album *Run Devil Run*.

Early in 1957 we finally gave up on skiffle, and focused each concert on the band's music and a blues slot for Ottilie. Consequently, Johnny Duncan left and set up his own band, the Blue Grass Boys, which included a few very well-known jazz musicians, Denny Wright on guitar, Lennie Hastings on drums and Jack Fallon on bass. Denis Preston produced his records, and in June 1957 he made Johnny's one and only hit, 'Last Train To San Fernando', which reached number two in the charts.

We stayed with Denis Preston ourselves for some time, first recording for Pye and later transferring to Columbia, which was then part of EMI. At the time, Mike Daniels and Humph were being produced by Denis for EMI's other imprint, Parlophone. My main criticism of Parlophone was that their recording techniques made all the bands sound the same. I think our records sounded a bit more individual because at least to start with they were engineered differently. We made the first records at IBC studios in Portland Place, and they were engineered by Joe Meek. Indeed Joe travelled with us to Berlin to record our concert there for Denis in May 1959. In due course we moved to the studio that Denis built, Lansdowne, near Holland Park. It had been designed by the Scottish jazz clarinetist, Sandy Brown, who was also a professional acoustic engineer. Despite being a fine jazz musician, Sandy had made the studio impossible to play in. The acoustics were so dry that we could not hear one another properly. And eventually, when we left Denis, it was at least partly owing to the difficulty of recording in that studio because, naturally, he wanted to make all his own records on the premises.

The other main reason that we parted company was that Denis became quite cynical about the business. If I wanted to spend more than half an hour recording a track, he'd have none of it. He'd say, "Come on Chris, let's face it, in thirty years' time, we'll both be sitting back on the sofa with a glass of brandy, playing Duke Ellington records. So don't worry too much about this piece. Just play what's going down well in the clubs." And that was his philosophy. But it didn't square with the level of attention we were giving to our live shows.

In 1956, we had started playing Sunday concerts in big halls across the country, and from the following year, we largely stopped playing the smaller jazz clubs and were able to focus on playing in theatres and concert halls. This was the unintended consequence of the Lord's Day Observance Society. Under the Lord's Day Observance Act as it stood at the time, it was illegal to wear costume on stage on a Sunday. You couldn't have a play presented on a Sunday, for example. And nor could you have the variety shows that were a great part of the seaside tradition all round Britain, unless the acts were not wearing their costumes and dressed in ordinary clothes instead. So at many of these seaside theatres, where a new crowd of holidaymakers had turned up on a Saturday, they decided to put on concerts to keep the new arrivals entertained on a Sunday.

Even then there were rules. Harry Gold's Pieces of Eight, for example, used to wear tartan dinner jackets. That counted as a costume, and so they were not permitted to play Sunday concerts. But we wore lounge suits and we began to be offered plenty of bookings at those seaside theatres. The instinctive thing with the band, at that time, was to spread out and fill a big stage with six people. It was an amazing effect. Plenty of the beat groups had their rhythm section grouped centrally on stage and just the singer moved about. But we spread the whole band out across the stage and the front line in particular could move about freely as we played, keeping a bit of variety going. It was perfect for concerts and people loved it.

The natural consequence of playing Sunday concerts in seaside resorts during the summer season was that we began to get offers to play in theatres all over the rest of the country during the winter. We jumped at this opportunity to get out of the clubs. Physically speaking, to play music in the discomfort of a jazz club is very difficult. Plus it's hot, the audience is noisy, they're drinking, and in those days smoking as well. The sound was often terrible and the acoustics rotten. Also, if you've got a glass of beer in your hand, you can't applaud. So despite our popularity in the clubs, a lot of the time it felt as if we had very little reaction.

Obviously you don't go out solely to demand applause but, when we played in the theatres, we got it. Lots of it. However, the main thing was that we could hear each other properly on stage, and we could make a lovely sound. Try that in the 100 Club. It's terrible – totally impossible. The Marquee was nice to play in, later on, but by and large clubs did not give us the same advantages that we had in theatres or concert halls. I mentioned earlier our annual concerts in Liverpool. We got to the Empire by way of some smaller theatres, where we were booked by a local promoter called Albert Kinder. He started us off at the Pavilion Theatre, then we moved to the Playhouse, until by 1958 the only venue big enough to accommodate our following was the Empire. In 1958, 1959 and 1960, all 3,000 seats sold out in an hour. The Empire shows were promoted by Louis Buckley, a small man who drove a large Rover. I remember that when he was sitting in the car you could barely see the top of his head over the steering wheel.

Our experience in Liverpool was typical of what was happening all over the country. Everywhere we went it was the same. An extraordinary number of people came out to see us. But as I said earlier, it's important to remember that we really didn't have any competition. Acker Bilk joined Ken Colyer shortly after we parted company with Ken, but then he went back to Somerset and didn't start his Paramount Jazz Band as a fully professional group until October 1957. Kenny Ball started up in 1958 after a spell with Terry Lightfoot. Humph's band was never fully professional, so he did far less travelling than we did. Alex Welsh and Mick Mulligan weren't really playing the size of venue that we were. So, in effect, from when we started the band until late 1957 or so, we had the field to ourselves and our success was, in some ways, stupefying. At the height of our fame, some promoters were trying to encourage me to do two houses a night in some of the bigger theatres, but I disagreed. I wanted people to come and get a full concert of all our music, not just an hour of the hits.

The other thing I insisted on was to have a day off pretty regularly. Perceived wisdom in the industry was never to turn down a job, because you never knew if it would be offered to you again. But I believed we needed time off so that we could continue to do the best job we could on the music and keep our interest up. I also reckoned that playing a bit less would help keep everything sold out, because it would – in effect – create demand. So by the mid-fifties we were working about five days a week. We graduated from staying in digs to staying in hotels when we travelled.

I remember our first visits to Manchester, when we played at the Bodega Club in 1954, which was on Cross Street more or less under the *Manchester Guardian* building, and opposite the Royal Exchange. It was probably the hottest place I've ever played in. We got £35, for the whole band, to drive up there, stay in digs, and drive back the next day. In those very early days, Jim Bray still had his huge Humber Super Snipe shooting brake with a wooden body that had room for six people in it – just! The sixth seat was in the very back behind the rear seats, but you could smell the exhaust fumes there, so Lonnie tended to buy his own ticket and go up on the train. We all played poker a lot in those days when we travelled, so the three on the rear bench seat would play all the way. But within a couple of years we'd be going to Manchester to play in a theatre, drive there comfortably in separate cars, and stay in a decent hotel.

Each year we also increased the time we spent touring abroad, so that our two weeks in Denmark in 1954 had become twenty-nine weeks abroad by 1959. The real jump in our overseas travelling was in 1958, when we took Sonny Terry and Brownie McGhee with us and played several dates in Germany. I still meet large numbers of German fans who don't remember Sonny and Brownie being with us at all on that first German tour. It was our band that they had been waiting for. Consequently, we were filling big halls there and that first tour in 1958 created a demand for us to return and play some really big venues again in 1959 and 1960. Nevertheless, I should say that, at the time, the audiences absolutely loved Sonny and Brownie, when they got the chance to hear them. But in the longer term, when it came to remembering the impact of their concerts, maybe it was a question of language. Sonny and Brownie's act, being based on blues songs, relied on a knowledge of English. Plus I was limited by what I could say in German. I wanted to try and explain a bit more about the music and didn't just want these to be concerts where people turned up and went away. I wanted them to realise that this was special music and there was something in it of value and interest. For the most part our normal band concerts were instrumental – plus Ottilie's songs of course – but the instrumental sections could communicate in any language. Over the course of the next ten years when we were on tour there, I worked out enough of the language to announce the concerts in German, which helped build a bond with the audiences. But there was no way I could have done that in 1958.

Right after our work with Big Bill, we decided to seize every opportunity both at home and abroad to play with more genuine jazz and blues musicians, and to try to communicate our excitement about that to our audiences.

As Lonnie Donegan found out to his cost when he supported Lonnie Johnson in 1951, the ban on members of the American Federation of Musicians (AFM) playing in Britain that had been introduced by the UK Musicians' Union in the 1930s was still in force. We would really have liked to have real jazz musicians come over from America to play with us, just as Big Bill had done, but they were not allowed to. On top of that, the Musicians' Union in Britain in the 1950s was communist, which didn't help matters when it came to dealing with the United States. I went to see the General Secretary of the Union, who wielded enormous power at the time, almost like the Teamsters in America, and I tried to persuade him to let Louis Armstrong come and work here. "If we can get him to come and play solo with a British band, that would be fantastic! We'll all learn so much about the music, and the public has a great taste for it now. We'll get lots of work out of it, and it'll be good for all of us."

He said, and I kid you not, "Why do you always want an American trumpeter? Why don't you get a Russian trumpeter?"

However, we discovered, quite by chance, as a consequence of Big Bill's visits, that the majority of singers in America, blues or folk singers and so forth, could not join the AFM because they weren't classified as "musicians". They had to join the American Guild of Variety Artists, if, indeed, they belonged to a union at all. The Variety Artists' Federation in Britain had no dispute with its US counterpart. The American Guild did not care a damn about their artists coming over to play here, nor did it prevent them from having work permits. All it required was two per cent of their income as union dues.

Once we knew that, the question was, who else were we going to get? One of our first thoughts was that many of the great blues artists who are still playing might not be accustomed to playing in front of white audiences. This might actually put them off from giving of their best. We did not want to embarrass them, or have them not sure quite what to do, even if all they needed to do was what they normally did to satisfy a black audience in Chicago or New York. But we knew that Sister Rosetta Tharpe had been playing in clubs with mostly white audiences, singing with Lucky Millinder's band and Cab Calloway's Orchestra. So clearly she wouldn't be worried about that. As a result, in 1957 we asked her to come over.

The first day we met her, for a concert at Birmingham Town Hall in late November, she brought in the charts from Lucky Millinder's band, which was a sixteen-piece group. Now collectively we couldn't read music, hardly at all, let alone when the parts are lying on the floor, because we didn't have music stands. So I thought what are we going to do?

I said, "Sister, would you play a number and we'll just join in." And she played 'Every Time I Feel The Spirit'. It was absolutely, mind-bogglingly wonderful. The best, most immediate, unexpected experience ever. She acted as if she'd found a band she'd never heard before, but which she needed to have all her life. You can hear the fire of her performance and the incredible reaction of the audience on the recording of the concert we played with her at the Free Trade Hall in Manchester a few days later on 9 December 1957. One critic wrote, "She combines the rhythmic drive of a dance band vocalist with the fervent appeal of one who sings in prayer". And that just about sums it up; we ended up doing both 'Old Time Religion' and 'When the Saints Go Marching In' twice, before the audience would let us go.

At the start of the tour, there were a few stories in the press that questioned the motives of a singer and a jazz band performing gospel numbers in concert halls and getting paid for it. I wanted to quash that cynicism, and I called a press conference at Sister Rosetta's hotel. While talking away to the reporters, she got out her guitar and started singing. They immediately understood that she was a sincere character, and gradually they drifted away, without picking up the story any further. She was a genuine, decent person doing what she did best, and, of course, the minute they realised that, she was of no interest to those sections of the media that had initially raised the issue.

We had the most marvellous tour with her. She and Ottilie got on very well together. It was almost the same relationship that Sister Rosetta had had back in the States with Sister Marie Knight for years. Some people said, "You've already got a singer. Surely she and Ottilie will be at each other's throats as rivals." But that was stupid and ridiculous. They sang beautifully together, and got on well off stage, too. In fact at times we had trouble persuading Sister Rosetta to sing on her own without having Ottilie there as well. We did about four weeks with Sister Rosetta, playing virtually every night. Critic Bob Dawbarn wrote in the *Melody Maker*:

> Sister Rosetta was in great voice throughout. She has incredible control of the vocal smears and swoops which characterise her singing, which somehow combines power and sweetness. She can wring the last drop of drama from a song while singing like a female Jimmy Rushing. Her effect on the band? . . . They swung as they have never swung before.

It was during that tour that Graham Burbidge joined the band on drums, and Ron left to join Kenny Ball. Graham's arrival was the beginning of what

John Lewis once described as the best rhythm section he'd heard in Britain, with Eddie Smith on banjo, Dick Smith on bass and Graham.

One reason we chose Sonny Terry and Brownie McGhee for our next such tour in April and May 1958 was that they had worked on Broadway shows including *Finian's Rainbow* and *Cat on a Hot Tin Roof*. That type of work had already taken them outside their normal black environment. In other words we felt they'd be familiar with working with people like us, and playing to concert audiences like the ones we had in England and Europe. Brownie was a very nice man, lovely to work with and a very good musician. He – and Sonny, his musical partner – really justified the choice that we made, now that we realised we could bring members of the Guild of Variety Artists over to Europe ourselves. Like Big Bill and Sister Rosetta, they were people with whom we wanted to work, in order to get closer to the music and to learn more about playing it right. If you play with such musicians you learn in the same way that kids in New Orleans always did, by being in direct contact with those who developed it in the first place.

Sonny was nearly blind, and Brownie led him around, although Brownie himself walked with a stick as he had suffered from polio as a child. To describe them, Brownie used to quote the rather archaic words from the Bible, "The halt leading the blind", but he was always energetic, saying "C'mon, Sonny, let's do this . . . let's do that!" Sonny would reply, "You're just jealous of me 'cause I'm a better blues singer than you are!"

Years of performing had made Brownie such a seasoned professional that he seemed to worry very little about appearing on stage. "Don't be too serious," he'd say. "Just do the songs." This was something Ottilie found hard to understand because she (like all of us) was very serious about performing the blues. He adapted what had originally been a twelve-bar blues, 'Cornbread, Peas and Black Molasses', to the metre of Rudyard Kipling's "If", a poem he admired. Yet, despite his outwardly hard professional attitude, Brownie was actually so sentimental that when he got home to the United States, on his next record for Folkways, as part of his ordinary recorded output, he did a song about the trip and about the band, 'Memories Of My Trip'. He went through all our names and thanked us for having had such a good time. Actually, the names posed a problem for the sleeve note writers at Folkways because they tried to write down exactly what he'd sung. So they refer to a mythical character called "Big Gilman" whereas – as you can hear on the track – what he actually sang was "Dick, Graham, and Eddie". And Ottilie was transformed into the blues singer "R. B. Patterson"!

At the time, we thought "Oh, that's nice," but as time went on, and we toured with many other musicians from America, Brownie remained the only one who actually thanked us in this way, and so it meant a lot to us. The other real memory of the trip is tied up in the line from that same song, "I saw Berlin". Recently I found a photograph of Sonny and Brownie plus the band, descending the steps from a Constellation airliner, after landing in Berlin just before our first concert there. In those days following the Berlin airlift, all flights from the West had to land in the cramped airfield at Tempelhof, which was squeezed into the urban area of West Berlin, so when Brownie sang "I saw Berlin" he had genuinely seen it from about 100 feet above the city.

On our concerts with them, we normally arranged things so that Sonny and Brownie did a set on their own, between the band numbers, and then we'd all join together for the finale. But during the period that we were on the road with them, we were also doing a weekly BBC radio series, called *Chris Barber's Bandbox* which went out every Monday. So we invited Sonny and Brownie along as guests every week while they were with us. They did some songs on their own, but as the show was named after the band we tried to play as much as possible, so we also ended up doing several pieces with them. Most weeks from mid-April to mid-May 1958 we followed up a few short pieces by them with a couple of longer numbers featuring all of us.

Working with them on the road we'd really developed a feel for one another's phrasing and we were starting to sound very good together. One of the songs we broadcast is a lovely one written by Tampa Red called 'When Things Go Wrong With You, It Hurts Me Too'. It was originally recorded by lots of people in the 1940s, including Tampa Red himself, and Sonny and Brownie knew the song well. So we did that one, with some nice harmonica playing from Sonny, and Ottilie joining in the vocal.

Just as Big Bill had done, Sonny and Brownie also did spirituals. We still had the underlying feeling left over from Big Bill's reaction to Mahalia Jackson that some of the blues people did not want to get involved with spirituals, and in later years when Jimmy Witherspoon sang a spiritual with us on a concert that was something which would once have seemed most unlikely. A favourite that we did with Sonny and Brownie was 'Do Lord, Do Remember Me'. On concerts and on one of our broadcasts Ottilie would sing a chorus, then Brownie would do the next chorus and then all of us would join in singing. It was a wonderful experience playing with them, and it meant an awful lot to us.

By 1957, I had become part of an organisation called the National Jazz Federation, and one of its goals was to accelerate the rate at which American musicians could visit. Gradually the Musicians' Union was thinking about relaxing the rule about Americans playing in Britain, and the scheme they came up with was to allow them in, if an identical number of musicians from the UK was contracted to perform in the States. This exchange system was difficult because when it started there was virtually no demand for British bands in America at all. I remember going to sign contracts for an exchange in front of a Union delegate at the offices of the agent Harold Davison, and then quietly tearing up the agreement afterwards once the business had been seen to be done by the official.

However, the upshot of this was that several American small groups were finally able to come and play in Britain in the late 1950s. It is important to think back to that time and realise that, before this, it had been quite simply impossible for English audiences to hear at first hand bands such as the Gerry Mulligan Quartet or the Modern Jazz Quartet, despite the fact that French and German audiences had been able to hear them for years as there had been no such restrictions in those territories. Through the National Jazz Federation, I came to meet the members of the Modern Jazz Quartet. Its pianist John Lewis and I became lifelong friends.

One day I was having a chat to John, who liked all kinds of music, including Chicago blues, and he asked me, "Who have you brought over here?"

I said, "Sister Rosetta Tharpe, Sonny and Brownie."

He said, "Why don't you bring Muddy Waters?"

I said, "I don't know how to reach him. What do you do, send a postcard to Stovall's Plantation or something?"

John laughed and said, "No. He's got a Cadillac and an agent!"

I discovered later that Chess, his record label, had bought him a Cadillac because their rival company Dot had bought one for Fats Domino. And Muddy didn't like the idea of receiving inferior treatment from his label. In fact he never used the car! Anyway on John's recommendation we booked Muddy to come over to the UK in October 1958. Again it was wonderful. A fantastic experience.

By this time we weren't nervous about playing with legendary figures. We also felt quite confident about *how* to tackle playing with Muddy. On his own records he was mainly accompanied by just bass and drums. There were horns on some records, often just a clarinet or saxophone, and I suspect most bands like ours would not have known what to do with numbers played like that. But we did.

His schedule was so tight that we had no time to rehearse with him before he joined us for the first concert at Newcastle upon Tyne, on a Sunday night. That wasn't the original intention, because he should have had the Saturday to acclimatise after arriving, but he was invited at rather short notice to headline at a jazz festival at Harewood House near Leeds. So he and Otis Spann went there first and found themselves working with the Jazz Today Unit, which was a modernish mainstream band. It included trumpeter Kenny Baker, altoist Bruce Turner, and other similar players, but although they were a fine band, and all good musicians, they weren't really well-versed in the kind of blues that Muddy played.

So on the Sunday in Newcastle, he and Otis just turned up, not really knowing what to expect. After a hurried chat we told him that we would go on and do a set, and then he would join us after a number or two in the second half. He heard us playing New Orleans jazz in the first half, and didn't say much about it in the interval. He didn't say anything either way to indicate that he liked or disliked what he was hearing; he just asked what we'd start with. I said, " 'Hoochie Coochie Man'."

He said, "Yeah."

I sang him the opening riff and he asked, "What key?"

I said, "A."

He just said, "Okay."

So we went out to do a couple of songs, and then we called him on. In that theatre, there were windows in the door that led on to the stage, and as we played we could see him and the pianist Otis Spann peering through those little windows and watching as we played our traditional jazz numbers. Then I announced them, and as they came on stage we played the opening riff. Their faces lit up like watermelon eaters! They knew at once we were on their wavelength, so we kept playing and they came out. We dropped the volume right down for them, and it was the most impressive, exciting feeling. They hadn't expected us to know or care about their music. We had a really great time with them both.

I remember some critics said that Muddy played too loudly, but I never experienced this. I played with him on tour, and then sat in with his band quite often, and you could hold a conversation two feet in front of his amp and hear each other talk. The same year that Muddy came over, in 1958, we launched the Marquee Club in London. My business partner in the new club was my old friend Harold Pendleton, who had done so much to help get us going. Harold had been working with the Alex Welsh band, and similar groups, after we'd begun playing in concert halls and theatres and more or less stopped playing in clubs. We were talking one day in London and he said he wanted to open another jazz club, and I said, "Find one!" because actually I wanted somewhere else in London to play that wasn't the 100 Club. I just don't like the place, even when working with famous people. I start to play there, and after a few notes I wish I hadn't. Having no band room was a nuisance, but you can live with that. The problem is that the acoustics were – and still are – awful. In its heyday in the fifties, there was nothing in that club but the bare walls and the pillars. And it was always so crowded. Terry Lightfoot set the record, squeezing in 1,300 people. There was no licensed bar down there in those days, just a little coffee stall, that's all they had.

So Harold kept looking and he finally found what would become the Marquee, which was in the basement of the Academy Cinema in Oxford Street. It was on the other side of the road from the 100 Club and about 25 yards nearer Oxford Circus. The place was a function room that was used for wedding receptions and parties and such like, with a bandstand. We called it the Marquee because it had one of those striped awnings that the Americans call a "marquee" around the top of the stage. We started on Wednesdays and Saturdays and then we added Sundays, and then gradually added other days, until we had it all the time. But the point was to find a place in London where we could play decent music and make it sound like decent music. Harold and I co-owned the club.

In 1964 we ran into a problem with the Marquee because the owner of the Academy Cinema was looking at the costs of running the business in central

London, with rents going up and so forth, and he came to the conclusion that he needed to reclaim the basement in order to open a second screen. Having found somewhere with good acoustics, which was comfortable for the audience and where we enjoyed playing, we did not know what to do. Then Harold discovered that the cinema owner (who had other movie houses in London) employed an estate manager, and somehow he persuaded him to look for somewhere to move the club. Just in time, very shortly before our notice was up on the original Marquee, he found something suitable, at 90 Wardour Street. At the time, it was the central London store for the stock of all Burton's tailoring, and it was full of hundreds of suits. If it had a problem as a club, it was that outwardly it was just a door – there was no street frontage. But we could live with that, because nobody had previously realised just how much space there was inside, and how it could be reconfigured as a club.

Harold took on the lease and we reopened there. In due course, after a couple of years, the engineer Philip Wood came along and built a recording studio behind the club, running through into Richmond Mews. It was run as a going concern for over twenty years, from 1966, by Spencer Brooks.

Harold and I also owned the Reading Festival, because we started that through the National Jazz Federation. As well as bringing in American visitors through the NJF, another of the reasons we started it was to rescue jazz from the hands of Lord Donegal and Jimmy Asman and the NFJO, the ones who'd brought in Lonnie Johnson and Ralph Sutton, during the Festival of Britain, without thinking of the consequences for local musicians. They had never tried to tackle the union problem, or to work out how to break down the stranglehold on preventing Americans from playing in Britain. Overall, they were really hopeless, which is a shame because with the Marquess of Donegal's political connections he might have tried to do something.

The Marquee house record, which I think we achieved by presenting Jimi Hendrix, was just over 1,100. But then along came the GLC (the Greater London Council) and fire regulations. Suddenly it all changed and the capacity of the Marquee was limited to 400. And not only that, if there was a fire and the fire chief wanted to get in there, somebody had to come out first, so that the club was never over the legal limit.

My band didn't play there all the time because by 1958 we were travelling so much. So other bands would come in on other nights. Harold and I also set up a management company based on the club with some of the groups that we knew. The Moody Blues signed up with us, and so did several other bands of the time including Procol Harum. One of them, which played at the club a lot, was called the T-Bones, which had nothing to do with trombones, but was a group with organ, guitar, bass and drums. The organist was a young fellow called Keith Emerson, who was to become rather well-known with Greg Lake and Carl Palmer. But at that time he was a devotee of Jack McDuff and Jimmy McGriff. I used to go and sit in, and even did a few gigs as a soloist with them which I enjoyed very much. Their vocalist Gary Farr was not much more than a passable singer, but the rest of the band were fine players – in particular Alan Turner the drummer was very good indeed. When Graham Burbidge was about to leave my band, I wanted to get Alan to play with us, but in the end we got Pete York. Alan was a great drummer but he gave up music in the 1980s and went into the garment trade, which was a shame. I did a week with the T-Bones in Biarritz once, just playing in a club, and I really liked doing the bluesy sort of music they played.

When my band wasn't out on the road, on our nights off I'd drop in to the Marquee and see what was going on, and sometimes sit in. Friday night was blues night, and usually it featured someone like the Yardbirds. I have a picture somewhere of me, Jeff Beck and Ronnie Wood playing there one Friday in the Jeff Beck group. Rod Stewart sang, Ronnie played bass and Mickey Waller was on drums. On another occasion, in the mid-sixties some time, I played there with Eric Clapton and Stevie Winwood on a fundraiser for some other musicians who had been involved in a terrible car accident.

Our first office, for the Marquee, the agency, the band and the NJF, was in Great Chapel Street, on the ground floor of a building a couple of streets away from Soho Square. The magazine *Jazz News* was based there as well, which was also our company. We ran *Jazz News* for quite some time, and Harold and I tried everything with it, from weekly to fortnightly, to monthly. But we always lost about twenty quid an issue. We didn't put a lot of money into it, but we couldn't make it a success, despite jazz's popularity at the time. We tried it in newsagents, which didn't do any good. Val Wilmer took some great photographs for us, but none of it worked. The publication was a joint effort by Harold and me with Ted Morton of the 100 Club, but that was one venture that simply did not take off.

After that we moved roughly a block away to an office that was upstairs on Dean Street in Soho, above what is now the Pizza Express Jazz Club. We were based for quite a while on the floor immediately over the restaurant. In those days, before Peter Boizot's pizza company moved in, there was a coffee bar on the ground floor. I remember it well because it was one of the first ones in London that had a proper Italian Gaggia steam machine installed.

From 1964 the band office was above the Marquee itself. There was a cut through from Dean Street, via Richmond Mews, if you came in through the back door via the Marquee studio, into the main building on Wardour Street. I came through one day in the mid-1960s and there was this group practising something in the studio. I wasn't sure who they were, but they were going over and over this piece of music again and again. They kept stopping in the middle all the time. I eventually asked what was going on. It was The Who and their manager Kit Lambert, who was making them rehearse their miming routine for when they went on TV, doing 'I Can't Explain'. It was very sensible because it meant when they went up to Manchester to record *Top of the Pops* they would know exactly what to do to look convincing, rather than a less punctilious band such as Manfred Mann, who just waved their hands in the air and made no pretence at playing the song.

Thinking about films and television, going back to the year we originally launched the Marquee, in the autumn of 1958 we took part in making the movie *Look Back in Anger* for the director Tony Richardson. It opens in a jazz club with Richard Burton as the leading character Jimmy Porter, playing the trumpet with our band. We were offered the chance to appear in the movie because, as I mentioned earlier, we had made a film in 1955 called *Momma Don't Allow*, which had been shot at the Fishmonger's Arms Jazz Club in Wood Green. It was an experimental movie for the British Film Institute, which had been jointly directed by Tony Richardson and Karel Reisz. It's a very atmospheric film, and a good evocation of what one of the jazz clubs we had been playing at regularly was like at the time. Tony liked our work on *Momma Don't Allow*, and so when he wanted to create the jazz club scenes for John Osborne's angry young man at the beginning of his feature film he immediately thought of us. In most films of the period, what you see looks nothing like a real jazz club, but everything about that opening title sequence of *Look Back in Anger*, from the lighting to the placement of the audience, is just right and makes it one of the most convincing jazz sequences in all of cinema history.

When we started we had no idea that every scene you see in a full-scale movie is actually mimed by the actors to a pre-recorded soundtrack. If you look closely at the band immediately after the titles, Richard Burton is the only one who looks as if he is actually playing. He put a valve down for every note and puckered his lips convincingly. They were actually all the wrong valves, but it didn't matter because it looked the part, and he was moving with the music. The rest of us are looking slightly puzzled and worrying about whether we're playing the same notes as we did on the soundtrack recording. We were playing 'Don't Go Away Nobody' which has only a minimal tune, yet, when we met two years later, Richard sang me the two choruses he played, note perfect. In other parts of the film, Jimmy Porter, who is a rather annoying character, plays the trumpet all over the place, in the street, in phone boxes, that sort of thing. Pat Halcox recorded all those little bits for Richard to mime to. It paid off for him because, in 1962, Tony Richardson asked Pat to play the jazz sequences behind Tom Courtenay's cross country scenes in *The Loneliness of the Long Distance Runner*. The rest of that score is by John Addison, but Pat's sequences are the musical highlight of the film.

Having got on very well with Richard Burton on the set, we discovered that he was very keen on doing something with jazz and poetry. However, he said he didn't want anything to do with effete modern poetry, but that he'd rather declaim Shakespeare, or something comparable, in rhythm. His intention was to follow up our collaboration on the film, but we never got round to it. Which is a shame because it might have been an interesting meeting of styles and genres.

However, not too long after that, Ottilie did record some Shakespeare. She was very keen on words, which is one of the reasons she was so good at singing the blues, because every word always carried just the right weight of meaning. She wrote settings of four lovely Shakespeare pieces that she played with the band in 1964, including a very up-tempo version of the song from *As You Like It*, 'Blow, Blow, Thou Winter Wind'.

It was the 400th anniversary of Shakespeare at the time, and a lot of attention was paid to Cleo Laine's record from the same year called *Shakespeare and All That Jazz*. There was comparatively little interest in Ottilie's album. Personally I found Cleo's versions to be rather delicate, whereas Ottilie's songs were very down to earth. She certainly believed that Shakespeare himself was very down to earth, which was the starting point for her settings. The best one is the sonnet number 29, "When, in disgrace with fortune and men's eyes, I all alone beweep my troubled state". She did it as a gospel piece, and she based the style and feel of it on a record of Mahalia Jackson, singing 'I Can Put My Trust In Jesus'. Johnny Parker joined us to play piano on Ottilie's version so that we could get as close as possible to that American recording, which I think had Sonny White playing piano for Mahalia.

Later Ottilie did a fantastic album called *Spring Song* in 1968 for the producer Giorgio Gomelski, on which she wrote the settings and Richard Hill did the string arrangements. Some of the guys who went on to form the band Blue Mink were on it including bassist Herbie Flowers and the drummer Barry Morgan. It's a marvellous record, although it's very serious. There are translations of Latin poetry by Tertullian and others, and she also plays a slow waltz piece on the piano referring to Mrs Pankhurst and the suffragettes. The best of the Shakespeare pieces has John Wilbraham – who was principal of the Royal Philharmonic Orchestra at the time – on Bach trumpet, and Sheila Bromberg playing the harp. All the players were marvellous, but those two stood out. There's a somewhat lugubrious song on the record called 'The Bitterness of Death', based on a 2,000-year-old poem. When Giorgio released it, this song was very adversely reviewed by Ian Anderson. Ottilie wanted to include it because she thought it was really sad, and was as straightforward about it as that. Overall, though, the record is really first rate, and proves what an articulate and sensitive artist Ottilie was. Unfortunately, the year after it was made, Giorgio had a breakup with his backers and distributors at Polydor, and his Marmalade label, which issued the record, closed down and that was the end of it. They never came to a subsequent agreement, so anything that was originally issued by Marmalade Records can't be released by anybody else. As a result, the only existing copies of *Spring Song* are the LP copies sold at the time, and it has become a real rarity.

At the end of the 1950s, not long after making the movie with Richard Burton, we began to collaborate occasionally with the Jamaican alto saxophonist Joe Harriott. In fact, Joe was around and about in London for a long time before I really thought much about working with him. We knew some of the modern players at the time, probably more than most of the traditional bands did, partly because we were interested, but partly also because my first band had played at Studio 51 and we'd made a lot of long-term friends there. Joe was playing with several of these people such as Tony Kinsey from around 1954, then he did a stint in Ronnie Scott's big band, and he formed his own quintet in 1958.

When Harold initially founded the Marquee, we played there every Wednesday, and that was all. As I mentioned, additional nights were gradually added, and Saturday was a modern jazz night. By 1959 the regular band was Joe's, with Shake Keane on trumpet and Coleridge Goode on bass. The supporting band might have been Mike Garrick or Tubby Hayes, but I know that it was on one of those Saturday nights that I first really heard Joe properly. Then we ended up doing a BBC *Jazz Club* broadcast together. At that time, my band was also still playing a monthly session at the Recital Room at the Royal Festival Hall – what is now called the Purcell Room. It had started out, organised by Harold, not long after we had parted company with Ken Colyer, and we had played there virtually every month thereafter.

I know, for example, that we played there one night in 1957 during the time the Eddie Condon band was in town. I don't think, when it came to the press reception that same evening at the start of Eddie's tour, that anyone had quite alerted the promoters to the amount the Condon band was capable of drinking. Anyway we were due to play at the Recital Room that night, and Pat didn't show up. He finally appeared at about ten o'clock, having come from the reception, where he'd joined the Condon band in slightly more than a drink or two, caught the tube, and fallen asleep. He woke up at the very end of the Northern Line in Morden, and had to come all the way back again to Waterloo. Meanwhile, a couple of members of the Condon band turned up at our concert way before he got there, having been brought straight from the reception, and apparently stone cold sober.

At those monthly gigs, we had lots of guests, mainly, looking back on it, saxophone players, including Don Rendell. But strangely I don't think Joe Harriott was ever one of them. On the other hand, I know he did come with us on a couple of riverboat shuffles to Margate. The system was that you'd go out there from London on a steamer, and then change boats for the return voyage, with a quick break in between for a cup of tea. Consequently, people who went out on the first boat would have a different band coming back, and the same thing applied to the audience on the second boat. Usually it all went well, and the bands swapped easily. One time, I missed the departure of the first boat because the universal joint on the prop-shaft failed on my 1938 Lagonda LG6, as I was driving to the quay. So I didn't catch it, but I finally got there just in time to get the second boat, so I went out with that, and, of course, came back on it with my own band that had sailed out on the first boat. The year after that breakdown, Joe Harriott came with us. I remember having terrible trouble persuading him to leave the café where we swapped over in Margate, and join us for the return journey. Eventually he emerged and we just made it onto the boat. After that adventure he played with us quite a few times. Listening again today to the BBC broadcast that we made, I wonder now why I didn't offer him a full-time job with the band. He wasn't getting much work at the time, and we got on well. I suppose the reason I didn't ask him was because I wanted to do things that I was sure would work with the public as well as musically, and not take a risk on something that might not be a surefire success.

Joe played New Orleans music in a very good way, without relinquishing the bebop style that was his natural musical identity. It was interesting and different, and yet it was a wholehearted contribution to the ensemble. Maybe the best example is the Palladium concert we did, where all of us played his tune 'Revival'. That was just fantastic.

Years later, of course, I did add a permanent extra reed to the front line. After Ian Wheeler had left the band and John Crocker joined, Sammy Rimington came in as an extra reed player, and did very nicely, and when he left we got Ian back again alongside John Crocker. Sammy said that he didn't like being in a "big band" because he didn't get enough time to play solo, although it was actually only an eight-piece group!

4 Petite Fleur

When we came to record 'Petite Fleur' in 1959, our third ten-inch LP with Pye was due to be recorded. So I said to Monty, "It's your turn." I'd played a solo on the first album, Pat had taken a solo number on the second, and now it was his chance to have the spotlight. He said, "I don't know anything suitable." We told him to go home and see what he could come up with, and we'd talk about it tomorrow.

The next day he turned up and said: "I've got this tune. Sidney Bechet plays it with this French band." He started playing it. It took us a while to work out the chords, which turned out to be in A flat minor, the relative minor of B major. Sidney Bechet didn't do it in that key, of course, but Monty's record player was running fast and he simply learned it off the record note for note. Actually that's why we sold millions of it and Bechet didn't, because the sound of the piece going from A flat minor to that B natural key is marvellous, it's one of *the* keys, whereas Bechet going from G minor to B flat sounds dull by comparison. It's a tiny point but it makes all the difference.

When our record of 'Petite Fleur' became a hit in America, it was on a label called Laurie, run by brothers Bob and Gene Schwartz. Basically at that time, if the American arm of a British record label did not want to or could not issue a disc in the United States, the recordings went through a sort of clearing house company in New York, and the Laurie label bought a lot of its catalogue from them. According to our agent Abe Turchen, behind the scenes Laurie was actually masterminded by Dick Clark, the man known popularly as "America's Oldest Teenager", and the host of the country's longest running television variety show *American Bandstand*.

Clark had been hauled before the Senate committee investigating Payola, the practice of plugging a record in which the DJ or presenter had a financial interest, without declaring it on air. Shortly before our record came out, he had been forced to sell his minority holdings in several other record companies, by ABC television, who wanted their host to be seen as "clean". But because publicly Laurie was backed by the millionaire Allan I. Sussel, Clark continued to be the brains behind that label. Oren Harris, the Democrat president of the enquiry, acquitted him from any wrongdoing, calling him a "fine young man".

However Dick Clark knew exactly how to sail close to the wind, and we promoted the record on Laurie by playing 'Petite Fleur' on his television show *American Bandstand*. That was very unusual, to be playing what was essentially a Dixieland number on a mainstream variety show, which at that time was mainly full of rock and roll acts. Sadly, unlike *Ready Steady Go*, the British television pop show, nobody has bought the rights so that the material from *American Bandstand* can readily be seen again today. My main memory of it was playing in front of a crowd of rock and roll kids who hadn't the faintest idea what to do with themselves while they were listening to a jazz number.

On that same tour we appeared on the *Ed Sullivan Show*. We got that gig owing to the help of Abe Turchen whose main job was Woody Herman's manager. Later, Abe was the man largely responsible for the mess Woody got into over taxes with the IRS, but when we were on tour he was a powerful figure. He had kept Woody working all the way through the decline of the big bands at the end of the 1940s and into the 1950s. Unlike Louis Armstrong's manager Joe Glaser who sat back waiting for the phone to ring, Abe got on the phone and made calls to book the band. But he had a system to keep costs down because, with the United States being so big, calls were expensive in those days. The idea was that Woody or his drummer who was road managing the band would place a person-to-person call to Abe; they would get a message saying that Mr Turchen was not available at the moment, but could be reached at such and such a ballroom in such and such a place on Tuesday 13th. That way, the band got the information for its date sheet while it was out on the road, and the call did not cost either side a penny.

Our 1959 tour came at the time when a lot of West Coast studio musicians were getting disenchanted with the American Federation of Musicians, the main musicians' union. A breakaway group was forming the Guild of Musicians, which was a problem for all the big television and radio companies who had binding agreements with the AFM. Neither the AFM nor the networks wanted to have to renegotiate everything.

So Abe Turchen rang up the AFM and said, "If you don't get Chris Barber on the *Ed Sullivan Show*, Woody Herman will join the Guild of Musicians." So the union *told* Ed Sullivan to have us, when the actual exchange agreement with that selfsame union specifically did not allow us to play on TV! If you think about it, that was amazing. At that stage of the tour, we were in Toronto, but we left our cars at the airport and flew down for the day from Canada to New York to do the show. That said, Ed Sullivan was a nasty piece of work. He reminded me of Captain Queeg, the obsessive, unpleasant character in *The Caine Mutiny*, who is constantly compressing a pair of ball bearings in his hand. From his body language, I'd swear that Ed Sullivan was doing something similar.

At first they only wanted to give us twenty seconds: "Play your Gold Record and get off." In the end they compromised on two and a half minutes, and we played a very short version of 'Diga Diga Doo', and then an even briefer version of 'Petite Fleur' which Sullivan talked all over. Luckily we worked it out so that Monty didn't get stuck because, having learned the tune by ear, he was fine if he started at the beginning but if we asked him to pick it up from the middle he couldn't always find it again. There was an odd assortment of people on the show that night. They had Fred MacMurray (who had played the saxophone with Paul Whiteman), and Jane Russell, who sang a spiritual. And us.

I don't think we got the worst treatment from Sullivan among visiting British acts, however. A few months later we were playing in Sheffield, and in a restaurant before the show I bumped into Jimmy Jewel the comedian, who had just been in the States with his double-act partner Ben Warriss. They were Britain's leading comedy act at the time, and as well as regularly topping the bill at the London Palladium, they had a really popular radio series called *Up The Pole*, where they lived in a fictional house at the North Pole. So they arrived to appear on the *Ed Sullivan Show*, and, Jimmy told me that night, Ed having first told them at rehearsal that their time on air could be no more than eight minutes, he introduced them on air by saying: "From England, Jules and his Walrus. You've got two minutes."

The reason we had been lined up for television appearances by Abe Turchen in America is that in the winter of 1959 we had been selected under the Musicians' Union agreement as an exchange act to work in the United States so that Woody Herman's band could play in Britain. This time, it was not a fake contract for the purposes of inveigling American artists into Britain. Woody's Anglo-American band did indeed play in the UK, and from the recordings I've heard it was excellent. Meanwhile, we set off in late February for a tour of the States and Canada that would stretch well into March.

Our own concerts went well, and we had a remarkably positive critical reception. John S. Wilson, the critic of the *New York Times*, described our music as "full-blooded and buoyant jazz that is definitely superior to that of any equivalent band in this country". He praised the breadth of our repertoire, pointing out that, unlike most revivalists, we did not just do 1920s classics and pieces played by present-day New Orleans musicians such as George Lewis, but that we performed Ellington material and even pieces by the MJQ. He finished by describing our "compelling ensemble playing", and going on to say, "it is in its ensemble playing that this band shines, and it is, in this sense, one of the most genuine jazz bands heard on a New York concert stage for a long, long time."

It's still possible to get a flavour of that first American tour because one of our concerts in late February in Detroit was recorded, although it was issued as a bootleg, the label claiming it to be by the "All American Ramblers". I found a copy on sale in Joe's Record Shop in New York on our way back to London at the end of the tour. It was quite clearly us, as we played 'Bobby Shaftoe' which I don't think any other bands, let alone American groups, were doing at the time, and a couple of the other tracks on the label were mis-named. While we were in Canada I also came across an EP, apparently by the "Danton Phillips Sextet". It turned out to be our recording of 'Savoy Blues', cut in two, with one half on each side of the record!

On this first visit, we did not play in Chicago, but we passed through the city and actually had a little time off there, between concerts. Our tour manager took us to see the Sears Tower and some of the famous buildings in the Loop. The previous October, when Muddy Waters had been playing with us in Britain, he had told us to come down and hear him if we should ever be in Chicago. As it was only four months later, we figured he would remember us, and so we got taxis to take us all down to Smitty's Corner, at 35th and Indiana, which was the club where he played when he was in town. We came in, and Muddy was immediately very welcoming. He announced us to the audience as his friends from the "State of England", and of course he wanted us to get up and play.

On that first US tour we were travelling together in a large station wagon, and it had a trailer that we pulled behind it to carry all our instruments and equipment. Having come down to the club by taxi we had none of our instruments with us. So without further ado, Muddy announced us as singers. He didn't really bother to ask. He already knew that Ottilie sang the blues, and he thought the rest of us could make a reasonable go of it. As Ottilie said later, "Singers — you can't say you left that instrument behind! It's your throat!"

Muddy's own band at that time was just about the best band he ever led, with Otis Spann on piano, who had toured with us in Britain, Pat Hare on guitar, Jimmy Cotton on harmonica and Francis Clay on drums. It was a beautiful band. Ottilie started to sing Big Bill Broonzy's tune 'Southbound Train'. It was a song she'd sung with Big Bill himself not all that long before, and she launched into it with "I wonder why that Southbound Train . . ." And the entire audience raised their right hands and said, "Yeah!" That was really heart-warming because it showed that she had conveyed not just what the words were, but what they meant. The idea is that you don't want to go back down there to the South, but somehow you're drawn to it. That audience wasn't joking in any way. If Muddy had sung the same song himself he would have got the same reaction.

That night was the first time we met Jimmy Cotton and we really took to him. In fact Jimmy did most of the singing because Muddy's band were on from 9 pm until 3 am, and they did a forty-minute set each hour, with Muddy coming on to sing the last number or two of each set. Jimmy and Otis Spann did the rest of the singing. A couple of years later, Lord Edward Montagu asked if we would do something at the Beaulieu Festival. I said I'd come if I could do something different, and suggested I bring Jimmy Cotton over. He travelled over to Britain for a few weeks during which we did the concert at Beaulieu and also made a recording. We did eleven titles, eight of which came out on two EPs. Two of the others are not so hot because I'm playing guitar alongside Alexis Korner, but there was a rather good version of 'Love Me Or Leave Me' that only went unreleased at the time because it had a tiny technical glitch. With modern technology we sorted that out, so in 2000 we finally released that song by Jimmy with some fine vocal and harmonica playing.

By the time Jimmy came over to the UK we had already played with my full band at Smitty's Corner. In the autumn of 1959 we were back in the States, and Muddy arranged to bring us into the club, where we played our usual stuff. We got a standing ovation. And that was from Muddy's regular audience because nobody else knew that we were coming, as it wasn't widely advertised. The crowd was made up of older black Americans, first-generation immigrants to Chicago from the South. The place only held about sixty people, and Muddy used to say about them, "My crowd drinks whisky!"

In 1960, we were back in Chicago, and Ottilie and I stayed at Muddy's house on South Lake Park. One night during our stay Muddy had a gig in Gary, Indiana and I went along as a member of the band. We travelled in his Chevy station wagon with Muddy, Killer (his bodyguard, who wasn't really a bodyguard at all) and Jimmy Oden, who, after having had a bad car accident a couple of years before, had stopped performing as "St Louis Jimmy" and devoted himself to writing new material for Muddy to sing. He had become a sort of mascot for Muddy.

We got to the club, which was a very smart place, and I played the first set with the band. It was a similar pattern to Smitty's, in that Muddy only came on to sing the last couple of numbers in each set. I looked around and everyone was extremely smartly turned out, beautifully dressed. It was a very cultured club, and it struck me, as it often did during those years, that only black people in America had real style. Anyway, at the end of that first set I came down from the stage, looking for the toilet. I had to squeeze past a group of around eight people who were standing at the back, again extremely smart, and chatting amongst themselves. As I went by, a girl leaned back from the group, pulled my sleeve, and said, "Hey, are you Chris Barber?"

I said, "Yes, I am."

She said, "Is that your record, that 'Petite Fleur'?"

I told her, "Yes, it is."

She said, "I don't like it!"

It came from an era of music that probably her parents couldn't even remember, so there was no reason she would like it, I suppose. But it was put very frankly, directly, and so nicely!

Because our first American tour in early 1959 had gone very well, Harold Pendleton at the National Jazz Federation, and Abe Turchen, got together to book a longer and more ambitious six-week tour in September and October that same year. It was a marvellous time to be working in the States, as a lot of jazz was still going on and we were often working alongside well-known American bands so we got to meet and hang out with many legendary players. Our anticipation of mingling with and hearing so many fine musicians began on our journey from Idlewild Airport (now John F. Kennedy International Airport) into Manhattan to get to our hotel on the first night, 18 September. We drove past Jimmy Ryan's club, which was then still in its original location on 52nd Street, and we saw Wilbur De Paris and his "New" New Orleans Jazz Band billed on the marquee outside. Sadly we were unaware at the time that the band's fine clarinetist, Omer Simeon, a veteran of some of Jelly Roll Morton's best recordings, had died in the Harlem Hospital less than 24 hours before we arrived.

We had met the De Paris band (with Omer) on our first visit, and they greeted us very cordially when we went down to the club again that night. Garvin Bushell was playing clarinet and, more unusually, oboe, in Simeon's place. After hearing a set most of us then walked downtown the four blocks or so to the Metropole Café on Seventh Avenue and 48th Street, where there was music every afternoon and evening. Whichever band was playing was ranged in a long line above and behind the bar. That night there were several pianists taking part, Sammy Price, Dick Wellstood and Claude Hopkins. Sol Yaged played clarinet, Hal Singer (whom we'd met before, but who was now sporting a rather Mephistophelian beard) played tenor sax, and Benny Moten played bass. The drummer was the twenty-three-year-old Rufus "Speedy" Jones who was already showing the talent that was to bring him work with Count Basie and Duke Ellington in the years that followed.

We found out that earlier that same day, during the afternoon, we'd missed hearing Fats Waller's former clarinet and saxophone player, Gene Sedric, and the legendary New Orleans drummer Zutty Singleton.

At that point the Metropole had jazz on two floors, and upstairs we found Max Kaminsky leading a Dixieland group, with George Wettling on drums, and, more surprisingly, Charlie Parker's one-time bassist Tommy Potter. Dick Wellstood dashed between venues to play piano for this band. The Kaminsky band alternated with Gene Krupa's quartet, which featured the British-born pianist Ronnie Ball, whom I knew from his early days playing modern jazz at Studio 51 in London, before he moved to New York in 1952 to study with Lennie Tristano.

I went on from the Metropole to Condon's, which was then a short cab ride uptown to 56th Street. I already knew some members of the band because they had toured the UK in 1957, and that night they were joined by Louis Armstrong's former pianist Dick Cary. They invited me to sit in, and while I was playing, Monty, Pat and Eddie Smith went off to Nick's, another famous jazz club down in Greenwich Village, where the widow of the founder, Nick Rongetti, gave them a very warm welcome. She told them that she had already heard of the Chris Barber Band. They listened to a short set from the interval pianist, Hank Duncan, a very fine stride player, whom I got to know a couple of years later when I recorded with him. Before we turned in for the night we all met up again at Central Plaza, where a jam-session band led by the trombonist Big Chief Russell Moore (and with the actor and trombonist Conrad Janis also making his presence known) was blowing lustily and somewhat raucously into the small hours.

Ahead of our arduous round of travelling, we had another day to get acclimatised in New York. We looked in on the Metropole and Ryan's again, but Ottilie and I decided to go uptown and catch the "Gospel Caravan" at the Apollo Theatre in Harlem. We had been to the Apollo on our first visit and loved the atmosphere of the place. This time the audience was still more responsive, even during the movie that was shown before the live acts came on stage. Once the gospel part of the evening began — it was scheduled to run for an hour, but ran over double that time — the audience became yet more animated. There were several great gospel groups, among which I remember the Spirit of Memphis, the Clara Ward Singers, and what was, for us, the most exciting of all, Professor Alex Bradford at the top of the bill. We would later invite him to come and work with the band in the UK, but that night his group was the climax of two tremendously exciting hours.

After a day and a half in New York, the tour began with a long drive to Pittsburgh. After 400 miles on the road it was just a stopover that night, with no performance for us, and no music to be heard, before we set off the next morning for Huntington, Virginia, where we were playing our first concert opposite what we ended up calling the "Famous Jimmy Dorsey Ghost Orchestra". (Jimmy himself had died a couple of years earlier, in 1957.) It was not a particularly memorable concert, and we had an early start the next day for the 520-mile drive into Canada, for a gig at Hamilton, Ontario. We finally arrived at 1.30 am.

The concert was to be at the Westdale Hotel, where we played to many noisy jazz fans. We felt they were very enthusiastic but not always likeable. A lot of them were originally from Britain but they didn't behave with much dignity. However there was a treat waiting for us on the pavement outside the Westdale when we arrived there — none other than Mr and Mrs Jack Teagarden. We had met them when Jack and Earl Hines toured Britain in 1957 under the auspices of the National Jazz Federation, and they were there to invite us down to another club in Hamilton, where Jack had opened the previous night. We visited that club en masse when we had finished our concert, and his group made very pleasant listening. We particularly liked the playing of his pianist Don Ewell, who encompassed everything from Jelly Roll Morton to stride. He was to become a lifelong friend of Pat Halcox. They used to play chess by post, with games lasting over a year as their letters chased each other round the globe. Pat made one of his first records independently from my band in 1971 when Don came to Britain and recorded a quintet album, featuring Pat alongside John Defferary, Jackie Flavelle and Barry Martyn. We were reunited with Don in 1980 when he came to play in Britain, and did a number of concerts including one at the 100 Club in Oxford Street with most of my band. Sadly he was taken ill during that tour, and did not return to England again.

At Hamilton, we discovered that Jack and his band would be opening in New Orleans the same night as we were to play a concert there, much later in our tour. So we all agreed to meet up again in the Crescent City.

The next morning, it was off for the 400-mile drive to Springfield, Massachusetts. For this trip, unlike the previous one when we were in one station wagon with a trailer, we had hired two new Chevrolet shooting brakes. It was much better than travelling by coach, and, because there were two cars, the seven of us could split up from time to time along the way and do different detours, for sightseeing or meeting friends. Springfield was a rather unpleasant industrial town, so it hardly lived up to its name, but it was the setting for a three-day jazz festival, running at the Eastern States Exposition.

We played in a large tent theatre which, surprisingly for the time, was just about perfect for sound and lighting. But the most memorable aspect of the festival was that we played five split concerts with the Woody Herman band. He was now back in the States after his English tour, and the version of his orchestra that Woody brought to Springfield was basically built around the rehearsal big band run by the pianist Nat Pierce in New York City. There were several outstanding players as well as Woody and Nat. In the trumpet section were Reunald Jones and Howard McGhee, Dick Hafer played tenor sax, and on bass was an old friend, Major Holley. Major had actually lived and worked in London for much of the mid-1950s, as a studio musician for BBC television and radio. During that time, he spent as much time as possible playing and recording with local bands in and around London. He'd played with the maverick drummer Phil Seamen, and recorded with Joe Harriott. Major's nickname was "Mule" and his catchphrase was, "I needs to be be'ed with!" Woody's drummer was a young man called Ben Riley, who later became famous as a member of the Thelonious Monk quartet, and to our surprise he asked us all for autographed photos.

For several of our concerts, Ben Riley was in the audience, as were Howard McGhee, Reunald Jones and Nat Pierce, and it was thrilling for us that American stars wanted to listen to our music. McGhee paid Pat a great compliment by urging him to come down to one of the local jazz clubs and sit in.

After the festival, our drivers set off by road in the Chevvies to cover the 3,116 miles to San Francisco. We had a more leisurely trip, taking the train back to New York, and then flying from there to the West Coast the following day. We made the most of New York City, again doing the rounds of the music venues. That night one highlight was hearing the portly clarinetist Cecil Scott playing a set at Jimmy Ryan's with the pianist Don Frye and Zutty Singleton on drums.

Because it was our first visit to the West Coast, the flight across the United States was actually very thrilling, just watching the vast land-mass of America unravelling beneath our plane. Our route over New York State, parts of Pennsylvania, Ohio, Michigan, Illinois, Iowa, South Dakota and Wyoming was spectacular, from wild open country to the big cities we passed including Detroit and Chicago. We crossed the great divide, and as the sun started to set the mountain scenery took on a fantastic blood-red glow. By the time we were over Salt Lake City it was a rather eerie twilight, and the mountains and salt flats looked like something from a lunar landscape. Once darkness fell there was not much to see until the twinkling lights of San Francisco came into view.

Once we had found our hotel there was a night of jazz activity ahead of us. First, we set out for Club Hangover, on Bush Street, not far from Union Square. There, the resident band was led by Earl Hines, who was on dazzling form. The group was excellent too, with Muggsy Spanier, Darnell Howard, Jimmy Archey and Earl Watkins. Their bassist, the venerable Pops Foster, actually fell asleep on the stand while they were playing.

The interval pianist was Ralph Sutton, whom I had heard in 1951 on the London concert with Lonnie Johnson, and he was talking enthusiastically about returning to Europe, possibly to live there, and maybe settle in England. This did not, in the end, come about, but he was to be a frequent and welcome guest to Britain in the years that followed. Ottilie went her own way both on that first night and on our following "rest day" in San Francisco. She hooked up with an Irish friend, and we eventually found them in a Scottish bar called the Edinburgh Castle singing loudly and partaking of Gaelic refreshment!

On the second day everyone else went out and about as well. Monty, Pat and Eddie went to hear Marty Marsala's band, and were very impressed with the blind clarinetist Vince Cattolica. Eddie went to the Red Garter club, where the band consisted of four banjos, tuba and piano. Apparently the highlight of his evening was when one of the (Italian) banjoists picked up the bagpipes and played 'Scotland the Brave'. We also took advantage of the perfect weather to drive North and over the Golden Gate Bridge to take a distant view of San Francisco, which we all felt was a charming and relatively dignified city, with a feeling of permanence about it that was not often the case in 1950s America.

Our first West Coast concert was going to be at the second Monterey Jazz Festival, located some 124 miles south of San Francisco, and we set off there on 1 October. The festival had been launched the previous year, with Louis Armstrong, Dizzy Gillespie and Billie Holiday topping the bill, and it was advertised as a "sylvan setting with the best jazz people in the whole world playing on the same stage, having a whole weekend of jazz." There was a big open-air arena with a permanently roofed and well-designed concert stage. As one entered the festival grounds there was a row of horse stalls to one side, which we later discovered had a certain significance! We did our own rehearsal, and then for a dollar went in to watch the public rehearsal on the main stage. There was a specially convened big band which was being conducted (simultaneously, it seemed) by Woody Herman and John Lewis. There were numerous specially written arrangements so that the band could back the star guests, Coleman Hawkins, Ben Webster, J. J. Johnson and Ornette Coleman. Ornette was very much a new name at the time, having only just released his first records, but John Lewis, the festival's music adviser, thought very highly of him, and this was to be one of the first major festival concerts of his career.

When we arrived Ben Webster was blowing his way through Hawkins's parts, as Hawk had not yet arrived, and indeed did not do so until midnight. Then we met several of those who were taking part, including the composer, conductor, and former Miles Davis French horn player, Gunther Schuller, who was to present some of his modern jazz compositions. At the same time we met Victor Feldman, an expatriate British musician, and one of the brothers who had played at the precursor to the 100 Club, who was playing piano and vibraphone in the big band. In due course we retired to our rooms in the hotel, looking out over Monterey Bay and Santa Cruz, with the distant sound of seals barking as we went off to sleep.

The next day the festival grounds were really bustling with activity. I found the big band still running through parts of the programme, but also when I first got there the vocal group Lambert, Hendricks and Ross were up on the main stage rehearsing with their trio. I discovered that they were to be the musical masters of ceremonies, introducing each act by their best known number, with specially written words. For us, to the tune of 'Petite Fleur' they sang,

> *Here comes, from an Ancestral land*
> *Straight from London to you*
> *Chris Barber's band.*

Ottilie was not too pleased when their lyric for her announced her as "from Dublin's fair city", which was particularly odd, as Annie Ross's forbears were Orangemen, so it's hardly a mistake she would normally make. Actually I don't think it occurred to her because Jon Hendricks had come up with the lyrics, and to him Dublin was synonymous with Ireland, just as London is synonymous with England. However, in the long run we took the compliment of being given a musical introduction in the spirit in which it was meant, and we managed to get hold of one of their lyric sheets as a souvenir.

That evening was our big moment. We got to the festival ground at 7.30 pm, to discover that the big room behind the stage was still being used for a press reception, and the dressing rooms had not yet been built. That's when we discovered the significance of the horse boxes, where all the stars including the great Lizzie Miles had had to change the previous year. It was the same for us. Despite the reception over-running, the show started more or less on time, and after a brief speech by Jimmy Lyons, who organized the

My father, Donald Barber

Chris Barber collection

My mother, Hettie Barber, during her tenure as Mayor of Canterbury, around 1973

Chris Barber collection

Me and my sister Audrey, just before World War Two

Chris Barber collection

My 1950 band (musicians l to r): Chris Barber, trombone; Ben Cohen, cornet; Brian Lawes, drums; Keith Jary, trumpet; Ferdie Favager, banjo; Roy Sturgess, piano; Alex Revell, clarinet; Alexis Korner, guitar

Chris Barber collection

My band, a little later in 1950 (l to r): Chris Barber, Ferdie Favager, Jeremy French, Roy Sturgess, Alex Revell

Chris Barber collection

Riverboat shuffle; musicians include (l to r): Chris Barber, Alex Revell, Humphrey Lyttelton, Bernie Newlands, Owen Bryce

Chris Barber collection

Ken Colyer's Jazzmen, 1953: Monty Sunshine, Lonnie Donegan, Ken Colyer, Ron Bowden, Chris Barber, Jim Bray

Johnny Chown

The reception in my bedsit in Bayswater after my wedding to Naida (l to r): Ron Bowden, Chris Barber, Ottilie Patterson, Beryl Bryden, Pat Halcox, Naida

Chris Barber collection

Arriving in Berlin, 1958 (l to r): Dick Smith, Chris Barber, Eddie Smith, Monty Sunshine, Sonny Terry, Pat Halcox, Graham Burbidge (at foot of stairs), Brownie McGhee

Johnny Chown

With a New Orleans legend: Dick Smith, George Lewis, Pat Halcox, in Leicester, 1957

D. G. Wills

Autograph hunters and Sister Rosetta Tharpe

Johnny Chown

Muddy Waters, "St. Louis Jimmy" (Jimmy Oden), Chris Barber and Ottilie Patterson at McKie's Disc Jockey Show Lounge, Chicago, 1959

Chris Barber collection

Arriving in the USA, 1960: top: Harold Pendleton, Graham Burbidge; middle: Monty Sunshine, Eddie Smith, Pat Halcox; front: Chris Barber, Ottilie Patterson

Monty Sunshine, Pat Halcox, Joe Harriott, Eddie Smith, at the Marquee Club, 1960

Terry Cryer

On the *Ed Sullivan Show*, 1959; Jane Russell and Ed Sullivan either side of Chris

Steve Oroz Associates

Chris Barber's American Jazz Band: Chris Barber, Ed Hall, Hayes Alvis, Joe Marshall, Sidney De Paris, Hank Duncan

Chris Barber collection

Chris Barber's Jazz Band, in a promotional still from the 1963 film *Übermut im Salzkammergut*: Ian Wheeler, Dick Smith, Chris Barber, Pat Halcox, Graham Burbidge, Eddie Smith

Chris Barber collection

Chris Barber, Ottilie Patterson and their dog Willie-Mae at Drumalta, Northern Ireland, late 1960s
Chris Barber collection

Pat Halcox and Chris Barber, 1970
Chris Barber collection

The band at Brands Hatch early 1970s: John Crocker, Jackie Flavelle, Pat Halcox, Graham Burbidge, Chris Barber, John Slaughter, Steve Hammond

Chris Barber collection

Graham Hill and Chris Barber, Nürburgring, 1964

Chris Barber collection

Chris Barber and cyclist, during the six-day cycle event at Halle Münsterland, 1975

Chris Barber collection

Jackie Stewart and Chris Barber, late 1950s

Chris Barber collection

Ken Tyrell, George Harrison and Chris Barber, 1994

Chris Barber collection

John Lewis, Mirjana Lewis and Chris Barber, 2000

Chris Barber collection

Dr John and Chris Barber, late 1990s

Chris Barber collection

My daughter Caroline, wife Renate and son Christopher, 1991

Chris Barber collection

The eight-piece band on the road in Germany, 1994: Pat Halcox, John Crocker, Paul Sealey, John Slaughter, Ian Wheeler, Alan "Sticky" Wickett, Vic Pitt, Chris Barber

Chris Barber collection

Chris Barber and Kate Gray

Chris Barber collection

The Big Chris Barber Band: John Defferary, Paul Sealey, Vic Pitt, Colin Miller, Pat Halcox, Chris Barber, Mike Henry, Bob Hunt, John Slaughter, Nik Payton

David Redfern

event, our singing compères came on to introduce us. We played for the first hour of the evening and we were very well received, finishing off with three band numbers and an encore from Ottilie. After us came Lizzie Miles, and, to accompany her, the festival had engaged Burt Bales. He was well-known in the area, having played with the local revivalist bands of Lu Watters and Bob Scobey. He often worked as the intermission pianist at Club Hangover, as Ralph Sutton was doing during our stay, and he frequently played there with Lizzie Miles.

However, Burt was highly inebriated when he came on stage, and, to say the least, there were some discrepancies of tempo between them. Yet Lizzie Miles was a veritable triumph. She sang all her well-known numbers, with her usual inserted verses in French. Following her came George Lewis and his New Orleans band. There was the familiar rhythm section of Alton Purnell, Lawrence Marrero, Slow Drag Pavageau and Joe Watkins, but in the front line (billed as Buddy Bolden Jr.) was the trumpeter Andy Anderson, a great brass band player and the composer of the song 'Chant of the Tuxedos'. On trombone was Bob Mielke, a local San Franciscan, who played very well, and turned in a memorable solo on 'Tin Roof Blues'.

The next artist to appear was the most successful of the evening, Earl Hines, with Vernon Alley, bass and Mel Lewis, drums. Earl was in even more brilliant form that he had been at Club Hangover, and played as well — if not better — than any time I ever saw him. After playing for thirty minutes and then a couple of encores, the trio was augmented by Ben Webster, Coleman Hawkins, Roy Eldridge, Urbie Green and Woody Herman, to create the Festival's All Star mainstream group. They had never played together before as a band but they did remarkably well, despite covering some pretty well-known ground. Shortly after midnight they were joined by Jimmy Witherspoon, the last star of the show. The piano and front-line accompaniment was tremendous, especially Coleman Hawkins, but I felt Spoon might have been even more successful with a more rhythm and blues style drummer. At one o'clock everything wound up, and there was a glorious melée backstage of musicians, journalists and hangers-on of all types.

The next day some of us went sightseeing on the Monterey Peninsula. Ottilie and I visited an old friend from London, Roland Thorpe, who was a record collector. He had moved out to California in 1948. While we were spending time with him the rest of the band went along to an avant-garde concert, with specially commissioned works from Gunther Schuller and John Lewis among others. When I got to the show ground, I was pleasantly surprised to see and hear an unannounced visitor, the blues singer Jesse Fuller. He was originally from Georgia, but had been living in San Francisco for a while following a whole variety of careers from barrel-making to woodcarving and from film acting to welding. He had been stationed by the organisers in one of the bays of the open-air art exhibition, where he played as a one-man band. As well as playing guitar he had a kazoo and harmonica, a hi-hat cymbal, and an amazing invention called the fotdella, which was a box, strung with six bass strings, that he could play with his feet. I had heard of him because he had made his first records the previous year at the ripe old age of sixty-two, but it was great to hear him in person, singing blues and skiffle to a very appreciative audience. I later found out he had left his full-time occupation on a shoeshine stand for the day to come into the festival grounds and perform.

The evening concert opened with the festival big band under Woody Herman's direction. The MJQ followed Woody, but their set was rather unsuccessful because there had been a mistaken announcement of an interval, whereas the concert carried straight on, so half the audience was leaving and others coming back in a rush as the quartet began their set. The following act, Lambert, Hendricks and Ross, was tremendous entertainment, with Jon Hendricks's slick vocal dexterity stealing the show. The evening rounded off with Cal Tjader joining forces with Herman for some Latin jazz, plus guest appearances from Ernestine Anderson, who was not very impressive, and Jimmy Witherspoon, who was, but not as brilliant as on his outstanding set the previous night.

After Monterey, we set off on the road again, for a four-day journey to Chickasha, Oklahoma. En route we took in a show in Las Vegas by Sammy Davis Jr., who was fantastically good. Probably the best single entertainer I have ever seen, he was singing, acting, impersonating, dancing, playing vibes and getting away with tremendously racially-inclined jokes. He even contrived to look like Jimmy Cagney and Frank Sinatra in his imperson-ations. The following day our route took us close to the Grand Canyon, so we went to see it just an hour before sunset, and, without doubt, it is one of the most thrilling and remarkable places on the face of the earth. From there we pressed on to Flagstaff, Arizona, and then into New Mexico. Some towns marked on the map were just a single shop or "trading post" in the desert, whereas biggish towns had a couple of filling stations as well!

I bought a cowboy hat in New Mexico, and so did Eddie Smith and Ottilie. But we felt rather inhibited wearing them in Albuquerque, once we finally arrived there after our trip past the Petrified Forest and the Painted Desert. Nevertheless, Ottilie was in geological ecstasy about all the physical wonders of the landscape. The final day of our trip to Chickasha was a mere 530 miles from Albuquerque, crossing Texas into Oklahoma. When we arrived at 8.30 pm, everything was very quiet. But the next day, 8 October, we turned up for our engagement at Oklahoma College for Women. Amazingly, the college supported its own sixteen-piece modern jazz all-girl big band, and we went along to one of their open rehearsals, which was pretty impressive. The concert that night was open to the public as well as college students, and it went very well. Because of the average age of the crowd it was the closest we had come on the tour so far to playing to a young audience like the ones at home.

The next night we were just twelve miles away, at Oklahoma State University in Stillwater. The university had a state-of-the-art student union building, which included a hotel for visitors to the campus, such as our band. They held a formal reception for us in the Chinese lounge, one of several in this union complex, but the refreshment was not as exotic as the décor, since we were simply offered cookies and fruit punch. The students put on a talent show, and our concert followed straight on from that. The evening wound up at about 11.30 pm, and at some point during the festivities I was made an honorary life member of "Epsilon sigma epsilon" – the student fraternity connected with entertainment.

When we left Stillwater the next day, it was apparently the day of one of the biggest football matches in the calendar. Everybody had been wearing orange and black lapel badges or cards the night before and many of them read "Yea, Cowboys! Tromp Tulsa!" Although we were off on the road towards our next destination at Wichita University by the time the match started, we learned later that the Stillwater "Cowboys" did indeed "tromp" Tulsa.

Our next concert in Wichita was the first return to a venue that we had played on our previous tour. It was great to see many of the same people we had met before. Once again we were royally received, this time in a gracious lounge in a new building that had been constructed from scratch since our last visit. The concert went even better than the one in March.

After playing that concert our cars went their different ways again. Some of the band went in one of the shooting brakes to Sioux City, where the Turchen family lived, and they were well entertained and fed into the bargain. Ottilie and I drove to Kansas City, where Dinah Washington was playing in the huge municipal auditorium. It was built to hold an audience of thousands, but she was playing to just a few hundred. This was a shame because she sang really well, but she and her trio were a bit lost in the cavernous space of the auditorium. She was supported by a rather dull house band that played for dancing.

Our next job was a couple of days later in the college at Grinnell, Iowa. It was a pleasant small town, and we played in the gymnasium of the college, which had lights and a good stage, but unfortunately there was a formidable echo and the amplification system did not improve matters. The main thing we remembered about Iowa was that you needed a permit to drink alcohol. When we returned to Britain the only member of the band who still had her permit was Ottilie. Eddie Smith teased her about being a state-registered drunk!

Our eventual destination was Chicago, which we reached by way of concerts at River Falls, Wisconsin (a return visit from March), Minneapolis (where we hooked up with trumpeter Doc Evans), and Waverly, Iowa (from where the girls' choir had visited England earlier in the year). Finally, we played in Monmouth College, Illinois, and drove the 200 miles to Chicago after our concert, in order to arrive before the last set at Smitty's Corner where Muddy Waters was just about to take the stage.

We were to return to Smitty's Corner the next night for the session I have already described above, but earlier in the evening, on 18 October, we went out and about to see what other music Chicago had to offer. Some of the band went to hear Art Hodes playing piano at the Café Continental. The rest of us went to the Red Arrow, where the band led by veteran saxophonist Franz Jackson was playing. Franz had played with both Fats Waller and Earl Hines, and he had recorded with Roy Eldridge. His own band included two veterans, Albert Wynn on trombone and Bob Shoffner on trumpet. Ottilie was invited up to sing a couple of numbers with the band and while she sang 'Careless Love' and 'Backwater Blues' it was quite a thrill to realise that Albert Wynn had spent two years playing with Ma Rainey and Shoffner had played with both Ma Rainey and Bessie Smith. They accompanied her beautifully, and seemed to enjoy it immensely. Al Wynn was particularly friendly, and he came with us to Muddy's club, where Little Walter was just beginning his set. Walter's harmonica solos were quite far out, often having a quite different number of bars from twelve, and changing tempo quite alarmingly during his solo breaks. Then it was Muddy's band and we went on last. We were still sitting up chewing the fat with Muddy, St. Louis Jimmy and other members of his band at six in the morning. Al Wynn said he had not been so well entertained, musically and socially, for years!

We flew from Chicago to Texas for a couple of days, playing in a beautiful festival hall-sized auditorium in Austin, and then at the South Texas State Fair Jazz Festival in Dallas. Both concerts were split between us, Woody Herman and another band. The Dallas show took place at the Coliseum Horse Arena, which had really excellent lighting and sound. Backstage it was even more quaint than Monterey, with live ponies and horses in the stalls, sawdust, and a very pricey saddle shop. We saw one listed at $1000, which in 1959 was a huge amount.

Back in Chicago we heard Bob Scobey's band, which was rather disappointing apart from the jovial Clancy Hayes on banjo and vocals. Art Hodes was on good form, but Ottilie and I, along with Eddie Smith, spent our evening off going back to Muddy Waters' club. This time we had the treat of hearing Little Brother Montgomery on piano, as unfortunately Otis Spann had been called away to a funeral. Robert Johnson's stepson was playing guitar and singing, and he was keen for Ottilie to join in with him. We also heard a young singer called Minnie Thomas. At that point she had yet to be recorded, but she already had the firm commanding voice you can hear on her discs, and she sang blues in a grand majestic manner, with lots of gospel type decorations and embellishments.

After Chicago it was off to Mount Pleasant, Michigan; Cincinnati, and Indianapolis. In Cincinnati we bumped into the members of the George Lewis band, whom we had last seen in Monterey, and had been travelling across the country as well. This was a curtain raiser for what was to be the highlight of our trip, arriving in New Orleans itself, which we reached by way of a rather lengthy flight via Memphis and Jackson.

Mike Slatter, who formerly lived in London, and who made some fine recordings of New Orleans musicians, greeted us at the airport, along with his American friend Ralph Collins. They took us to our hotel, which was called the "New Orleans" and situated on the corner of Canal and Saratoga Streets. We checked in, and then Mike and Ralph took us out straight away to sightsee in the French Quarter, which was by far the most picturesque place we'd visited in America (and probably outside America for that matter). We stopped by at the French Market for the traditional local fare of coffee and doughnuts, before making our way to the shop run by clarinetist Raymond Burke. It was a pretty murky little book-and-junk shop, and Ray was sitting on a stool on the sidewalk surrounded by heaps of old books. But in the inner recesses of the shop he had a collection of really eccentric musical instruments. He had made an instrument where he put two lengths of gas pipe of different bore together, so one slid inside the other, but they were relatively airtight. It created a slide clarinet, and that's where the term "gaspipe" clarinet comes from. It sounded a bit like a swanee whistle. Ray then dug out more weird instruments. Our visit finished with Pat playing an improvised horn of a shape so eccentric that it beat Dizzy Gillespie's any day of the week, and Ray joining him on bazooka, for a busk through 'Milenburg Joys'.

We moved on from Ray Burke to see Bill Russell at his American Music record shop. My first impression of Bill, whom we came to know well, was of a tall, amiable, but rather vague man, whose shop was a heavenly shambles of delight for the jazz enthusiast. There were violins, banjos, thousands of records, antique advertisements, and Mardi Gras souvenirs and invitation cards. One thing Bill had — in which I took a great interest — was the *Red Backed Book of Rags*, of which he had a photostat. It contained instrumental parts for several instruments. In due course, in January 1960, we recorded several of these, and I also used some of the parts as the basis for multi-tracking one or two of the rags myself to create an all-trombone front line.

After leaving Bill's shop we went looking up and down the streets at some of the famous places, but there wasn't a lot of time to see anything on that occasion because we soon had to get ready for our big moment — the concert at the Civic Auditorium. It was a strange feeling to think that part of this building stood on the site of Congo Square, which had played such an important role in jazz history. We knew that we were sharing the bill with Pete Fountain's group, but when we got there we discovered from the organisers, Harry and Doc Souchon, that Paul Barbarin's band would be on the programme as well.

The official programme was started off by the Barbarin group, then the British Consul General, the Hon. A. G. Maitland, introduced us and we played for an hour. After the interval, I was called back to the stage and made an honorary citizen of New Orleans and presented with a key to the city.

The rest of the band were made honorary members of the New Orleans Jazz Club, along with Jack Teagarden who was present, but he did not play on the concert that evening because, as we already knew, he was in town to play a club residency. The next part of the concert was by the Pete Fountain group, which overran considerably, maybe because their set was being recorded. We finished the show, but the highlight for us was the Barbarin band, giving us the opportunity to hear the city's real music played by real pioneers in the real place. Afterwards we went to the Dream Room, where Sharkey Bonano's band and Jack Teagarden's group were both playing. During that part of the evening I remember meeting the clarinetist Peanuts Hucko, who had driven 1,072 miles the previous day in order to get there.

The next day the *New Orleans Times-Picayune* in its midday edition carried a review of the concert whose headline said: "British Win Battle of New Orleans". In those days, before rolling television news, regional papers in the States used to produce more than one edition a day, each with a different front cover. These were known as "slip" editions, and maybe by the time of the evening paper everything would have been re-jigged to take into account breaking news stories. Fortunately, I went out and bought several copies of the midday edition because by the evening our review had been relegated to a little box, without the marvellous headline. I cut out the stories from each paper, stuck them on giant postcards of the city and sent these off to various British newspapers. The British Consul General, Mr Maitland, also sent a copy to the Foreign Office, reporting how successful the event had been. I know that the copy I sent to the music writer Patrick Doncaster at the *Daily Mirror* was reprinted in his column, and I think one or two other UK papers picked up the story. In the *Times-Picayune* report, from that midday slip edition, there were some nice photographs of the concert. One of them is a shot taken backstage showing me with the president of the New Orleans Jazz Club, Pete Miller, listening to Paul Barbarin's band. You can't see it in the picture, but I was really taken aback when he turned to me and said, "You gotta hand it to them niggers, they sure got that beat!" I don't think he was putting anybody down. It was very much the everyday language of white Southern Americans at the time. But if you'd been brought up in a left-leaning household as I was, which vehemently opposed any whiff of eugenics, then any prejudicial statement like that was dodgy. He was right, of course, that the band had a marvellous beat, but the way he expressed it really shocked me.

I think that visit also shocked some of the band as we experienced aspects of segregation quite unlike anything we had encountered in Europe. It was in New Orleans that all the guys in the band realised just the depth and breadth of the colour bar in 1950s America, although in some ways the city had been more integrated than most right the way through its history. For example, black musicians taught white kids about music at the Opera House. So in some senses it was not segregated in ways in which Europeans might use the word. But the social segregation was deep-rooted. I remember Graham Burbidge going white as a sheet when he discovered that black women had to use the gents' toilet at the airport because only white women could use the ladies'.

Otherwise, the time we spent in New Orleans after the concert passed a bit like a dream, really. I remember a late breakfast with Mr Maitland and Harry Souchon. While Maitland was Consul there, he always made a point of taking any British visitors out to one particular ante-bellum plantation, with its big house and cotton fields. No doubt he had some kind of tacit arrangement with the owners. Then I recall doing a television interview with the veteran *New Orleans Item* reporter "Scoop" Kennedy (who had published a guide to the city's eating places) and the broadcaster Mel Leavitt. After that, Ottilie and I dropped in to see Lizzie Miles whom we'd met at Monterey. At the time I noted that she was "shrewd, vivacious, voluble and full of praises for the band".

Once we left Lizzie, we tried to catch as much music as possible before our scheduled departure on a flight at midnight. The jazz historian and scholar Dick Allen was in town and showed us around various musical venues. He was an enormous fan of the *Goon Show*. We wondered how Americans even heard the programmes, but maybe he listened to them on the BBC World Service or possibly forces' radio. The trumpeter Alvin Alcorn was one musician we met then, who was a very sociable sort of guy, and who was to come to Britain with my band many years later. At some point on that visit I remember hearing the trumpeter Al Hirt, known as "Jumbo", whose technique was remarkable, but who did not combine his exceptional ability on the instrument with a comparable level of good taste, often sounding rather brash and raw. At the same time Pat and some of the rest of the band made their way to the Paddock Lounge to hear Thomas Jefferson and Andrew Morgan playing with some members of the Barbarin band.

Another treat for me was hearing Percy and Willie Humphrey at the Absinthe House with Sweet Emma Barrett on piano and Cié Frazier on drums. It was just a quartet, but playing really nice music. Many years later in August 1991 I recorded with Percy in New Orleans and it turned out to be one of the last recordings he made before he died, four years later. He wasn't terribly well at the time, but on the record he still sounded very much like his younger self, bringing back memories of that first visit. And it was a pleasure to work with him and Willie, along with Jeanette Kimball and Frank Fields, plus Barry Martyn on drums.

My main memory of that first meeting with Percy at the Absinthe House was that he was very friendly. In fact all the musicians we met and spent time with in the city were extremely friendly. One in particular was a pianist called Archibald. He was a fine rhythm and blues singer and player, a little bit in the Professor Longhair style, who had made some impressive records for Imperial at the beginning of the 1950s, such as 'Stack-o-lee' and 'Shake Shake Baby', but who was, by the time of our visit, earning his living working in a bar on Bourbon Street.

The friendliest musician of all turned out to be Paul Barbarin. After the concert he gave me some sheet music for some of his songs, to whom other people had added lyrics. I told him that we were using 'Bourbon Street Parade' as our theme song, and he was delighted, saying, "That's great!" Yet I think at the time many other musicians in show business in the United States would not have taken kindly to somebody else playing their theme, which they'd written themselves to play with their own band. Mind you, he did earn some money from it. Putting a song like that out on a record in America would not have made him very much because the mechanical recording rights are almost nil, but we recorded it several times in Britain and Europe where payments to songwriters are enforced by law. So in due course he would have received a sizeable amount of money.

We remained friends with Paul, and the next year when we came back to the city we recorded with him, on an album with Billie and DeDe Pierce. I don't remember if Graham Burbidge felt like taking the day off, but Paul was there for the session and ended up playing on all of it! It was done at Larry Borenstein's house, on the patio in his back yard, because this was in the days before Preservation Hall — which began in the art gallery that Larry set up on St. Peter Street. Doc Souchon was there with his guitar, Eddie Smith played banjo on one or two numbers, Paul Crawford dropped in and played a bit on trombone, but the centre of it all was DeDe's trumpet playing and Billie's singing and piano. It was recorded by Bill Russell who brought along a stereo tape recorder, although he had his own ideas about recording in stereo, and the results seem more like mono.

Our flight out of New Orleans on that first visit was a real let-down after the wonderful time we had had in the city. We were sent on a detour via Atlanta to Chicago, which cost the band a total of eighty dollars extra, which was a lot of money in 1959, and, after landing in Chicago at 4 am, we finally left for Toronto at 9 am. It was after midday when we finally arrived at our hotel. Somehow we roused ourselves after a sleep in the afternoon to play at the Eton Auditorium that night. We had performed at Massey Hall earlier in the year, but the Eton was a more pleasant environment in which to play, although the acoustics were very dry. Despite our long night and day, we dropped in after our concert to hear Wild Bill Davison at the Westover Hotel.

The last three days of October saw us in Buffalo, Hamilton (Ontario) and finally back in New York, for our last gig of the tour. It had been an eventful journey down from Hamilton, in driving rain, and we'd had to change a wheel on one of the cars, yet the thrill of being back in Manhattan was so great that we were soon out and about visiting Condon's, Ryan's and the Metropole.

During this very short time in New York, I organised a recording session with some of the surviving members of Clarence Williams's Washboard Band from the 1920s. I wanted to get as close as I could to the spirit of those old records but without consciously trying to recreate what had been done thirty years or so earlier. We'd met Cecil Scott, the reed player with Williams's original band, at Jimmy Ryan's and through him I was able to put together the rest of the group. Cecil taught music in Harlem, so he had a good network of contacts. He found Ed Allen, who had played trumpet on the '20s recordings, playing in a dime-a-dance hall. I was surprised when we called 'Royal Garden Blues' and he didn't know how it went. Then he told me that he used to learn the tunes on the way to the sessions in a taxi to the studio, and although he probably remembered the tunes, he didn't always recall the names. 'Royal Garden Blues' had also been known as 'Beer Garden Blues' at one stage, so that might also have explained why he thought he didn't know it. By 1959 Cecil Scott thought of himself as mainly a tenor sax player, and his intention was to play as close to Ben Webster's style as he possibly could. However, we persuaded him to play clarinet and revert to the kind of playing he had done at Ryan's. Floyd Casey had played washboard back on those '20s records, and he was so sure we must have made a mistake asking for him to play washboard that he turned up with a full drum kit. Fortunately, just in case we'd been serious, he had packed his washboard, and he was actually delighted to play it again after so many years!

We could not get Clarence Williams himself for this session, but Cecil put us in touch with Don Frye who had played with King Oliver in 1929, so he seemed to me to be a suitably authentic choice, and on bass we had the much younger Leonard Gaskin. I played on three of the tracks we made that day, but because I did not have the union's permission to record I limited myself to those few numbers, and put myself down on the ledger as "T-Bone Jefferson". The record came out as *Chris Barber Presents Harlem Washboard*.

Our final concert with my band was on the Sunday at Basin Street East on East 48th Street. It was normally closed on Sundays, but it opened specially for our show, and we were supported by the Chubby Jackson Trio. The event was promoted by Laurie Records, who had released 'Petite Fleur' in the States and, among other guests in the audience, they had brought in the entire Turk Murphy band from the West Coast.

A lot of friends turned out to meet us and hear the band at the club, including Zutty and Marge Singleton, and Leonard Feather. One very startling and rather tragic event happened when Max Roach came down to the club. He had been suffering from a series of nervous attacks, and occasionally had hysterics in public. Unfortunately, this was one of those events, and he lay down on the sidewalk outside the club banging his hands on the ground. In his state of wild panic the police were called, but fortunately he left before they arrived and there wasn't any kind of confrontation.

As late as 1959 flying back into Britain from the USA involved arriving at Heathrow's international terminal which was roughly where Terminal 1 is now. The customs area was a long shed parallel with the A4, perhaps twenty yards away from the road. It was quite long, and perhaps twenty feet deep. Along the centre line ran a trestle table from one end to the other. The customs officers stood behind it and the arriving passengers faced them across it. As we disembarked I was carrying a holdall containing some fifty 78s which I had found in the house where St. Louis Jimmy had rooms, a few blocks from the apartment of Butterbeans & Susie. The records had belonged to the landlady's son (who interestingly enough collected scent bottles). They were in a pile over two feet high, and not even in paper covers.

The owner (whose name I have forgotten) checked carefully to make sure I wasn't getting any of his favourites. The only one I had asked to buy and about which he had doubts over selling was an Okeh record of Clarence Williams's Blue Five with a vocal by Eva Taylor. His doubts were because he wanted to keep it for the vocal, which he liked. The rest of the pile included 78s of King Oliver's band and many excellent 1920s blues singers with accompanists such as Louis Armstrong. He wanted fifty cents each and, in fact, he got rather more because I was aware of the value of some of the discs.

Carrying the holdall, I approached the customs table and was asked if I had bought anything "over there". When I explained I had a number of thirty-year-old 78s, one of the customs officers said, "Hello Chris! Did you get anything good?"

No duty was charged!

All in all, that first full tour of America was extremely successful and it was followed up by a further lengthy visit in the autumn of 1960. We began that trip in Los Angeles, where Ottilie and I arrived ahead of the band. I was lent a Lotus Elite sports car by the local distributor for our few days off, and we enjoyed the sun and the atmosphere of the city, although Pat teased me when he arrived over the fact that I had already collected a parking fine.

This time our first concert was in a venue every bit as impressive as the Monterey Festival site, Massey Hall or the New Orleans Municipal Auditorium — namely the Hollywood Bowl. It seated 20,000 people, and we were on a bill with the Count Basie Orchestra, the Firehouse Five in full regalia, Teddy Buckner's band and the Louis Armstrong All Stars. It was quite daunting to go on after the first three of those bands, and to be followed by Louis, but we went on and — according to the set-list that Pat kept — played 'Panama', 'Chimes Blues', 'Stevedore Stomp', 'Lord Lord Lord', 'Blues Before Sunrise', 'Come Along Home To Me' and 'This Little Light Of Mine'. We went over time, because we'd been very late starting. I remember vividly as we came towards the end of our set, Louis Armstrong's voice could be clearly heard backstage saying: "Give the boys another number!"

The concert was reviewed by Paul Affeldt, a local ragtime expert and record collector, in his magazine *The Jazz Report*. He said:

> Chris Barber's Band was even more than I expected . . . they had a
> tough row to hoe in following the Firehouse Five, and when they
> kicked off on 'Panama Rag' there was a small amount of unease

and uncertainty. But they steadily gained confidence and soon had the entire bowl hanging on their every note. This group is true to what I've grown to expect from English bands, they were earnest, swinging and musicianly in their every note. There wasn't a second of sloppy or tired sounding playing here. This is a group that takes New Orleans jazz as seriously as Bolden himself must have and they played the most spirited and close-knit honest jazz of the evening . . .Also with them was one of the finest girl vocalists I've ever heard. Ottilie Patterson has a slightly hoarse, low voice, and the best grasp of the blues style I've heard in years. This was especially apparent on her great 'Blues Before Sunrise'.

So it turned out to be a pretty memorable evening, and both Joe Darensbourg and Teddy Buckner came round and complimented the band after the show. It was a great start to the tour, and we next played in — among other places — Las Vegas and Laramie. From there it was on to Boulder, Waverly and Chicago.

I've already covered our reunion with Muddy Waters in Chicago, and, apart from visiting his club and his home, we played our own shows at the Red Arrow Jazz Club in Stickney, just south west of Chicago and close to Cicero. It was a big club, seating about 350, and it was run very successfully by Otto J. Kubik. Don Ewell, whom we had met the previous year with Jack Teagarden, dropped in to say hello, as did Clancy Hayes. So again, after our social evenings with Muddy, Albert Wynne and Little Brother, we felt surrounded by friends and received a very warm welcome.

The distances we drove in America seemed even longer this time. In British terms, it was a bit like saying we'd start in Southend-on-Sea, followed by Inverness, followed by Penzance, and then Carlisle. That's what we were doing in the United States, more or less. On that tour we played at a resort hotel in the Catskill Mountains, and then set off for Toronto. Abe Turchen had contacts in the Catskill region so he was able to book us there, and one curious observation we made was that at that time these plush resort hotel complexes were virtually all Jewish owned. The history behind this was that on finding themselves unwelcome in previously established country clubs, the Jewish community built their own, only bigger and better. In the one we worked at, the Woody Herman seven-piece band was playing when we arrived on a bandstand in the foyer, and we played in the main night club opposite them for two or three evenings.

When we came to leave the Catskills, it was snowing. We had a long way to go so we thought we'd better get moving. We set off and averaged about ninety miles an hour the whole way up the New York State freeway as far as the Canadian border. We didn't see any other cars, let alone police cars, along the way. Apparently it was considered too dangerous for the police to go out on patrol because they figured you could not drive on snow. Of course one could and we did, but in my memory it seems like a scene from a science fiction movie where they hadn't brought in the actors, but they had got the scenery ready! There had been some road clearing done, although we didn't see a single snow plough, and to be honest the conditions weren't that bad. But they were bad enough for the patrol cars to stay safely in their garages.

We did have an incident with road clearing when we played a concert in St. Paul, Minnesota, a bit later on during that same tour. We had to drive down to Chicago from there, and some of us took the train, but the others went in the two cars. Pat Halcox and Eddie Smith drove the first of the station wagons, and they had been driving down a snow-covered main road when they decided to stop in a lay-by for a breather. A ploughing machine came down the road, failed to spot them, and dumped all the snow from the road over them and the car, almost burying them alive. It took them quite a while to dig themselves out and get on the move again.

Driving in America gave us some other really unusual experiences. We got stopped for speeding on the Connecticut Thruway. The patrolman was very nice when he discovered we were British, but he explained that on that section of road the limit was fifty miles per hour and we had been going well over that. I told him we were terribly sorry and had not quite realised the limits in the United States. So he said, "I've got a packet of ten tickets here for the Police Support Ball. It's ten dollars." So I agreed to buy them. The tickets looked like a book of raffle tickets and he tore off one and handed me the rest. In other words, I now had nine more tickets that I could use to get away with speeding were we to be stopped again, through having handed over the ten dollars.

During the Toronto stage of the tour we managed to hook up with Richard Burton whom we hadn't seen since filming *Look Back in Anger*. We were playing at Eaton's Auditorium, and he was starring in *Camelot* in one of the big theatres in town. He suggested we join him at the Variety Club, and we ended up by playing for the assembled company, while he sang a stirring version of 'Land of My Fathers'.

We worked our way south from Chicago via Indiana, Kentucky, Alabama and into Louisiana, before arriving again in New Orleans. This was the visit on which we recorded with Billie and DeDe, but it was also an opportunity to hear some of the other musicians who were active in 1960. The Octave Crosby band was on good form, and this time when we visited Bill Russell's shop there was a jam session in a nearby bar which gave us the chance to hear Ray Burke playing a real clarinet, alongside veteran trumpeter Johnny Wiggs. We managed to witness a street parade, with the Gibson Brass Band, and we also heard a fiery set from Kid Thomas, playing on the waterfront to entertain passengers on one of the Mississippi riverboats. Our own concert was once again promoted by the New Orleans Jazz Club, and this time we shared the bill with the trumpeter Tony Almerico and his All Stars, featuring the local hero "Buglin' Sam" DeKemel.

From New Orleans it was back to the Red Arrow near Chicago. Then we wound our way down to Maryland, and eventually arrived in New York. One of the places we played was a roadhouse at Niantic, out on the Connecticut shore. They had jazz there quite often, and we played in a room about the size of the present-day Pizza Express Jazz Club in London. The food was particularly good, because the old roadhouse had been taken over by two young chefs. They were sons of Greek immigrants from the Carolinas, but the two of them had just won a national competition to find America's new young chefs, and they were dedicated to providing fine cooking for the jazz club clientele. Sadly it seemed to us as if the majority of the customers just wanted to drink bourbon and eat a well-done hamburger. But we made the most of it, and they provided us with lobster and all the works. Consequently, we got on very well with the chefs. They told us that Dizzy Gillespie had recently been there with his quintet. They noticed that when one of the other members of the band took a long solo, Dizzy would go and sit at one of the customers' tables. Within a few seconds, a whisky would arrive at his side. Having heard about this, the band invented the scenario where Dizzy arrives at a table, settles down, shakes hands with the customers and says, "Hello, I'm Dizzy Gillespie, what am I having?"

We'd seen something similar ourselves, at Eddie Condon's club, where his money was made by going and sitting down with the punters, and encouraging them to spend more, usually by buying him a bottle of whisky. But there were two sides to Eddie. I remember sitting in with his band one night, when Rex Stewart and Herbie Hall were in the front line and the rhythm section was Gene Schroeder on piano, Buzzy Drootin on drums and Leonard Gaskin, who (although he'd played on the Harlem Washboard record with me) was a very ineffectual bassist in a club setting. I started playing and suddenly the rhythm section started to swing. I looked round and Eddie had picked up his guitar and joined in. From then on, with him there, every tempo was just right, and everything swung. His presence was subtle, but it made the world of difference. I knew what a fine player he could be, as, when his band had appeared at the Royal Festival Hall in 1957, I'd gone along to their late-night concert. The thing that sticks in my memory from that night was Eddie taking a half-chorus solo on a tune in the ballad medley. It was just perfect, and with the tuning of his four-string tenor guitar it had a very distinctive sound. He reminded me of Carmen Mastren, who was a true virtuoso. Eddie could certainly play and play well, when he wasn't coaxing spending money out of his club customers.

Our concerts this time were at the Central Plaza down in the East Village on 2nd Avenue and 6th Street. It was a very well-known venue that operated on Fridays and Saturdays, in a large ballroom on the top floor of a five-storey building. It mainly catered for a young crowd in their early twenties, who weren't so much jazz fans as simply out to enjoy the atmosphere of traditional jazz. It was run by Jack Crystal, who was the father of the comedian Billy

Crystal. We played there on both nights, opposite an all-star band led by the trombonist and actor Conrad Janis. His line-up was slightly different from night to night, but trumpeters Max Kaminsky and Herman Autrey, clarinetists Tony Parenti and Gene Sedric, pianist Claude Hopkins and drummer Panama Francis were among those who played.

We attracted our own guests, too. J. C Higginbotham came down to see us, but the high point was when Sister Rosetta Tharpe was reunited with the band, and sang 'When The Saints Go Marching In'. This brought the audience to its feet and made a fantastic end to a long and sometimes exhausting tour.

5 Harlem Bound

When the 1960 tour finished, Ottilie and I stayed on at the Wellington Hotel near Central Park for a few days, and took in more music. Being in America, it seemed to our friends and fans back in Britain that we must have had the chance to meet lots of musicians, people we'd idolised or learned the music from by proxy on recordings. Of course the festivals and big concerts in places like New Orleans did allow us to do that, but being out on the road for so much of the time meant we didn't really meet very many of them, given all the weeks we spent in the States. Usually we were playing somewhere that nobody else was playing. It's a bit like the 1960s in England where people would ask, "How is Acker Bilk?" And I'd find myself saying, "I don't know, because I probably haven't seen him as often as you have!" That changed in more recent times with the "Three B's" concerts, but we definitely did not see a lot of each other in the sixties, and the same was true of our heroes in the States, who were either out on the road like us, or playing in Chicago or New York when we weren't there.

So our precious time at the end of a tour, or when we had a few days in one place, gave us a real opportunity to hear other music, and to meet musicians and hang out with them. One musician who was especially nice to me was Zutty Singleton. He was playing drums on Monday nights, when the main band had its night off, at Jimmy Ryan's. It was just a trio with Sammy Price on piano and Tony Parenti on clarinet. Zutty had heard our band playing a set at the club a little earlier, and he came over and introduced himself, and said, "What I like about your band is there's no piano player. I hate piano players. They all lose time. You can't play with them – a band without piano is wonderful." Zutty had a habit of calling everybody "Face". Sometimes he would add a descriptive adjective, so Ian Wheeler, for example, whom he met on a later tour, he called "Mattress Face" because of his beard. Apparently this style of nickname came from Zutty's brother-in-law, the St Louis bandleader, Charlie Creath. When they were playing on the riverboats, people would come up to the bandstand and ask for requests. For some reason this always seemed to involve them coming face to face with Creath, at very close quarters, so he would describe them by their face. The minor variation, for obvious reasons, is that some people who came too close were nicknamed "Breath". Zutty was a most affable man, and an excellent player, too. I had enough of his records to know his playing well, but he was even more impressive in the flesh.

Some incidents concerning the musicians we met involved the practicalities of life in America. Earlier on the 1960 tour we arrived in Cleveland ahead of a job the following day, and we discovered that Ruby Braff was playing in a bar there, so we went to hear him. It was an excellent little quartet and we stayed for the last number, which predictably was 'When The Saints Go Marching In'. Ruby picked up the microphone to sing, and within two words the barman had rushed over and grabbed the mike out of his hand. In Ohio, the cabaret tax for singing and dancing was set at a higher rate than simple entertainment tax, and the barman was not going to risk sacrificing a higher percentage of his takings to the taxman! This experience made sense of all the stories in jazz history about people having to have cabaret cards that allowed them to work in places where singing and dancing went on.

There was a story that Miles Davis was unable to work in New York in 1959, shortly before our first visit, because he did not have a cabaret card. Ottilie and I were invited round to Sammy Price's apartment in Harlem, and during the evening we were speaking to Clarence Williams's grandson. He was a policeman who worked in the department that issued those cards, and he told me that Miles had never applied for one. If he had done, he would have been given one, because he was Miles Davis. But the Miles cabaret card story entered into the mythology.

The reason we were at Sammy Price's apartment was because we already knew him, and when we re-encountered him at Ryan's, playing with Zutty and Tony Parenti, he asked us round. I had first met Sammy in 1958 in Holland. My band had just started touring the continent extensively, our first German tour having been in May of that year. We returned to Europe in the autumn and arrived in Holland from Denmark to find Sammy and his band were staying in the same hotel. They'd been booked on a tour by the Catholic radio network KRO, but Pope Pius XII died in early October, just as they arrived, and so their concerts were cancelled. As a result, we spent more time with them.

A few years after our visit to his Harlem apartment, Sammy came to the UK to tour with Keith Smith and Sandy Brown. I recorded with them on a BBC *Jazz Club* session during that tour. I remember in those days the BBC Maida Vale studios had big cubes of copper sheeting brazed together that they used for ashtrays, and although they were hard to handle, I took one and used it as a mute. You can hear it on our recording of 'Tailgate Boogie' from that BBC session, which has now been issued on CD.

Through meeting the grandson of Clarence Williams at Sammy's home, a man who turned out to be very friendly and informative, we were taken out to Long Island to meet Clarence himself. I'd always thought that the 1920s drawing of him, with round spectacles and a particularly high-domed head that appears on some of his record covers, was a caricature. But it wasn't – it was exactly how he looked in old age. The person who opened the door when we arrived looked a bit like the cleaning lady in *Upstairs Downstairs*, certainly not dressed up or glamorous in any way, but this was the great blues singer Eva Taylor, Clarence's wife. She turned out to be very nice indeed, and he was extremely interesting. He didn't offer any great or profound insights, but we knew his music, asked informed questions about it and listened to what he said. It was such a thrill to be chatting to two such pioneers of jazz and blues. It was that meeting with them that prompted the Harlem Washboard session I mentioned in the previous chapter.

There was a chance to meet another pioneer during one of our breaks in Chicago. Abe Turchen's nephew, Dick Turchen, was travelling with us on behalf of the tour management. As an aside, I might mention that it was while he was with us that we discovered that one of the two new station wagons we had been using actually belonged to a member of Woody Herman's orchestra, who had left it in New York with Abe for safekeeping while the band was out on tour. We put about five thousand miles on the clock, and actually met the somewhat disconcerted musician owner when we played opposite Woody's band one night in Texas. We probably put more miles on the vehicle than we needed to because Dick wasn't very good at reading maps and always got completely lost in any American town that wasn't built on a strict grid pattern. He got hopelessly tangled up in Denver, for example, which has several blocks on the northeast side that run diagonally.

However, Dick was with us when we had a couple of days in Chicago. We were staying inside the Loop, and went to hear Bob Scobey's band at a local club. I wasn't much struck by the band, as I have already mentioned, but I did get the chance to talk to Bob who had been a founder member of the revivalist Yerba Buena Jazz Band on the West Coast with Lu Watters. I wanted to know why the two trumpets played in harmony all the time instead of either playing unison or alternating the lead, and keeping harmony just for the breaks, the way Louis Armstrong and King Oliver had done. He confessed he didn't know, but that it was "something Lu wanted to do, because he wanted to be like King Oliver." But the Oliver records Lu was talking about, with harmonised trumpets, were by the later band, the Dixie Syncopators, which was a bigger group with quite different instrumentation from the Yerba Buena Band. Anyhow, it answered my question!

Dick suggested that if we weren't too keen on Bob's band we should make our way north to Club 1111, where the New Orleans trombonist George Brunies had a band. George had been a pioneer in the twenties and was in Muggsy Spanier's Ragtime Band in the late 1930s, so we knew his work well from records. George had quite a decent Dixieland band, and in the interval Dick introduced me to him. On discovering that I was the bandleader who had recently had a chart hit with 'Petite Fleur', George said, "Ah, you can settle something for me. I've got a bet on with some of the band that it is Sidney Bechet playing on your record." I had to tell him that he was not correct and that it was Monty Sunshine. But I was amazed that someone who had actually played and recorded with Bechet many times could not recognise that this was somebody else.

The year before our first American tour, Jonah Jones, the former Cab Calloway trumpeter, had made an appearance on Fred Astaire's television show, playing muted trumpet with a rhythm section. This quartet format was to be his main occupation for the rest of his playing days, and he was very successful with a string of records for Capitol. By the time we arrived in the States it had become the cool jazz sound of the day, so everybody seemed to be trying to get in on the act. Over the course of our tours in 1959 and 1960, we heard not only Jonah himself, but Bobby Hackett (with Dill Jones, Tommy Potter and Gene Krupa) and Ruby Braff. Yet, oddly enough, the finest of all the trumpeters playing in this chamber jazz style was a musician who is hardly on anyone's radar nowadays, and that was Charlie Teagarden, whom we heard during a stopover in Las Vegas. He was far and away the best. He played in a club called the Silver Slipper, which was not on the strip but in the old town and was a good old-fashioned jazz venue. I think he had a full band in the summer season, but for the winter, when we were there, it was just a quartet, playing in this sophisticated Jonah Jones manner.

Even Max Kaminsky tried his hand at this style, one time when we were in New York, but we mostly tended to hear Max in larger Dixieland groups. He could never understand why we were interested in all these old records. Finally I explained that it was these records that had got us all into music in the first place, and I think that finally managed to convince him. I suspect Max's attitude was symptomatic of the whole jazz scene in America. I'd say that even in the 1950s, unlike Europe, outside a few big American cities nobody knew about it, cared about it, understood it or had ever really heard any jazz. At that time they might have heard of Louis Armstrong singing 'Wonderful World' or 'Hello Dolly', or his 'Now You Has Jazz' scene from *High Society*. But that would be about it. Even among those who did know about jazz they maybe lacked judgement about what was really worth hearing. I remember Conrad Janis telling me that when he had been at college in San Francisco all his college mates without exception went off each week to hear Lu Watters, whereas Conrad was the only one who went to hear Kid Ory who was also playing in town. Anyhow, our perceptions about the lack of interest in jazz on the American scene as a whole meant that the limited time that we had to hear music in New York, Chicago or New Orleans was even more precious to us.

Of all the bands we heard in New York the one that impressed us the most was Wilbur De Paris and his New New Orleans Jazz. It was quite unlike Eddie Condon's group, which was really a sort of jam session band that only came to life when somebody new sat in, or maybe for the one or two numbers in each set when Eddie himself took part. By contrast, Wilbur's was a real jazz band, working regularly together, and with a distinctive repertoire and approach to playing.

We'd seen Jack Teagarden's band out on the road and now in New York we saw them again at the Village Gate. That was interesting because Jack played so quietly you could hardly hear him, even though I was sitting a few feet in front of the stage. You could all too easily hear his trumpeter, Don Goldie, who confirmed my earlier impression that he was a second-rate version of Al Hirt – loud and tasteless. Great as Jack himself was, both as a player and singer, his band did not add up to a complete whole in the way that the De Paris group did.

Just as an aside, I should mention that the other group on at the Village Gate, playing opposite Jack Teagarden, was the Ornette Coleman Quartet. We were able to witness them at the very moment they were making a huge stir in New York, and the main thing I remember is the way the bassist, Scott LaFaro, followed Ornette. He listened so intently that he followed Ornette incredibly closely, and you felt all the time that they were playing a familiar tune you had never actually heard before, even though it was actually free improvisation. I was fascinated by Scott's playing because at times he would play long sequences of four-note chords on the bass, double stopping on all four strings at once, and at really high tempos. But his solo basslines were also incredibly good, with a flow that complemented Ornette's alto saxophone. When Dave Green – a huge LaFaro fan – later joined my Big Chris Barber Band he was envious of this opportunity I had to witness one of the greatest of all jazz bass players.

The Metropole was also marvellous, with Henry Allen and Buster Bailey. But the more we went there we had the feeling that Red Allen's act was about entertaining the people who just walked in off the street on Seventh Avenue. A lot of the time they were just playing what they thought would appeal to ordinary Americans. You did, nevertheless, occasionally get some real jazz fans there. In our experience they tended to arrive about one or two o'clock in the morning. On one such night there was a small group of enthusiasts who came in at about one and stayed until three, and among them was John Ringling North, of Ringling Brothers and Barnum and Bailey, the great circus proprietors. By then he was running Barnum and Bailey, but he knew all about the jazz that was being played.

In the interval on one session at the Metropole, I went up to Buster Bailey and said, "I've got one of your records with Red, called 'House in Harlem For Sale'. It's a beautiful recording . . ."

He said, "I can't remember that at all."

I said, "'Rug Cutter Swing' was on the other side."

"Oh, yes, I remember that one very well!"

I wondered how he could forget making such a wonderful record. Minor key blues are quite unusual. People don't play them that much, perhaps because they don't know what to do, although the answer lies in being repetitive over those minor chords. You can't do many of the normal things you might do in a solo, without taking it out of that minor context. And although I knew that Buster had made a huge number of records, I was surprised he didn't have any memory of this one that really stood out from the rest. Of course, it was great just to be able to hear Buster and Red Allen, and to meet J. C. Higginbotham. Every time he came over to our seats, because he was usually drunk, Higgy would crush my hand. I sometimes wonder if it was his crippling handshakes that have given me arthritis in later life! But take away our affection for the musicians, and the thrill of hearing people who had made such wonderful records in the 1930s, and there wasn't really much to the Metropole.

The De Paris band was a refreshing contrast. They played their own repertoire and weren't out to entertain in quite such an obvious way. They were serious about the music and they played it really well. There was Garvin Bushell on reeds, Wilbur on trombone and usually Sidney De Paris – or occasionally, if Sidney didn't feel like playing, Doc Cheatham on trumpet. Doc would take time off from his other job of playing lead in Latin big bands at the Paramount Theatre.

The idea came up on our 1960 visit that I might make a recording with some of the local musicians while I was in New York, and this time we'd do it properly with full union permission so that I did not have to adopt another pseudonym like T-Bone Jefferson! I definitely wanted to get close to the spirit of the Wilbur De Paris band. I immediately asked Ed Hall, whom I'd met at Central Plaza, to play clarinet, and then I asked Sidney De Paris to play trumpet and lead the band, which he agreed to do. One of them suggested Hank Duncan on piano, which was a fine idea, although Hank had been playing solo piano in various places around town for so long that his tempos had rather started to wander. Joe Marshall was recommended to play drums. He was marvellous, even more so when you realise that this was the first time he had ever played Dixieland. He was just brilliant, and later in his career he went on to join Dizzy Gillespie. Finally, we had Duke Ellington's former bassist Hayes Alvis, who played beautifully as well. Actually at the time, the way the original record was mixed on the day, I wasn't too aware of his contribution, but when it came out on CD with a bit of adjustment to the sound I was really able to hear how excellent he was.

The band really swings and sounds very unified, but later Ed Hall said to me, "If I'd known Sidney De Paris was going to be leader on the date, I wouldn't have taken the job." There's no denying Sidney was a bit difficult. He'd talk in conundrums, in little disconnected phrases. If he was trying to explain how he wanted us to play something he couldn't explain it straight out, but in a rather blurred way, saying he wanted a feeling of this or that. He also changed his mind all the time. But the results are okay – in fact more than okay – and I like the record, which came out on Columbia as *Chris Barber's American Jazz Band*, very much. Sadly the six tracks that were issued on the original record were all that we recorded. I think we reached the end of studio time covered by the union scale, and that was that.

Denis Preston had asked Stanley Dance, the British-born writer who was by then living in the States, to produce it. Apart from turning up on the day, Stanley didn't do a thing, not even taking pictures of the musicians, so if it had been left to him there would have been no visual record of the recording session. Fortunately a local photographer did show up and there are some pictures of us in the heavily curtained studio, with odd bits of paraphernalia tucked in the corners, such as a set of tubular bells! The place we made it was in the CBS studio building at 49 East 52nd Street, where they recorded everything from pop sessions to classical orchestras. There was no remixing, and it went straight down to a stereo master. Funnily enough the other main thing I remember from the day was meeting Milt Hinton in the lobby as he was coming in to do a session in one of the other parts of the building. I was told that he was so busy at that time he kept a bass at each of the main New York studios so he could manage to fit in several sessions a day without having to worry about transporting his instrument through Manhattan.

Less than a month later, when we were back in London, I recorded 'L'il Liza Jane' again with my own band, because I really liked the number, but Sidney had not managed to get the words right for the American recording. Try as he might he could not get it, and we eventually settled for one of his less jumbled versions on the record. When I came to redo it I just took the words off the famous Oscar Celestin recording, with Alphonse Picou on clarinet and Bill Matthews on trombone. Matthews was a marvellous player of New Orleans jazz, but somehow you don't see him mentioned very often, which is a shame.

Thinking of New Orleans musicians, through making the record with my American Jazz Band I got to know Ed Hall quite well. We'd seen him in London in 1956 with the Louis Armstrong All Stars, although we hadn't realised at the time that he was rather unhappy with Louis. The touring, and playing the same repertoire every night, was really beginning to get to him. Every time he gave his notice, Louis's manager Joe Glaser raised his salary, so he'd stayed on. When eventually he left he had the idea of going to work in Ghana, teaching jazz. That didn't work out, and by the time of our record he was back at his apartment in New York, which fortunately he had kept on when he went to Ghana.

After this, Ed began to work as a soloist, and just a couple of years after we recorded together in America he came over to play with my band in Europe, during November 1962. Ours was one of his first European solo tours. He was very direct, and said what he meant. One of Ed's categorical statements, which because it came from him I'm inclined to believe, was that Ian Wheeler (who had replaced Monty in the band by that time) played the traditional clarinet part on 'High Society' better than anybody he'd ever heard. There's a nice recording of the two of them together, done in London during our tour. I remember when discussing the old days, Ed talked about early trumpet players and he said that Buddy Petit, the New Orleans pioneer, could play "like Bobby Hackett only better". He was full of such insights on the dawn of jazz and a real Southern gentleman. He was also a motoring enthusiast and, among other things, bought the first XK 120 Jaguar to come to America.

I thought quite seriously about asking him to join us, but we weren't as well off in 1962 as we had been in the late 1950s, and secondly we foresaw enormous work permit and visa difficulties, were he to come to England semi-permanently to play. I think we might have found a way round it, but the problems seemed insuperable at the time. I had a lot in common with Ed, and I'm sure with his interest in sports cars he'd have wanted to go saloon car racing, which I was getting involved in. He had that in common with Wilbur De Paris's clarinetist, Garvin Bushell, who had grown up around sports car racing in Springfield, Ohio, and was at one point quite a successful competitor. But then Garvin was an exceptional man, having been one of the first, if not the first, permanent black members of a white symphony orchestra, playing oboe and bassoon. He played jazz on the bassoon too, really well, and in stark contrast to Illinois Jacquet whom I once saw trying to play the instrument at Ronnie Scott's but who really didn't have the first idea of what to do.

Another thing that came out of my visits to New York, as well as the association with Ed Hall, was the chance to tour and record with Louis Jordan. When Ottilie and I were there in 1961 we were surprised to see that the Apollo Theatre in Harlem was to feature Louis Jordan and His Tympany Five. I knew his work from records, and I also knew that the "Five" was often a somewhat bigger band, but I had no real idea that he was still playing. We were even more surprised when we got to the Apollo to see from the posters outside that the band would include "Handsome Sonny Stitt". I'm not sure that those who knew Sonny's excellent bebop alto and tenor playing would have chosen "handsome" as the first adjective to describe him, but he was a great musician, and we looked forward to hearing him in the group. I went round backstage beforehand to say hello to Louis Jordan, and discovered he had another legendary figure in the band, Teddy Bunn on guitar, who had famously recorded both with Sidney Bechet, and the Spirits of Rhythm. At the end of the show, Louis, his baritone player, and Sonny Stitt on tenor, all jumped up in the air and did the splits, beaming from ear to ear.

Louis had never been to England, and afterwards I asked him if he'd be interested in coming. He said he'd love to. So in late 1962, immediately following our European tour with Ed Hall, he came over to the UK and did ten days on the road with us. He had a whole repertoire of arrangements, which he wanted to do, so he guided us through them and we quickly learned the routines. At that time he was fifty-five and we were in our early thirties, yet it was like being dragged along by a wild horse. His energy and skill and the perfectionism of his playing were incredible. We made a record with him while he was in England released as *Louis Jordan & Chris Barber*, but one track was never included on the original album, which was a duet with Ottilie, singing 'Tain't Nobody's Business'.

Louis unnerved Ottilie totally because of his sheer panache, experience, knowledge, everything you can think of about being a performer. He really was as close to perfection as it was possible to be. He was the best presenter of a song by movement and action that I have ever seen. Yet he wasn't too serious; by contrast Ottilie sang quite seriously, with Louis interjecting his humour. The end results were actually rather good. After languishing in the vaults for years, when we compiled the archive anthology series *Lost and Found*, our record of 'Tain't Nobody's Business' finally came out in the year 2008.

Visiting the Apollo became a regular part of our routine whenever Ottilie and I stayed in New York, and we liked the whole atmosphere of the shows. People said, "Oh don't go to Harlem, it's not safe," but we never had any trouble. One of the finest concerts I remember there was hearing the Count Basie Orchestra. In those days they tended to have a band there for a whole week, but as part of the arrangement, the band – as it would have done in the 1930s – played between showings of a film. So Basie's band was the house band for that week, and the alto saxophonist Marshal Royal was actually running it as musical director or "straw boss".

Top of the bill was Aretha Franklin, and it was one of her first major appearances after the early successes she'd had on record. The compère was Red Foxx. I'd heard him once before at the Crescendo Club in Los Angeles, where his presentation was filthier than a warm-up from Bob Monkhouse. At the Apollo the audience would not have gone for that degree of smut, so he just told simple gags, but he was hilarious and his timing immaculate. The highlight of his act was when he sang 'Honeysuckle Rose' with the Basie band, in which he did one chorus an entire bar ahead on purpose. They stayed there and he stayed there. It took the audience about half way through to figure out what he was doing, and by then Marshall was standing up in the middle of the sax section, conducting, to make sure the band stayed put.

When Aretha came on, she did much of her set alone at the piano, but the Basie band accompanied her for some pieces. On her recently released album *Aretha*, which she did with Ray Bryant's band, the solo trombonist had been Quentin Jackson, who was in the Basie line-up. So he came down to the front and did some wa-wa trombone behind her singing, as he had done on the record. Introducing the Basie part of the programme were Lambert, Hendricks and Ross.

Another act I saw at the Apollo was Sam Theard, known as "Spo-de-odee", who called himself "Lovin' Sam from down in 'Bam". I realised on seeing him that he was the man from whom Champion Jack Dupree stole most of his act, and then got most of it wrong! Sam's act was made up of sketches rather like a certain era of revue, such as the Parisian film about a stage show, *Ah! Les Belles Bacchantes*, with lots of quite innocent humour, each piece ending in a punchline. He told the audience that part of his act was doing imperson-ations. Sam said "I've been in show business a long time, and I do 'pressions. Now most people do *im*pressions of people like Nat King Cole, but I'm gonna do 'pressions of people you ain't ever heard of!" And then he introduced a song by "Nat Cole's uncle's brother", called 'Ice Cole'. It was really just like very old-fashioned music hall comedy.

Champion Jack himself showed up in Britain at the end of 1959, which was just about the time he decided to leave the United States and settle in Europe. He'd been born in New Orleans, and spent part of his childhood in the same Colored Waif's Home as Louis Armstrong. He played piano from his early years, but he was also a cook and specialised in Louisiana cuisine. His nickname apparently came from a time when he tried his hand at prize fighting in Detroit in the 1930s.

When he settled in Chicago, just before World War Two, Jack became part of a circle of blues singers who lived and worked in Chicago, along with Big Bill Broonzy and Tampa Red. He was a sweet man, and had a marvellous voice. I think he was probably one of the last blues singers to have the quality of voice that Big Bill and the others had. When he was young he played the piano pretty well, as you can tell from the recordings he made in the 1940s. But as he got older he got less and less accurate. Many a song would end up in a different key from the one in which it had started. His playing was full of blues feeling, but definitely somewhat haphazard, although wonderful in its way.

In 1959, once he had arrived in Britain, we got the chance to have him as a guest on one of our radio programmes. Now this did present a slight problem because Jack would agree a list of songs in advance, but when it came to the performance he didn't always do what he said he was going to do. He told us he was going to sing 'T. B. Blues', which is a rather serious blues about tuberculosis, and, of course, tuberculosis had been a great scourge of working-class black Americans. It was very prevalent, and a suitable subject for a reflective blues. We were all there with suitably long faces as we expected him to start with this song, and then – as it was December – he suddenly burst into 'Merry Christmas Blues' which was exactly the opposite in feeling and everything. You never knew, with Champion Jack, quite what he was going to do next!

I mentioned that we worked with Professor Alex Bradford, whom Ottilie and I also encountered initially at the Apollo Theatre in Harlem on our earliest visit to the States. We first played together with him and his singers in 1962, when he was in London for a production called *Black Nativity* by Langston Hughes. I like gospel music very much indeed and I realised from the moment I first heard him that Brad was a very good choirmaster and had an exceptional gift for getting choirs going. At the Abyssinian Baptist Church in Newark, New Jersey, he was the music man. After seeing him at the Apollo, Ottilie and I went to the church and heard the choir singing, and it was an absolutely beautiful sound. When *Black Nativity* came to London, I saw it twenty-two times. I'm not a practising Christian, but the effect that this show had on me was equivalent to when I read *Really the Blues* in 1942 or '43. I had got hold of one or two gospel discs in my early record buying days, such as Sister Rosetta Tharpe with the Sam Price Trio, and gradually I had built up from this starting point into quite a decent collection. I got interested in gospel quartets, and the early records by the Blind Boys of Alabama. (Of course, like a lot of long-lived groups, there were different "blind boys" as the years went by.)

My first live experience of gospel music was Mahalia Jackson at the Albert Hall in 1951. That led me to get hold of many of her records, and to explore some similar singers. But it was just a curtain-raiser to the first-hand contact with gospel that we had at the Apollo in New York. Going to the first house of that Sunday performance, when we first heard Alex, was not unlike being at church. By the evening, with all the singing and showmanship, they were pretty much tired out. But the opening performance was electrifying. On the bill with Alex and the Bradford Singers were the Spirit of Memphis Quartet and two other groups, plus an older lady who was a solo singer. We saw the show through twice. This kind of experience helped in Ottilie's quest to find better songs to sing with us because she was always looking for more interesting material than the kind of 'Won't You Please Come Home Bill Bailey?' songs that most jazz bands did with their singers.

Seeing *Black Nativity* live at the Criterion Theatre in the West End was a whole different experience again and, as I said, completely inspired my subsequent interest in performing gospel material. The show – which ran for quite a while – proved that there was a ready market in Britain for gospel music on stage. In October 1962 we made some studio recordings with Alex, plus his singers Madeleine Bell, Robert Pinkston, Bernie Durant, Jr. and Kenneth Washington.

I wondered if the first three songs that Brad and his singers recorded with us would interest his record company, Vee Jay, in Chicago. So in due course, over the Christmas holiday in 1962, I took the recordings across to Chicago. The firm was being run by some young black businessmen who were trying to put the company on the map. What they were doing was not exactly Tamla Motown, but that was certainly the kind of sound they were after. I played them the songs we'd done with Alex and they said, "We don't know what to call it. Who will we sell it to? But we have to have it!" What happened, of course, was that they really *didn't* know what to call it or who to sell it to.

Owing to their interest, we arranged to record again with Brad. By this time the *Black Nativity* show had transferred to Paris, and we actually went to Paris to meet him and work out what we would record together. He and the singers came back to London in January 1963 to make the records at Olympic Studios, which were then off Baker Street. While the singers were back in England we also got the chance to play a few concerts in which the band supported them. Kenneth came back to Britain again in 1966, when we worked with him as a solo singer.

For the sessions at Olympic studios we worked with Barbara Gardner, who was a black journalist whom Vee Jay had asked to produce the album. She sat there during the recordings. We were there for two days: the first day we had all the singers with us, and the second we had just Alex and the band. When the results got across to Vee Jay it was not long after Sister Rosetta Tharpe's records had begun to be reissued on LP. As a supposedly positive thing, Vee Jay had coined the phrase "pop gospel". They applied it to Sister Rosetta, and it was also used by the people marketing the Ward Singers, when they forsook their church audience in the early 1960s and started to play at clubs in Las Vegas and the like. So they put our album out as *Pop Gospel Live in London*, which meant it didn't sell any copies at all. Bradford fans didn't want it because of the "pop" appellation, as he stood for "proper" gospel – the real thing rather than some pop version of it – and jazz fans didn't want it because it was gospel. It did come out in England as well, so there were actually two versions of it. It's a beautiful record but it virtually disappeared at the time and had not been out again until a CD appeared in the 1990s. It contains some gorgeous music because Alex was such a skilled arranger. With Madeleine Bell as lead voice, she took the role of a big band lead trumpet, almost, and the effect is fantastic.

We were reunited with Alex Bradford in 1974, when we did what we called our "25th Anniversary Tour" with him as a solo guest. (We must have taken my first 1949 recordings by my semi-pro band as the starting point in calculating that particular birthday!) Touring with Alex Bradford was a marvellous experience, and it resulted in us really finding out much more about how gospel singers work together. On this tour we had Ray Nance and Alex together, and each played one half of every concert with us. 'Couldn't Keep It To Myself' was the song that Alex would finish with, which I believe he wrote. He'd go out into the audience singing, and then come back up on stage and start again. It calls for a group of backing singers to accompany him all the way through. With a band like mine we're not really used to doing the kind of vocal backing where you have to sing out, sing strongly and incisively all the time. But I have to say that we did exactly that, and the results came out in 2010 on the *Memories of My Trip* anthology. We're proud of it because it's a hard thing to do, and it's part of learning about the music properly.

After recording with us in 1963, Kenneth Washington was left behind in Britain with the rest of the Bradford Singers when Alex went off to Australia. Madeleine Bell found work easily, singing backings for Dusty Springfield, and then working with Blue Mink. But Kenneth did not have a lot to do, and so he sang quite a few concerts with us. When he worked with us again in 1966 I remember telling him, whatever he did, to keep his return ticket to the States. But at some point he must have cashed it in because I think he found it quite difficult to get back, and I know at one point after his return he had to take a job in a New York restaurant. But he had a fine voice and was a good gospel-style singer.

One thing he did with us was 'If I Had A Ticket'. I had an old Columbia record from 1926 or so by the Rev. T. E. Weems, whom Rosetta Tharpe told me had been her pastor. It was interesting because it had a backing group on it singing like an African choir in parallel fourths. We'd done a version of it ourselves, with me singing the vocal rather than Ottilie, unfortunately, and then Kenneth sang it with the band. But I had a feeling it could be done a slightly different way, so I recorded it again with Kenneth backed by me, Pat and Ian, plus Keith Emerson and the T-Bones, who used to play at the Marquee.

Over the years we went on to play with a number of other distinguished American visitors to Europe. Some, like Louis Jordan, we met in the United States, but others were musicians who had elected to base themselves in Europe. Recently, along with the recordings I made with Ed Hall, I had the chance to release sessions with Albert Nicholas and Joe Darensbourg, both great Louisiana clarinet players. Albert Nicholas was a very dignified man who had decided to live in Europe in the mid-1950s. I first met him in Basel when we were playing there in 1966 or '67. We kept in touch and finally managed to arrange to have Albert as our guest at a concert in Geneva in the Victoria Hall in 1968. Swiss Radio broadcast it, and gave us a recording. Until very recently I had no opportunity to make sensible use of it, but in 2012 I released the whole session. We had very little chance to rehearse, but that is not evident from the recorded results.

Another former member of the Louis Armstrong All Stars, Joe Darensbourg was touring Europe in 1974 with Barry Martyn's Legends of Jazz, and afterwards he stayed on for a bit longer in the UK. A recording session was put together by Dave Bennett, at his home in Basingstoke, and this gave Pat and me the chance to play alongside Joe in very relaxed informal surroundings, with Richard Simmons on piano, Terry Knight on bass and Dave Evans on drums. It's quite interesting to note the difference in style between those three esteemed New Orleans clarinetists, Ed Hall, Joe Darensbourg and Albert Nicholas. In contrast to the others, Albert was a very just-so and exact player, perhaps with a little less fire and invention in his playing, but he really loosened up on a version we made of 'C-Jam Blues', just as Ed Hall had done on 'St. Louis Blues'.

Both Ed Hall and Joe Darensbourg had been in the Armstrong All Stars, and so too had another of our guests, the trombonist Trummy Young. He really only came on tour with us in 1978 by accident because we had planned to bring over Roy Eldridge. I called the tour "Swing is Here" because I wanted to revive the Gene Krupa record of that name, with Roy on it, which has the best developing series of archetypal swing riffs I've ever heard. Then it turned out that Roy had contracted hypertension, and his doctors told him he couldn't risk travelling. I originally had another pianist in mind, but he couldn't do it either, so John Lewis came on board and he suggested Trummy. Just before the tour was due to start we still didn't know if Trummy was going to come, but we ran into a couple of fans who said, "Oh, we've heard Trummy's coming!" They'd read it in the *Watchtower* because Trummy was a Jehovah's Witness and he'd put it in the paper as a news item. So then we knew for sure he was going to be there.

We began the tour with both Trummy and John Lewis, and after four weeks or so John had to go back to New York, but Trummy stayed on with us. One of the gigs we did was the Mulheim festival in Germany. On the main tour Trummy had done his Armstrong features, and 'Margie' from his Lunceford days, but on this festival gig, after a raucous trombone duet on '12th Street Rag', he did a beautiful version of 'Georgia On My Mind' which I'd not heard him do before. It also had some brilliant alto sax from Sammy Rimington whose short stay in the band coincided with the tour, and some excellent Johnny McCallum guitar as well.

Before John Lewis went home, we'd had an interesting time playing music that he'd written for a musical. 1978 was the period when Broadway musicals such as *Ain't Misbehavin'*, *Bubbling Brown Sugar* and *One Mo' Time* were beginning to do rather well, and somebody thought that it would be timely to do a musical on the life of Mahalia Jackson, whose work was still immensely popular in America. She'd been born in New Orleans, and the producers thought it would be good to have a New Orleans jazz band on the stage, just as they did in *One Mo' Time*, backing up an actress who would recite and sing material from various stages in Mahalia's life. John was commissioned to write the music. It was first performed as a workshop version of the show (with lyrics written by Don Evans) under the title *Mahalia* in 1978. Eventually it was to have a short run at the Billie Holiday Theater in Brooklyn in 1986 under the revised title *Blues for a Gospel Queen*, but at the time he came over to work with us John had not managed to get the show put on beyond the original workshop.

We thought the music he had written was too good just to leave lying about, so we played some of it on our tour, including a pair of pieces that went together called 'Home' and 'Folks'. When we began rehearsing it, I asked John what kind of sound he had in mind, and he said, "I want it to sound like a good properly-played New Orleans band, so I made it sound like your band." That was a great tribute to us, but by 1978 our band had changed quite a bit from the original six-piece New Orleans line-up with which we'd begun; there's more about those changes in the next chapter.

Along with the jazz musicians we invited to tour with us, we still kept up our connections with the blues. By 1964, my good friends Horst Lippman and Fritz Rau in Germany had begun running a festival of American blues every year. This meant that there was the opportunity for more great blues artists to play in Europe, as well as return visits for some of those who had played with us already. This led to some concerts in Britain, in which the National

Jazz Federation presented a package of some of the artists who had appeared in Germany, and in that same year, 1964, I had the honour of introducing one of those concerts. One of the performers on the bill was a very striking gentleman indeed – Sonny Boy Williamson II. His real name, I believe, was Rice Miller, but he took Sonny Boy Williamson's name when the previous holder of the name (and famous blues singer) died. He was a great artist and a fantastic harmonica player. A bit like Little Walter, he treated the harmonica as if it was a kind of alto saxophone and with us he really liked to take solos on all kinds of material. He did Louis Jordan numbers, and one speciality for his instrumental prowess was the 'C-Jam Blues'. He lived for a while in London, staying in Giorgio Gomelski's flat, and I remember he had these amazing two-tone suits made for himself while he was there. The jacket might be white down the left side and brown down the right. The trousers would be the reverse, the left leg brown and the right leg white. He also wore a bowler, or as he would call it, a derby hat.

He was also a prodigious drinker. I remember sitting in our hotel in Nottingham during the tour and watching a waiter making for the lift with a tray of four quadruple scotch whiskies in tumblers. I asked what the drinks were for, and he said "Sonny Boy's breakfast"! But that didn't take away from his superb performances. He had a low story-telling voice and a real ability to put across atmosphere in the blues. This wasn't quite always the case, because he had worked with the Animals and the Yardbirds when they were just starting out, and he had a habit of stopping them in mid-performance and saying, "What's the matter with you? Can't you play the blues? You're playing it all wrong!"

He never did that to us, I'm glad to say. I think it helped that he was a Louis Jordan fanatic, and we could play those numbers as he wanted them. He was very, very gifted. Among the musicians who went on to perform his material, after that tour he did with us, were John Mayall's Bluesbreakers, Led Zeppelin, Van Morrison and The Who.

That same year, the National Jazz Federation launched its first festival, at the Twickenham Athletic Association. In due course this moved location to become the Reading Festival, but that first year it was at Twickers, close to Richmond in Surrey. We weren't allowed to play on the rugby pitch itself, but we did have a big stage set up at the ground on which my band and some of the guest artists played for a jazz night. Meanwhile an array of other musicians played in the clubhouse, including an up-and-coming group called the Rolling Stones.

Our outdoor session involved some special guests, including Humphrey Lyttelton and Ronnie Scott – probably the only time the three of us ever played together on stage at the same time – but the highlight was a reunion with Jimmy Witherspoon whom we'd first met on our American tour in 1959. Jimmy was to work with us again – notably in a broadcast we did for Dutch radio in 1980. He was one of the great charismatic blues performers, as we had witnessed at first hand when we saw him for the first time in Monterey. He was a really powerful singer, too, as well as being a very witty character. My favourite recording with him is a version we did of 'Tain't Nobody's Business' in 1980 which seems to roll all his best qualities together into one performance.

Another blues musician we came to work with was Chester Burnett, better known as Howlin' Wolf. We didn't meet him in person on our late 1950s and early 1960s tours to America, but one thing I did manage to do in Chicago was to pick up several of his recordings that he had made for the Chess label, on 78 rpm discs. In 1964 he came over to Europe for the Festival of American Blues, after which he came to the UK from Germany and played some dates with our band, at the Marquee and also on Eel Pie Island. I particularly remember his theme tune 'Howlin' For My Baby'. He used to prowl around the stage like a gorilla with his harmonica in his hand, and he seemed to be putting the evil eye on people, but it turned out this was just a bit of fun. Off stage he was a surprisingly quiet, moderate person, and one of the loveliest people I ever met. He came to dinner with Ottilie and me several times. Over the years we'd invited many of the band's guests to join us for dinner at home, but the only one of them who ever said grace before the meal, quietly and sincerely, was Howlin' Wolf.

Wolf's own records usually didn't have horns on them, but we devised riffs to play behind him that all seemed to work. Some of them almost sound like Beach Boys phrases behind his vocals on pieces like 'Take A Walk With Me'. Wolf didn't play guitar with us; indeed he still seemed to be learning the instrument, practising scales and so on, on an acoustic guitar, an hour or so before the gig. But he had with him one of the greatest of all blues guitarists, Hubert Sumlin, who played in his band back in the States, and let's face it if you have Hubert in your band, why bother to play guitar yourself? Hubert was one of the few players with whom we worked who had a signature song – a piece so well-known that you just have to play a note or two, and everyone knows it and falls into place around it immediately, and that was 'Dust My Broom'. It's an achievement that's rare enough in show business as a whole, but particularly in the blues. Players like these gave us – and our audiences – a wealth of experience and a real connection to the heart of the music that meant so much to us.

6 There'll be Some Changes Made

We had not been back from our autumn 1960 visit to America more than a couple of months when Monty Sunshine left the band. The rest of us shared a desire to get into certain areas of music that weren't really Monty's forte. We hadn't made up our minds about who to get, apart from deciding that we were after somebody who would be more interested in our forays into blues and other repertoire. In due course, it was agreed that Monty would leave at the end of December 1960, and soon afterwards he went on to form his own band, which began working a month or two later.

Ian Wheeler agreed to join us, but just as he was about to arrive he had a car crash. He had spent six years with Ken Colyer by this time, and consequently he'd become pretty well-known, but he'd left Ken earlier in 1960 and set up the short-lived band he co-led with the trumpeter Ken Sims. The accident happened in the Sims-Wheeler Vintage Jazz Band's American estate car. The crash was on the East Lancs Highway near Liverpool, and Ian was injured – badly enough that he couldn't play for about a week and a half.

We were still working almost every night, so various people filled in. Alex Revell did a couple of gigs, Don Lydiatt from the Merseysippi Jazz Band did a couple, and Wally Fawkes joined us for the rest. Wally had played with us occasionally before, when Monty had been unable to make it. I remember in particular a Big Bill Broonzy Memorial Concert at the Dominion in Tottenham Court Road, and Wally played on that, sounding very good. But because Wally, under his pen-name Trog, was a very well-known full-time cartoonist by this time, there could never have been any question of him being a regular member of the band.

Once Ian had recovered from the car crash he joined us, and immediately you could hear the difference. He brought a freshness to the band's sound, and was also good at tackling the blues numbers on alto saxophone or harmonica. We recorded with him at the London Palladium just a couple of months after he arrived, and whether he was playing with the full band, or duetting with our special guest Joe Harriott, he sounded completely at home.

Funnily enough, Ian had hardly played the alto saxophone with Ken Colyer. This is odd because Ken Colyer himself actually played the tenor saxophone. In his later years Ken would turn out to play it with various New Orleans-style brass bands, so he clearly wasn't completely anti-saxophone. Indeed in 1953 when we went to Denmark with him, despite his awkwardness in conversation, I really got to know Ken quite well, and he was very broad-minded about jazz. He listened to a much wider range of music than the traditional style with which he is usually associated, and was a particular enthusiast for Lester Young's playing, not least because Lester originally came from New Orleans. So Ken wasn't really against saxophones, but what he wanted from his own bands was for everyone to play together in the way you should for that collective front line to work. Ian's six years of doing this with Ken meant that he was excellent at fitting in with me and Pat in the New Orleans style, but in a supremely musical way. He always sounded like himself, and – like Monty – was immediately recognisable for having his own distinctive musical personality.

Ian was also a very remarkable person away from music. He had a talent for designing and making things. In 1960, using spare parts that mainly came from radio shops, he had built himself from scratch a radio-controlled model aeroplane that worked. He designed all the controls and how they linked to the various flight surfaces. You couldn't buy such a model at the time. He was always devising things, although he tended to lose interest once he had made a working prototype. He was very keen on kites, and he succeeded in making a helicopter kite. It flew somewhat in the manner of an autogyro, and nobody had ever made one like it before. He got an offer from the big toy maker Mattel, who said they would pay him 5% of the retail price on every one they sold. He refused the terms, saying he'd rather make them himself and take 100%, but, of course, he never got round to making a single example to sell. All of us in the band believed he would have become a wealthy man if Mattel had been allowed to take up his design.

He did sometimes take his fascination with fixing things a little too far. He mended his broken spectacles and – on one occasion – a broken tooth with Araldite. But when he turned that practical bent to things like sports cars, of which he had a few at various times, he was brilliant. Unfortunately Ian smoked incessantly, and that is ultimately what brought about his death. He'd lost one lung to tuberculosis before he joined Ken, back in the early 1950s, so throughout all of his professional career he was operating on just one lung. By the end, he suffered constantly from emphysema and weighed eighteen stone, entirely through his own choice. We had a reunion with him at the Edinburgh Festival in 2010, and he played absolutely beautifully, but he had to be helped off stage at the end. He knew just what had to be done to play well, and did it, but how he managed to live as long as he did in the condition he was in,

I just don't know. He could not give up smoking, and he liked a drink. But I was glad we had the opportunity for that final reunion, and also that some of his finest playing has been preserved on CD – such as 'High Society' which I mentioned in the previous chapter, alongside Edmond Hall guesting with the band, or his duet on 'S'Wonderful' with Joe Harriott.

Right through the period of our early visits to the United States, the band remained on a co-operative basis. But in 1962, as the economic climate changed, so, too, did the financial structure of the band. I kept it going for as long as I could as a shared endeavour, but it began to be much harder to get sufficient work. Oddly enough, just at the time we were starting to find it difficult to get our usual level of gigs, the first Ball, Barber and Bilk "Three B's" album was put out by Pye, and it actually went into the album charts. It certainly helped to keep our name in the public eye, but ironically, both Acker and I had left Pye some years before, when we both signed to Denis Preston and he took us to Columbia. So there wasn't a track on that hit album by either of us that was newer than five years old at the time, although Kenny Ball's tracks were pretty current as he was still with the label.

The *Best of Ball, Barber and Bilk* notwithstanding, in 1962 it started to get very tight, financially. It became so that we couldn't get a run of concerts on a tour that joined up in such a way that we could keep travel and accommodation costs down. I remember we were in Scotland, in the middle of a short series of dates north of the border, and things were not going too well. There was one, if not two members of the band who, because it was a co-operative, were not disposed to let me run it. In effect I *was* running it, because nobody else was prepared to put in the hours, but whenever we tried to discuss it there was a lot of talk along the lines of "What you need to do is take full-page adverts in the press!", which was not helpful.

On this particular tour, we were sitting down talking it over and I said, "We as a band have a £1000 overdraft, and we're carrying the full debt at present. So anyone who wants to have a seventh share of the band can pay me £150, and they can have it." But nobody bought it. In my view that wasn't sensible. It wasn't that I was trying to get rich by it. Indeed, in the economic downturn in the 1990s I nearly quit. But I thought it was a reasonable offer to share the debt to keep the thing co-operative. So as a result of that conversation I took the band over, along with its debts, and said to everyone, "I'll pay you the same money you're getting now. You'll have a reasonable weekly salary, and if we do a very lucrative gig abroad with lots of additional cash, I'll share it out, exactly as we've done up until now."

My initial thought was, on the basis of three long tours in America and two short ones, that we should go to the United States for a year. I knew, from the reaction we got in ordinary towns, that the country was ready for us, and I felt strongly that we'd have comparable success to that which we had achieved in England with "trad". We would have had to go and live there, but unfortunately the band didn't want to go to America, nor to live there for any length of time. Three members in particular just could not be persuaded to go. If I'd have said "Go to Azerbaijan!" I could have understood it, but if you're a jazz lover, to be living and working in America, and successful, would seem to me to be a natural thing to do. We wouldn't have been quite on the scale of the "British invasion" rock and pop groups who went and did exactly that a few years later, as our music was on a somewhat smaller scale. From the outset, their music was part of a big business, aimed at youth. Youth in America still had a problem with jazz in the sixties, because it was only played in bars they could not go to. But even so, I knew that there was potentially a very strong public for us and what we played. However, apart from occasional short tours, America was not to be the answer, and we remained based in England, but turned our attention instead towards Europe.

By 1964, as the business continued to fall away, we were no longer playing the big theatres and concert halls in Britain, and we were working at places like the George in Morden. This type of large roadhouse pub with a big function room that doubled as a medium size concert hall was the kind of venue we'd left behind ten years before, although we'd never actually played at the George itself in earlier times. In England our work had become mainly restricted to clubs of that size. Then our German manager, Karlheinz Lyrmann, got back to us, and said "There's a promoter over here doing concerts with the Dutch Swing College, and he's looking for another band to work with."

It was on a fee basis and the money was reasonable, so I said, "Yes, okay." Quite suddenly, we had a lot of work in Germany, back in the kinds of large concert hall we used to play in Britain. Also, for a short time in the mid-sixties, we had a lot of work in France. That came up somewhat unexpectedly, all of a sudden, and compared favourably to Germany in terms of audiences, venues and enthusiasm. However, it came to an abrupt end in 1968, when, as a consequence of the student protests in Paris and attacks on the police, the French government withdrew all funds from student unions. Almost all our concerts in France had been for student galas and festivals, and they usually involved signing a contract some months ahead. Once the guarantee of funding from the state was withdrawn the student unions could no longer sign long-term contracts with our management, or anyone else's.

Nevertheless, what was on offer in England during the mid-sixties was nothing to compare with what we were able to do on the continent. There were several large UK clubs where we still played quite often, and we did some concert halls and theatres too; indeed we retained a particularly loyal concert audience in Scotland. But with a majority of the jobs in Britain being in clubs, compared to playing concerts in Germany, it was obvious we were going to go there.

The demand when we first went to Germany had been so great that I think the people who ran the concerts did so on the principle of "make all you can as quickly as possible and then forget about it". They did this rather than thinking of building a long-term audience, or thinking of how to make the demand continue for longer. We did think about this, and one way of doing it was to keep a broad repertoire and also alter the sound of the band as time went on. Ian's arrival is one example, but there were others.

From the very beginning of the band we always adhered to the idea that we were not only going to play pieces that had been recorded by King Oliver, or Bix Beiderbecke, or any of those early heroes of the music. Playing "Bernie's Tune" with Ken Colyer was one example of this attitude, but there were more as the years went by. To our regular audiences these additional pieces didn't sound that different, because our original line-up was always clarinet, trombone, trumpet, banjo, bass and drums. I was never the arranger that Bob Hunt is, who plays with my big band now, but if I had been, I suspect I'd have been cleverer about our Ellington arrangements. Nevertheless, we played the likes of 'Stevedore Stomp' and 'Double Check Stomp' and so on, which were not the ordinary fare of New Orleans revival bands.

Although we'd worked with Muddy Waters, and other blues artists, I don't think our general public noticed we were doing anything different until we recorded Joe Harriott's 'Revival' in 1961, at the London Palladium. As a result of the LP of that concert, Columbia started getting lots of dealer requests for a single of 'Revival'. The concert version was well over four minutes long, and Denis Preston, who was most uninclined by this time to do things the way I wanted, should have told them that singles were just like EPs, and they could release the concert track in its entirety as one side of a 45 rpm disc. But he just wouldn't do it, saying that despite all my power as a best-selling recording artist, Columbia would not go out of its way for me, in order to issue a longer-than-normal single. So we had to go and record it again as a two-minute version. When we were scheduled to do this, unfortunately Joe Harriott was not about, so we did it as best we could, with Ian playing the alto part. I'm certain that to get the perfect take we played it through something like sixteen times. As a result, because of making so many takes, and without Joe's personal intensity, the issued single version lacks the feel that had made the concert album so popular and so great.

Even so, the single still made the top forty in the charts, and we played it on at least three *Sunday Night at the London Palladium* television shows as a consequence. But, without Joe, there was still too much of a trad sound in the band, whatever we did. Nevertheless 'Revival' was a signal that my band was going to play different music, and try things that were definitely not traditional jazz.

Quite early in the 1960s, Ottilie began to find she had difficulty performing, owing to her health, although she still liked doing it, and in her heart singing was all she wanted to do. She suffered from what amounted to psychosomatic catarrh, her nerves bringing about a condition that made singing more and more difficult for her. This really became a problem in 1962–63, which was when she first attempted to take time away from singing in public, in order to try and recover. Promoters, particularly in the UK, would ask, "Will Ottilie be there?"

If I said "no," then they wanted to postpone the booking until I could confirm that she would appear. The band didn't realise quite how difficult things had become. She wasn't temperamental, exactly, just in a bad state of mind, which was something she could do very little about. She had also suffered from mild epilepsy since her teens. Although I never saw her having a "grand mal" fit, she often suffered from "petit mal" seizures. These only last a few seconds, but they can seriously affect the confidence of anybody who has to appear on a public stage. This made it very hard for me, both living with her, and also trying to run the band and our careers. I did my best to find the right balance. In retrospect, I think she successfully managed to do a remarkable amount of work, even in that difficult time, and she remained very popular. Had she not carried on appearing with us, there might not have been sufficient work to keep the band going. It wasn't so much a question of whether the band was good, or not so good, it was just that promoters did not want us without Ottilie Patterson.

With the occasional short break, Ottilie managed to sing more or less full-time up until the start of 1964, but that marked the beginning of a period when she sang a lot less. She continued to make occasional appearances with us, and I think she still genuinely wanted to sing as much as possible. Even when our marriage broke up, some years later, she was still saying, "We'll be back together again with the blues." When she eventually divorced me it was on condition that I would not stand in her way if she wanted to come out and sing with us. In the end she did do this several times in the early 1980s, eventually finishing for good in 1985–86.

The first time she withdrew completely, however, was when she gave up singing with the band in 1966–67 and went to Ireland. Some school friends of hers had a farm there, and adjacent to their quite modern house was the traditional old farmstead with whitewashed walls and a corrugated iron roof. She stayed there, and I went over to be with her as often as our touring work would allow. Then in 1972 we bought a beautiful house in Rostrevor, County Down. It's very rare in Northern Ireland to find a regency mansion, because there weren't many built there during that period, but this was a very attractive one. It's a lovely place with a six-acre garden, and the original plan was for her parents to move in and live in the sizeable gate lodge, so that she would have company when I was on the road with the band. At the last minute, her mother would not go, perhaps because of the increase of what were known as "the Troubles" at that time in South Down. Nonetheless, Ottilie and I lived there together for some time. I had to drive to the airport in Belfast and leave the car there in order to fly to work, wherever the band was playing. This left Ottilie by herself, and as time went on she became quite scared, as the local area gradually acquired a reputation for IRA activity.

As a consequence we sold that house and bought a bungalow in Bangor, County Down, for Ottilie to share with her mother. In due course they sold that and moved to St. Albans, where her mother had some Latvian friends. After not getting on very well with them, Ottilie moved up to Ayr, to live near her sister, and she spent the rest of her life in that area.

While Ottilie was singing less with the band as the sixties went on, we were constantly making other changes to what and how we played. Mostly these were not huge sudden alterations, but small ones that brought in new ideas here and there. There were also some changes in personnel. Eddie Smith was replaced by Stu Morrison at the end of 1964. Stu had played banjo with Ken Colyer occasionally, but before he joined us he'd been playing in the Mike Cotton Sound. He was a good singer – with a real interest in the blues – and he sang quite a bit with us. Latterly, Mike had encouraged him to switch to bass guitar, so he joined us in order to return to playing banjo and guitar. Stu had also been a successful racing cyclist at one point and, as a result of that enthusiasm, I briefly found myself sponsoring a professional cycling team.

By the time Stu joined us we had already made a much more fundamental change to the band, by adding a blues guitarist to the line-up, alongside the banjo. After hearing how Muddy Waters sounded with us, and having had other American guests such as Sister Rosetta Tharpe and Brownie McGhee play guitar together with our usual instrumentation, I felt we needed the sound of a blues guitarist to broaden the range of what we could do in concert ourselves. So, in August 1964, I brought in a guitarist for our album *Good Morning Blues*, called John Slaughter.

This came about because I'd known, ever since Alexis Korner played his partly inaudible unamplified semi-acoustic guitar with my first band, that the electric guitar could potentially be a strong ingredient in our sound, and by mid-1964 I was looking around in earnest for a suitable player. I called some of the musicians on the blues scene in the UK, and by chance I happened to phone John Mayall, whose Bluesbreakers played regular sessions at the Marquee. John and his band had just done a tour of the UK with John Lee Hooker in June, and so he knew exactly the sound I was after. As it turned out, his regular guitarist Roger Dean had been taken ill a couple of nights before I phoned. His place had been taken at short notice by a young friend of the Bluesbreakers' drummer, and John Mayall thought this promising guitarist might possibly be able to provide what I was after. That was how John Slaughter first came to play with us, and he joined the band in August. Apart from a break from 1978 until 1986, John was in the band until his death in 2010.

It wasn't easy going with some of our audiences. Those who just liked the more traditional jazz sound could not see the point, but usually once they had heard what John could do they changed their minds. On what was probably his first tour to Switzerland with us he was booed by some sections of the audience at one concert, who hung a huge banner over the balcony saying

"Chris Barber's Beat Band". It was a bit like the Birmingham audience who did a similar thing when the alto saxophonist Bruce Turner joined Humph, only their banner said "Go Home Dirty Bopper". This sort of audience only wanted to hear us playing New Orleans jazz along the lines we had been doing for the previous ten years. I told them that the blues was an integral part of our music and that the guitar was therefore an integral part of our band. I think the worst reaction to John's presence was in Nuremburg. As the band went off the stage one by one, when we got to John they booed. I did a Nazi salute to the crowd (something for which, in the Germany of the time, I could have been arrested) and I said to them that we'd recently fought a war about tolerance, and I felt they were not being tolerant. Afterwards, backstage, a tall, blond German man thanked me for saying that. Then he asked if I'd sign a book for him. It was a copy of Charles Delauney's *Hot Discography*, printed illegally in France during the war. The man had been an officer in Paris at the time, and he had somehow acquired it, and then kept it with him despite the Nazi regime's official opposition to jazz.

To start with, John just played on the blues feature numbers, but as 1964 gave way to 1965 he played on just about everything we did, adding rhythm guitar along with the banjo. Because bringing John into the band involved the electric guitar becoming an integral ingredient in our sound, it prompted us into thinking seriously about the way the band sounded to audiences. In the early days we just used whatever PA system was in the clubs or halls where we played. And that remained true throughout the fifties and into the early sixties, although Dick Smith did use a bass amplifier. So to start with we got a basic amplifier for the rest of the band and some mikes. But then I went to Ralph Cornforth, who was a bit of an electronics wizard, and he put together a proper sound system for us. As time went on he worked out ways of getting the mixing desk further from the band so the result could be as perfect as possible from the audience's point of view. By the end of the seventies we had a fully professional system and to this day we are still the only British traditional style band that travels with an international quality sound system and our own lighting engineer.

John Ryan, our roadie, had worked with various groups handled by the Marquee booking agency before he joined us. He was used to working with sound, and he would set up and operate our system for us. However, I remember once in 1976 when we were playing in Kitzbühel in Austria, shortly after the Winter Olympics at Innsbruck, a particularly virulent strain of flu was doing the rounds, which became known as "Olympic flu" and several of the band contracted it. By the time we got to our next gig in Basel, at the Casino, half the band and John were completely out of action, so I remember on our concert there setting up the mixing desk at the side of the stage, close to me. I played bass and trombone, and did the sound mixing!

Shortly after John Slaughter and Stu Morrison joined the band, Dick Smith left. He had been having some trouble at home with his children, not least because he was away a lot with us. So he decided he had to give up doing all the travelling and be at home more. So we had to find another bass player. Initially I asked Mickey Ashman to come back and rejoin us because he knew about the music. He was with us for a while. We also briefly had Denny Coffey, but then in May 1967 Jackie Flavelle joined. I must have first heard him some years before that, during one of my visits to Newtownards with Ottilie, so by 1967 I was already aware of Jackie playing double bass and then bass guitar with various showbands. That year we were in Ireland on tour, and Jackie was in the particular showband that played support to us at a gig in Ballycastle. John Slaughter and I heard what he did during their set and thought he'd be right for us.

Consequently, Jackie left Northern Ireland. He and his wife moved to London and he joined the band. He was very reliable, and played accurately over every chord sequence, because his long period of time in the showbands had given him a great store of musical knowledge. To start with he played string bass with us, but the thing he did best was bass guitar. When he joined he had a fretless Ampeg, exactly the same type of instrument that Rich Danko plays in The Band. You could hit it quite hard without producing a long sustaining note. In 1968 he said he was fed up with carrying his string bass around and that he thought the sound coming out of the amp was more or less the same. So he asked us to do a blindfold test and tell him which one he was playing. We couldn't tell the difference, so he played the bass guitar all the time from then until Vic Pitt joined us ten years later.

Bringing in John Slaughter on electric guitar and now having an electric bass meant that by 1967 the band was rather different from the line-up with which we'd begun. We played more blues and gospel material in our ordinary sets, and at this point we began adding material from quite different sources altogether.

For example, as we were working more and more in Germany, at one point we happened to be in Dusseldorf. We had an evening off and went to a Hungarian-style restaurant in the Aldstadt district. This was a place called Czikos, and one reason we liked it was that, most times we went there, a Hungarian band would be playing. On this occasion, however, there'd been some confusion with the bookings, and instead of a Hungarian group there was a band from Macedonia. It had a cimbalom, clarinet, bass and violin, and they were all really impressive musicians. The violin was playing an oom-cha-cha second part while the clarinet played the melody.

This Macedonian music – in effect more or less the same as Bulgarian music – immediately grabbed our attention because it involved really unusual time-signatures. It was rather as if you were walking along the pavement taking regular sized steps and then quite unexpectedly you would trip over because the kerb or the next paving stone was not where you expected it to be. I got the clarinet player to write one of the trickier pieces out for me. It is in 21/8, and he wrote it out as a series of quavers in one long bar, although in Western music terms it equates to a bar of five, a bar of seven and a bar of nine. It intrigued Ottilie and me, and also Pat, and we started discussing how we might introduce something to our repertoire that was a bit like that. So first we made something out of the tune that had been written down for us, and we called it 'Czikos' after the restaurant, although it seems to have been a folk song originally. We played the theme in 5/7/9, and then into 4/4 for the central part and then back to the unorthodox metre again. Then we went into 9/8 for the last part and the improvisation, and that became a regular part of our repertoire. I loved playing it.

When we got back to England shortly after that, we were working down in the West Country, near Minehead, and at the time I had an American car with a Pioneer eight-track sound system on which you could actually record things. As I was driving along I thought of a tune and hummed it into that machine. In retrospect, I realise it was partly based on Jimmy Giuffre's 'The Train and The River', although my tune was in 5/8 which that one isn't. Later, I jotted it down from the tape and we tried to play it, eventually creating another finished number. I called this one 'Battersea Rain Dance' because one of the first times that we played it at a gig, in Battersea Park, it rained. Ironically, the open-air bandstand we played on, which always seemed to get soaked whenever we played there, ultimately burned down!

The time-signature experiments went on with another original piece, 'Ubava Zabava', which has a similar set of bars of different lengths to 'Czikos'. When we played in America at the Washington Jazz Festival opposite Don Ellis, he had just had a big hit with 'Bulgarian Bulge', a piece I think he'd worked out because his pianist was originally Bulgarian. However, 'Bulgarian Bulge' is just basically the same as 'Ubava Zabava'. We made more of a rock arrangement out of it, but his solution to how to improvise over such a complex metre was the same as ours – you ignore it and play over the rhythm *a capella*. You can't actually improvise on the metrical structure of the song because it's too restrictive. I remember playing 'Ubava Zabava' in 1970, the year when Harold Pendleton had to move the National Jazz Festival from Windsor, where it had been after Richmond, to Plumpton Racecourse. We played on the Sunday of the festival, and after us was the band of the day, Yes, and we got just as good a response from the audience as they did.

This Balkan material was a long way from some of the things we were still doing as a traditional jazz band, and equally quite different from the gospel singing that we did, with the whole front line harmonising in much the same way that Alex Bradford had done with us. One example of that kind of gospel music was a Staples Singers number called 'I'm Goin' Home on the Morning Train', which was also known as 'Get Right Church and Let's Go Home'. In fact one of our more unusual Columbia recordings from 1964 was 'Morning Train' because the session took place before Pat was able to get back from his summer holiday, and so I got Jimmy Deuchar and Ronnie Scott to round out the band. We made a rather good version of 'Hamp's Blues' with them as well.

We almost got that version of 'Morning Train' to become the new theme for the television show *Ready Steady Go!* because the journalist and writer Bob Bickford took our record, which had a really strong soul feel to it, to ATV. However, when she heard that it was by Chris Barber, the producer Vicky Wickham decided not to use it. However, soon after that it did get featured on television because we ended up miming to it on *Thank Your Lucky Stars*. I remember that Ronnie Scott was not available on the day of the filming, so I hired Don Rendell to come in and mime to Ronnie's solo.

At the same time as adding our first Balkan pieces and the gospel numbers, we were also including in our concerts Horace Silver's 'Song For My Father', which took us a while to work out for the front line, but which the rhythm section got straight away.

And then Giorgio Gomelski turned up. I've mentioned him before in connection with Ottilie's records. He had been born in Georgia, and travelled all over Europe before spending his teenage years, during the war, in Switzerland. Later he had to do his national service in the Swiss Air Force; although he was quite a good pilot he deliberately failed his flying test so that he would be discharged early. His mother (who was originally from Monte Carlo) came to work in London, and sent him the *Melody Maker* every week, from which he learned English, or at least his own idiosyncratic version of it. Having already promoted jazz events in his home country in the early 1950s, he arrived in Britain with the intention of making jazz movies. He started out doing subtitles for foreign films, but from the outset he wanted to become a director. In order to be recognised as a director there was a catch-22 – you had to have made a film first. So he worked out how to get finance for a movie that would get him qualified as a director. In the event, his first two movies were of our band. He went on to expand his activities into producing records.

By the time we got involved in recording for him in the late 1960s he was already working with our Marquee agency, managing the Yardbirds, and he had also set up the Crawdaddy blues club in Richmond where the Rolling Stones got their start. More importantly for us, he founded Marmalade Records which had begun to record people such as Brian Auger, John McLaughlin and Soft Machine. Giorgio became the *eminence grise* behind our recording career for the next few years, once we signed with Marmalade.

We'd stayed with Denis Preston until 1962, first with the contract under which his Record Supervision productions were sold to Pye and then on a similar arrangement with Columbia. As I said earlier, we parted company with him because we didn't like recording in his Lansdowne Studio owing to the acoustics. Our next few discs were mainly done directly for Columbia. We also put out some records on the French Vogue label, but these were sessions that we recorded ourselves at the Marquee Studio, which I produced and then sold to Vogue. This was because, until the work dried up with the 1968 riots, we needed something to sell to go with our frequent tours to France. I did not explain earlier why we had cracked the French market around 1962.

Prior to that time, any requests for us to play in the country had been referred to Hugues Panassié, who published *Le Jazz Hot*. He did not like trad bands in general, mainly because (a) we were not black and (b) we were British. For years he managed to block requests for us to play in France by telling enquirers that we did not want to play there. Then quite suddenly we started to get bookings.

I soon discovered that our new-found advocate in France was none other than Panassié's great enemy, Charles Delauney, who coincidentally was the accountant for Vogue Records. Immediately Vogue brought out our recordings, and we also got the benefits of their advertising, which included giant posters all over Paris and other major cities. After our first modest success with the label, we made an LP for them called *Chris Barber Dans le Vent*. It literally means "in the wind" but it's also a popular expression meaning we were "the height of fashion"! Then we got together with Barry Martyn's band to record an EP for Vogue of Beatles tunes in the style of a New Orleans brass band. We did 'Can't Buy Me Love', 'From Me To You', 'I Saw Her Standing There' and 'She Loves You'. They sound very good, and I'm surprised more people haven't thought of playing those pieces this way.

We signed with Giorgio in 1967, once he had got his label up and running, because not only had he a distribution deal with Polydor, but they were putting money into the label. This was to pump-prime his investment in artists, and also included paying to hire the Advision studio off Bond Street. Later this was to backfire because even though Giorgio had a huge hit with Julie Driscoll, Brian Auger and 'This Wheel's On Fire', none of the profits from that record found their way back from Polydor to Marmalade. So in the end they shut Marmalade down saying that it had made no money, and that's why, as I mentioned earlier in connection with Ottilie's *Spring Song*, nothing that was issued on the label is available now. Giorgio eventually walked away when Polydor refused to settle with him. So all the material we did for Marmalade remains unobtainable to this day.

When we first started working with Giorgio all these problems were in the future, and he was full of ideas. He really encouraged us to do the wide range of music on *Battersea Rain Dance*, with 'Better Get Hit In Your Soul' by Mingus and 'Dancy Dancy' by John Handy, as well as the Balkan title track. And he also enthused over getting in Brian Auger and Paul McCartney for the song 'Cat Call'. This album called *Battersea Rain Dance*, which was made over the course of just over a year from June 1967 to the end of July 1968, really moved us into a lot of different areas. It also saw the departure of Ian Wheeler and the arrival of his replacement John Crocker, although Ian was to rejoin the band later.

Not long after *Battersea Rain Dance* had appeared, a man walked into the Marquee one night, while we were playing, and said he'd like to produce a record with us. So I followed it up the next day and discovered his name was Steve Hammond. He'd been with Chris Farlowe, writing songs with him, and he'd also written 'Gemini' for Eric Burdon and the New Animals' album *Love Is*. Steve had grown up in Canada, playing clarinet in a school jazz band and guitar in a rock group, so he had a huge range of musical interests. This was helped by the fact that he'd been in high school with most of the members of The Band, but when Rick Danko and the others went off to the USA, Steve returned to London, where he'd been born. (Indeed, when talking about his early childhood, I discovered that although everybody called him Steve, he was actually christened Stephane, after Stephane Grappelli.)

Steve had a group of musical friends around London who were, in our terms, pretty far out, but he brought them to work with us. They included Peter Robinson, from Quatermass, who was a very good musician and a fine pianist. Then there was Paul Buckmaster, who played the cello. Not long after he first worked with us, Paul got a call from Miles Davis asking him to come over to New York to do some of the arrangements for *On The Corner*, but when we met him he was best known for playing with Sounds Nice and the Third Ear Band. He wrote a piece for the first record that Steve produced with us. It was called 'Shoeman the Human'. He also developed some music with us for a piece called 'O'Reilly' that can best be described as "free trad". It's on the second Steve Hammond album we did. On that, the very talented Ann O'Dell played electric piano with us, and among the other guests Rory Gallagher played guitar.

I should mention here that we did a few live concerts with Rory in the years that followed, including a 1990 session at a theatre in Swindon that happened to be recorded, on which I played bass along with his blues guitar. In contrast to Muddy Waters, Rory really was loud. Like some other British blues players, he aimed to get a slightly distorted guitar effect by using volume, whereas Muddy seemed to have some knack of twisting the string that produced a similar sound at little or no volume. But Rory really was very good, and played and sang really well. The Irish connection was very strong, and when he sang Leadbelly's 'Out On The Western Plains' it really sounded like an Irish song. It was a shame we lost him in 1995, aged just forty-seven after an unsuccessful liver transplant.

Steve Hammond ended up being a staff arranger at Paramount Pictures working on a huge range of movies, before he also died extremely young following a heart attack in 1989. Before he left Britain, he not only produced my albums *Get Rollin'* and *Drat That Fratle Rat*, but he played banjo and – from time to time – electric guitar with the band. He took over from Stu Morrison in 1971 and stayed until Johnny McCallum arrived in 1973. If Steve had chosen to stay around with us a bit longer he'd have been of great benefit to the band, taking our ideas even further than on those albums he produced, yet without dispensing with the traditional background of jazz and blues.

Those three Marmalade/Polydor albums, which are all pretty hard to find now, were really all down to Giorgio. He fired us up with enthusiasm and encouragement in the first place, and then put in the money to promote the records. In terms of what we had done before, these were novelty records to some extent, and they needed extra promotion on a big scale. I was sure they would sell if the public actually knew about them because the music is very catchy. But it didn't really catch on with the general public, and this is at least partly because it needed Beatles-level promotion.

The closest we came to the Beatles was our single 'Cat Call' with Paul McCartney, from the *Battersea Rain Dance* album. Paul was there when we first recorded it at the Marquee studio as a jazz tune. We were still learning how to play it, and that version was never released, but Paul and his girlfriend of the time, Jane Asher, were there in the studio. When we redid it for the album Paul was part of it because we decided to do it like the end section of 'All You Need Is Love', with all kinds of bands playing different tunes and people singing and shouting. And doing cat-calls. The idea was that the underlying little tune would get jazzier and jazzier, whereupon the producer (Giorgio) comes on the talkback and says, "Stop! Stop! Stop! Chris, can you play it slow?" So then we start playing it slow, and as it gets groovier, that's where all the shouting and singing and so forth comes in, like that second bit of 'All You Need Is Love'. And it all came about because, as I said earlier, I met Paul when he bought a house from a friend of mine near Lord's cricket ground.

I mentioned that Steve Hammond was replaced as a regular member of the band by Johnny McCallum. Johnny had a shared background with Jackie Flavelle in Northern Ireland. Indeed their musical roots were from playing together in an Orange marching band. Johnny played snare drum in that group, and he is to this day a superb snare drummer, particularly in a New Orleans parade band. Jackie had played the flute, back in those early days in Ulster. There were two flautists in the band, one was Jackie and the other was James Galway, who went on to become a rather well-known player of the instrument! (I should say in passing that James Galway's brother George is a jazz saxophone player.) Anyway, Jackie put me in touch with Johnny McCallum, and he proved to be an ideal addition to the band, playing very deft single string solos on the banjo, and also playing guitar. He's a great fan of Tal Farlow – not that he played like Tal with us – but his musical tastes were very broad and this helped bring variety and interest into the band during the mid-seventies.

After Sammy Rimington and Pete York left the band in 1979 we settled into the front line of myself, Pat, Ian Wheeler and John Crocker, with Johnny McCallum and John Slaughter on guitars, Vic Pitt on bass (who replaced Jackie) and Norman Emberson on drums. This line-up had very few changes through the 1980s, except Roger Hill joined when John Slaughter took some time out from the band. A good example of the sound of the 1980s band is on the album *Barbican Blues* recorded at the London concert hall in 1982.

At the end of the decade, Norman was replaced by Alan "Sticky" Wicket. In the early 1990s, Sticky left for a while to be replaced by Russell Gilbrook, but then he returned to the band again. He has often rejoined us since for subsequent reunions of the small band.

One advantage of the eight-piece band in the 1980s, given Johnny McCallum's skill as a snare drummer, was that it was relatively easy to turn it into a New Orleans-style parade band. Vic switched from bass to sousaphone, and Norman played bass drum, while Johnny played snares. John Slaughter or Roger Hill usually played additional percussion. Our interest in this style of music had been there for many years, and I've already mentioned our get-to-gether with Barry Martyn for French Vogue, playing brass band versions of Beatles songs. That had been in 1965, but the experience which really got me enthused about playing this type of New Orleans parade had been three years earlier, in Washington DC, when we went there to appear at President John F. Kennedy's first ever Washington Jazz Festival.

The newly-formed Preservation Hall Jazz Band was also on the bill, with Willie and Percy Humphrey, and to publicise the event the Eureka Brass Band (which also featured Percy and Willie) was to march through the streets up to the White House. The organisers, who included Doc Souchon from New Orleans, invited our front line to join the Eureka for the march. We'd known about this music from a distance, and we'd had a limited chance to hear it on our previous visits to New Orleans, but we were overjoyed to be asked to take part in a proper parade and really learn how the music works from one of the greatest of all the brass bands. This was so important to us that it made us look for opportunities as the years went on to repeat the experience.

As the Eureka paraded through Washington DC that day in 1962, I joined the trombone section, playing alongside Oscar "Chicken" Henry and Albert Warner. Dick Smith took many photographs of the occasion, with the Eureka playing at its best, and Percy Humphrey leading on trumpet. There were many of the other stars of Crescent City jazz in the line-up. I think when we got to the White House that all of us in the band rather hoped JFK would come out on to the balcony and wave, but sadly he did not appear.

Our own attempts to play this music on a more regular basis date to a collaboration with Van Morrison in 1976 when he asked us to come and help make a record. Dr John, whom we didn't know at that time, was producing the album for Van, and he wanted to include the old New Orleans brass band number 'Oh Didn't He Ramble'. They'd originally tried to make it with various session players but that hadn't really worked, although those musicians included some black American rhythm section players who'd just assisted with a recent Rolling Stones tour. They were very good, so they stayed on to join us. They were guitarist Marlo Henderson, bassist Reggie McBride and drummer Ollie E. Brown. From our band, Pat Halcox, John Crocker, Johnny McCallum and I came in, and Dr John played the piano. When Van's record company heard the results of all the sessions there were a dozen or so normal Van Morrison bluesy ballady songs, and this one New Orleans marching band track, so they didn't use it at the time! I happened to keep a copy of the backing that we made, and in 2010 Van came back to the studio and recorded his vocal so that it was finally put out on record for the first time that year.

After that, we began to play this style of music a little more often. I put together a parade band for the 1978 Reading Festival, where we were joined by New Orleans trumpeter Alvin Alcorn who was touring with us at the time. The following year in New Orleans I raised the prospect with Dr John of coming to Europe to work with us, and at the same time, we thought of bringing along the drummer Freddie Kohlman. He was one of the best drummers in the city, but not very well-known outside New Orleans or Chicago where he had previously spent many years playing in the house band at the Jazz Ltd. club, backing everyone from Billie Holiday to Sidney Bechet.

In 1980, it finally happened and Dr John and Freddie Kohlman came to Europe for the "Take Me Back to New Orleans" tour. We added some extra musicians from the Inter Cities Jazz Band to create a full-size parade group, with Teddy Fullick on trumpet, Roy Maskell joining me in the trombones, and Dick Cook playing E flat clarinet, while John Beecham played tuba. Freddie Kohlman played bass drum and also sang some of his Louis Armstrong style vocals. Our sets opened and closed with the brass band, and then the eight-piece group was joined by Dr John, playing his special brand of piano and singing, including such Professor Longhair numbers as 'Ti-pi-ti-na' and 'Professor Longhair's Tip'. An album recorded in London at the time contains these songs, but also gives the impression of the parade band marching along and eventually fading into the distance. When Freddie Kohlman had to leave the tour early his place was taken by another great New Orleans drummer, and a real character, Chester Jones.

We were fortunate that in touring this show we had some help from British Airways who had just inaugurated a direct flight to New Orleans, and in April 1981 they flew us out there to play in the city. We played our scheduled concert at the International Hotel, but because the New Orleans Jazz and Heritage Festival was in full swing, at the last minute the producer George Wein added us to the official programme and we played a second concert at the Roosevelt Hotel. The critic and jazz writer Floyd Levin was there, and he later wrote: "Their spirited performance left an indelible mark on those who witnessed the event. It was probably the highlight of the entire festival."

We met Alvin Alcorn again on that visit, and while we were there we were also making a feature for BBC TV. When we played our festival set the only American on our part of the show was Freddie Kohlman, but Alvin wanted to join in with us too. He was very enthusiastic and a very good musician indeed. As we knew from his UK tour, he had a strange, laid-back way of playing which took a bit of getting used to, but was very effective.

On that visit I was staying in the Marriott Hotel on Canal Street, and playing in the reception lounge at weekends there'd be a trio of Alvin, guitarist Justin Adams and bassist Frank Fields. Alvin used to wander about during their sets and stop to chat with the audience, leaving Frank and Justin playing, and I got the impression the other two members of the trio occasionally got rather fed up! Of course you can't help being reminded of Alvin after his appearance in the Olympia Brass Band street parade in the 1973 James Bond film, *You Only Live Twice*. He plays the knife-wielding killer: "Whose funeral is that?" "Yours, if you like!" That movie was made a few years before we toured with him.

When we got together with Alvin and Freddie Kohlman in our brass band on the package show, they said, "We'll try and persuade one of the local bands to come and challenge you, because you're going to win!" It was a very nice thought, although sadly it did not happen.

Nevertheless, from then on, we regularly included some parade music in our sets, usually finishing with the band marching off stage. In 1982 we did a week at Ronnie Scott's in London, when Ronnie had run into some trouble with his tax affairs, and to help him raise the money he needed we came into the club. On our opening night we marched through Soho Square and down to the club on Frith Street, much to the bemusement of the locals and late commuters making their way home!

Another memorable session on which we played some brass band music was when we were reunited with Ken Colyer in 1984. He played some pieces with the eight-piece band, but he also joined us on some parade tunes. He moved to France soon afterwards but a record survives of one of our concerts from that tour, and – as ever – Ken played his very special brand of New Orleans lead.

1984 was also the year I started a very different project with Richard Hill. I first met him when he did some of the arrangements for Ottilie's recordings with Giorgio, and he is a very wide-ranging and accomplished musician whose work, by the mid-1980s, encompassed producing with Paul McCartney, writing the music for the West End production of the *Canterbury Tales* which ran at the Phoenix Theatre for five years from 1968, and plenty of film and television scores.

Richard had studied classical trombone and conducting, but he also played jazz trombone in Dave Keir's band. One day he and I got talking about jazz bands and orchestras playing together, and what the problems are in trying to fuse these very different areas of music. It used to be the case that anybody who knew about orchestral music didn't know about jazz syncopation. Although that's changing, I think we came to the view that when a group of jazz musicians is playing with all the intensity of syncopation that they would use in a normal performance, if you put them with symphonic musicians the symphonic players would have to adapt, so as to play in a way that works with what the jazz players instinctively do.

Then an opportunity came our way. The Dutch Swing College Band had recently done several concerts with the Royal Dutch Marinierskapel (their equivalent to the Royal Marines Band). It is a classical-styled military band, with reeds, brass and percussion, but no strings. The DSC Band had used stock arrangements, such as 'South Rampart Street Parade', where the band played something based on Bob Crosby's original and the orchestra played alongside them. When we were invited to work with them I asked Richard Hill to write new arrangements. He came up with several, and we did a series of concerts with them that worked very well.

Then Richard and I thought about expanding it to work with a full orchestra. One of the things we discussed was that whereas jazz and dance band musicians do not have syncopations written out – they automatically understand where they go in the parts – every bit of syncopation would have to be written out as precisely as possible for the symphony players. Richard worked out a method of doing this, and then he composed his own 'New Orleans Overture' for a symphony orchestra to play together with the line-up of our New Orleans Brass Band. Then he started out on a trombone concerto. The first movement is ragtimey in style, then there's a blues, of which the first chorus has no passing chords, but is based purely on the three basic chords of the traditional blues. Then each successive chorus adds passing chords that make it different. And the final movement has a sort of Charleston feel.

At the time we were always being asked if we could do more concerts in East Berlin because by the mid-eighties we had begun to play quite frequently in East Germany. So I suggested we might come and do this concerto with a symphony orchestra there. As it happened, this was quite a good move because, in the West, most symphony orchestras had been used to do backing tracks for pop singers, film scores, commercials and so on. But that had barely happened at all in the East, so in 1986 the Großes Rundfunkorchester Berlin jumped at the chance to do this piece with us.

We spent five days in Berlin. We did a normal band concert one night, and then we had two nights playing the concerto with the symphony orchestra, conducted by Robert Hanell. At first glance he seemed as precise a conductor as Klaus Tennstedt (who'd worked for years with the North German Radio Symphony Orchestra) and slightly remote, but then we saw that Hanell had a twinkle in his eye and it worked very well. We played in the showpiece concert hall of the DDR (the Deutsche Demokratische Republik), the Palast der Republik, and, being a radio orchestra, they were used to having each string player miked individually, so the balance between them and the band was excellent. As well as the trombone concerto we did Richard's 'New Orleans Overture' and he'd also done new arrangements of several other pieces including 'Mood Indigo', 'Harlem Rag' and 'Alligator Hop'. At the end, they joined us on 'Ice Cream'. For the last two choruses, Richard had written "Off beat handclap" in the string parts, and they all did it. The thing that most impressed me was the way Hanell had worked with the strings on the fast final "Stomp" movement. There's a recurring syncopation right through it, and he had rehearsed them during the week before, starting at half tempo and then speeding it up to get it exactly right. They were as together as any top-flight 1920s jazz orchestra. It was really a thrill to do it, and to have the orchestral musicians taking it absolutely seriously. No long faces, just real commitment. We did it again two years later with a few more orchestral pieces added.

We've always wanted to take every chance to do it again, but we've never had the opportunity to play these pieces in England. I gather that on one occasion Don Lusher did play one movement of the 'Trombone Concerto' on *Friday Night is Music Night* on the BBC, but not the whole thing. Richard Hill was friendly with a trombone player in the City of Birmingham Symphony Orchestra, and he got the orchestra to do the 'New Orleans Overture' while Sir Simon Rattle was still chief conductor. But we have not played any of this material in Britain ourselves. By contrast, we've played it several times in East Germany, in Nuremburg, and more recently in Denmark, with the South Jutland Symphony Orchestra and another brilliant conductor who understood exactly how to make it work rhythmically.

By the time those symphony collaborations began, we were spending the majority of our time in Germany, as we had been since the end of the 1970s, mainly because our German manager, Karlheinz Lyrmann, was a great guy and organised a lot of work for us. During the war he had been captured in Denmark by the Germans and interned in a prisoner of war camp. While he was in the camp the call went round, "Does anyone play chess?" As it turned out, he did, and so he ended up playing games with the camp commandant. As the war was drawing to an end he discovered that people were gradually being released from the camp and repatriated. He found out that the Germans were starting with those whose surnames were at the end of the alphabet, and so he put his name down as Zyrmann, and got sent home with a close friend whose name was also in that section of the alphabet. By the time he worked with us he had long been a very active figure in the German jazz scene and, through the German Jazz Federation, he had run a series of jazz band contests in the 1950s and 1960s.

As an aside, Klaus Doldinger told me that he won one of the first of those competitions with his band the Feetwarmers, back in the fifties, and the prize was a visit to America. The main sponsor was Coca Cola, so as well as New Orleans and Chicago the band went to Atlanta, which was the headquarters of the drinks company. In Atlanta they had a reception with the mayor, and that afternoon they had the disturbing sight of the mayor marching through the streets at the head of a procession with the Ku Klux Klan. Then they got to New Orleans and because they had met George Lewis in Europe with Ken Colyer, Klaus rang him and said, "Hi George, let's meet up and have lunch together!"

George's answer was one word: "Where?"

Owing to segregation it just wasn't possible in New Orleans at that time, but for a man who normally said very little, that was an unusually biting comment for George. The only possible place would have been in George's own house, but practically anywhere else was impermissible.

Anyhow, as I said, through the efforts of Karlheinz, we were working a lot in Germany, particularly in the Ruhr but with consistent touring all over the country. Consequently we often took some of our time off there, rather than rushing back to Britain, only to turn round almost immediately and head back to Germany again. I met Renate Hilbich there in 1974. We got chatting, went out for a meal, and then I started seeing her every time I was in Germany. She came to live in England in 1979 and our daughter Caroline was born in 1980. Caroline now lives in the United States, and works in broadcasting in Los Angeles. Renate and I were married in 1984, once my divorce from Ottilie was final.

Renate was born and grew up in West Germany at the time of the Wirtschaftswunder, when everything was being done according to the idea of the new Germany. In 1985 our son Christopher was born. By this time in the eighties the band always had summer holidays. These had begun some years earlier when other members of the band had school-age children and it continued thereafter. Pat, for instance, spent part of his summers on an island in the Mediterranean, but he also used to take a week or two of his vacation every year touring with his "Summer Band", which made a change from what we did with my band. Indeed this group had a very different sound, as it regularly included a piano. Most years the featured pianist was Johnny Parker, whom we'd known since before the time of Ottilie's arrival in London. Playing trombone was either the broadcaster Campbell Burnap, or John Beecham (when he was not on the road with the Kinks, whose brass section he led). John also doubled on the tuba, and had played in some of my New Orleans Brass Band projects. On drums Pete York often joined them, and other years another old friend Jimmy Garforth took over the drum chair. Back in the very early days of my band we had occasionally played with the altoist and clarinetist Bruce Turner, and he was a frequent guest in Pat's summer line-up. Another real difference between the Summer Band and mine was that it frequently appeared in concert with the vocal group Sweet Substitute. Consequently the repertoire was definitely geared towards standards and Tin Pan Alley material, although perhaps the most popular piece that they played was a punchy jazz arrangement of the *Flintstones* television theme tune. I did manage to hear the Summer Band on various occasions, but for the most part that time of year was a chance for me to get away and enjoy a family holiday. One year, during our summer vacation, Renate and I went to Florida to take the kids to Disney World, and we ended up going back there several times. Our son Christopher now lives there permanently.

I liked Florida, as there was plenty there to interest me. There's more later about my serious involvement with cars, but during one of our Florida holidays I almost bought a hot rod, of the kind that the band ZZ Top are always seen driving around in — basically a modified vintage Ford with a pumped-up suspension, big dragster rear wheels, the engine block sticking out of the top of the bonnet, and so on. In the end I didn't buy the car.

Renate and I were divorced in 1992. She returned to Germany and later moved permanently to Fort Myers in Florida.

In 1996 I married Kate Gray. Her daughter is the ceramic artist Catherine Gray. Today, Kate and I live in the Wiltshire countryside. It's a good base for all the continuing touring of the Big Chris Barber Band.

7 Automobile Blues

I remember when I was seven or eight years old, I started cutting pictures of cars out of magazines and newspapers. The ones I liked most were art deco: Delages and the late Bugattis – I should say the last "real" Bugattis, made in the factory in Alsace – all of them marvellous machines. So I became very interested in cars, though I don't exactly know why. The first family car my father owned was a Morris 8, and I know we went on holiday in it to the West Country before the war. It must have been 1938, and I remember it had a gravity fuel feed. So we had to go up Countisbury Hill near Lynmouth backwards. It's a one-in-four hill on the edge of Exmoor, just a few miles from the even steeper and more challenging hill at Porlock.

The next year we had a Hillman Minx and a caravan. We went on holiday to the same sort of area, and I learned to drive by taking the Hillman round the caravan site car park. After that, although I knew how to drive, I didn't have the chance to get any more practice because war broke out and I no longer had access to a car. But I liked cars and I kept up both my enthusiasm and knowledge about them throughout the war.

When I became a mathematics student and was playing with my first band, I didn't really think about having a car. For a start, immediately after the war there weren't many cars to buy, and in those days, especially if one lived in the London area, one just didn't have a car. Once we had the band with Ken Colyer, we began to travel a lot more. The first car I bought was in 1954, and it was a 1939 Triumph Dolomite 1.6 litre, which had a cast aluminium front grille. These were extremely prone to damage, but I found a place where you could go to get replacement ones, which came in handy when I needed to repair mine after a friend borrowed the car and dented it. I learned to drive by persuading any friends who had a licence to accompany me until I passed my test.

I know that when Ottilie arrived to join the band, at Christmas 1954, I met her off the train at the London terminus in the Triumph. Apparently I was a bit uncertain in my handling of it on the way home, or so she said.

Certainly by the time she arrived I had become seriously interested in cars. In the early 1950s some of the cars you could get looked a bit like the ones I'd cut out of magazines for my scrapbooks. After the Dolomite, my next car was a 1938 Lagonda LG6. It was a beautiful car – the last in the line of real Lagondas that had been designed by W. O. Bentley after he'd left the company that carried his name. It was a lovely-looking, long-chassis four-door saloon, and it was excellent to drive. I think it cost about £400, which was a lot of money back then, and indeed the Triumph Dolomite had not been cheap.

I drove the Lagonda to gigs quite often, and somehow or other, I got the offer of buying another one that was a bit older than mine, a 1934 LG 45 model, which I bought from Lord Swinfen for £135, which was comparatively cheap. It was a very nice car but a bit of a brute to drive. It was also designed by Bentley, so, like his own cars of the 1920s, it had the accelerator in the centre, the brake on the right, and a crash gearbox that was extremely difficult to operate. Changing up gradually was easy enough, but in most other circumstances, if I got out of gear while driving it, it was a case of stopping and starting up again. I never really got the hang of it. In some of the press articles about me at the time, the cars were nicknamed "Julia" and "Emma".

I sold the LG 45 after a while because I couldn't look after it properly, and in the end it was the same with the other Lagonda. We had no garage, and so the cars were sitting in the street. The bodywork on both of them was at least partly built of wood, and this began to rot as a consequence of being outside all the time. I still remember the number of my first Lagonda, JPD 952 and the older car was BPE 292. (FLO 489 was the Dolomite.)

Although I sold them, having the Lagondas further stimulated my interest in cars. I began to read about them a lot, and then for some reason I ended up going to a motor race. Up until that time I knew vaguely what motor racing was and what it involved, because during the war a lot of people talked about what used to happen, but obviously nothing went on at the track until the war was over.

When we first started the band the only one of us who could really drive was Jim Bray. He had his 1934 Humber shooting brake that was our first bandwagon, and he also owned the Rolls-Royce that had formerly belonged to King Zog of Albania. Dickie Bishop used to have this song:

Take Jimmy Bray now
He's got a Rolls-Royce
Just to give lifts to
Handsome young boys.

Of course that wasn't really true. I never saw Jim with a boy, or a girl for that matter, but he had a Black Shadow Vincent motor bike and the Rolls-Royce. It was a beautiful car – a twin-cowl open tourer. Somewhat in contrast to that, he had created our bandwagon from the old Humber Super Snipe estate car I mentioned earlier, by adding a functional, but not very beautiful, wrought-iron roof rack for the bass and drums. When he was loading it up at our usual meeting place outside the Rex in Soho, opposite an old NCP car park, there'd always be two or three little boys, helping him. But I never saw any hint of him actually laying so much as a finger on any of them. He was older than all of us, and quite different in many ways. He had a degree already, and that set him slightly apart from the rest of us.

However, as time went on we all started to drive, and then of course I had the Lagondas. After my initial experience of seeing a race, I gradually got more and more interested in motor racing, and I first went to Silverstone in 1956. It wasn't a Grand Prix as such, but among the competing cars were some that had been built for the Grand Prix circuit, including the original V16 BRM. This really piqued my interest, and in due course I decided to buy a car in which I could compete myself. This was December 1956, and I went down to the Car Exchange – a sports car dealership in Brighton that specialised in racing, run by Ian Raby and Bill Frost. They had a great reputation for the racing side of things, and from them I bought a Lotus sports/racing car: a Mark IX Lotus. It was a very nice car with a Climax engine, and it had won a trophy for its amateur driver the year before.

It was priced at £960. I had the money, and after buying it I drove the car back to London. I remember that for our Royal Festival Hall concert in December 1956 I rolled up at the stage door in it. By then I had already driven the Lotus enough to have decided that I definitely wanted to race it on the track as well as driving it on the road. I had got to know several people who were involved in racing one way or another. Being popular entertainers, we met a lot of other people who were in the public eye. Graham Hill, for example, wasn't a jazz fan, but he liked the atmosphere of the music business, so he became a good friend. From being around Graham and other drivers whom we met through the entertainment world, I began to find out about how to prepare the car for racing.

The Lagondas were looked after by a mechanic called Ernie Prior. He was a former RAF pilot instructor, who had actually owned and maintained his own plane before the war. It was a Tiger Moth, or something similar, I think. During the war he had taught pilots to fly Spitfires, but the RAF didn't let him go on missions himself, as he was too valuable as a trainer and mechanical expert. He was a delightful, intelligent guy, with a little mews garage near Paddington, not too far from where I lived at the time. So he also became my mechanic for the Lotus and looked after the car.

A Lotus Mark IX was completely open, with no weather equipment. So that it could race as a sports car it was equipped with two seats, but for the track it was in effect a single seater. It had a metal tonneau cover that locked into place over the passenger side. There was a small windscreen situated in front of you on the driver's seat. For road use I used to take the tonneau off and fix a second windscreen up, and Ottilie and I used to go to gigs in it, but there was no weather protection at all. It was never meant to have any. One time I left it parked up north near Stockport railway station, and then I picked it up to drive on to the next gig. I remember thinking it was like sitting in a bath and someone emptying more baths full of water over your head. But of its type it was a very good car. In the 1957 NJF publication *Jazz Scene* it was described as "sleek and windswept" which is something of an understatement!

To race on a full competition licence you had to get six signatures attesting to your competence. There was an RAC observer at each race and if you only held a provisional racing licence you had to get their signature each time you went out. You could only race in club events. It actually took me seven races to get my six signatures because in one of them I went off the road at Oulton Park. We were playing a concert afterwards at Longton Town Hall and when I turned up with a cut on the chin the band all laughed at me. But I got my licence, and in due course I moved on from the Mark IX and bought a Lotus Elite.

In retrospect, I don't think I ever had enough time to race properly. I didn't do it badly, but the friends I was comparing myself with were Jim Clark and Colin Chapman who were the top professionals of the day. So there's no comparison really. Nonetheless I went almost straight away from a provisional racing licence to an international licence, which meant I could race more or less anywhere.

The Elite was a beautiful design by Colin Chapman, a lovely car to drive, and quite exceptional in many ways because it was one of the first – if not the first – cars to be built without a chassis. It was a fibreglass monocoque, to which all the components were bolted. The two prototype cars they had built had just won the *Motor Sport* magazine trophy for GT cars. At that stage they had just made these two cars, and the guy who drove one of them, Ian Walker, was intending to sell his. So I said I'd buy it from him and offered him £1500, which was quite a price in 1958.

Colin Chapman said, "Don't do it. Don't buy that car! It's falling to pieces. We kept it together with string for the GT races. I'll sell you a new one for the same price."

So he did. I got the last prototype to be built before they made the ones to be sold to the public. Mine was a lime-green example, and I got it for exactly fifteen hundred quid. The retail price for the production cars was set at £1956, and it was Chapman's strategy that selling them through the retail market would help to finance his racing programme. Actually, this didn't quite work out as he had planned because, even with the higher list price, Lotus still ended up losing money on every one they built. In the end they constructed exactly 1,030 of them before the run came to an end, and they lost an average of about £100 per car.

Quite recently, I was talking to the man who had been the accountant at Lotus at the time. He asked me if I still had the invoice. I said, "No, I don't think there ever was an invoice." Everything with Colin Chapman was a handshake deal. He was dedicated to spending all his time developing cars for racing or actually racing them, and he needed all the money he could get to spend on racing. He didn't make millions in order to store the money up by investing in other expensive luxuries. It all went into the cars.

I sold my old Lotus Mark IX to the sports car garage that used to be under the raised section of the M4 just west of the Chiswick roundabout. I remember the last race I did with it before I sold it was at Aintree, during which the crown and pinion gears in the differential broke. The trouble with Lotuses of that era is that they were all made with proprietary parts, and the Lotus IX had a Morris 8 differential installed in it. The gear was designed for a 5.3 to 1 ratio in the Morris, but Chapman had it modified to a 4.5 to 1 ratio, which was much faster. With the original gears you'd be going at peak revs and only managing about 80 miles per hour, but the 4.5 to 1 ratio worked far better. When the Lotus IX was being built, Colin had only ever ordered a specific number of those modified parts, and they had run out. So when I replaced it after Aintree I found myself with a diff on which you couldn't possibly race. You could drive the car on the road, but there was no way it could be used for racing, so I got the Elite.

The first time I raced it was the Boxing Day meeting at Brands Hatch in 1958. There were five prototype Elites there, which were driven by Colin Chapman, Jim Clark, Mike Costin (a delightful man who was half of Cosworth Engineering), me, and one other guy. I recall that Chapman tricked Clark into letting him win the race, Costin was third and I was ninth. But there were thirty other cars in the race, all of which should have beaten us because they were much faster cars. I raced the Elite a bit after that, but I hadn't really got the time to devote to getting any better. It was just absurd, really, but I drove it on the road as well. I did about 25,000 miles during the time I had it.

The Elite was a remarkable design because, unlike most British sports cars of the time, such as Morgans or MGs, where there is nowhere to put your elbows, there was plenty of room in the Lotus. It seems to me now that there was more space in it than in a modern Jaguar. It was so easy and comfortable to drive – all in all a marvellous little car. Some aspects of it were a bit daft, as it was put together from all sorts of bits and pieces from other makes, but it really worked.

Unusually, in the summer of 1959, I didn't race at all during the holiday. In fact I borrowed Pat Halcox's car, which was an Austin A35, and went abroad in it. It was a Speedwell conversion – which was Graham Hill's company, actually – so unlike a normal A35 it went at about 90 miles an hour. I took it to Berlin. The German Grand Prix was being held that year at the Automobil-Verkehrs und Ubungs Strasse circuit, which was on the autobahn that runs south west from West Berlin until it joins the main autobahn. The cars ran down in one direction, then round a sharp loop and back up the other carriageway. There was a big banked loop at the top end by the city which was very exciting. Stirling Moss was there in a Cooper, but Tony Brooks won the race in a Ferrari. Although I was following racing that summer I wasn't really taking part.

Then, at the beginning of 1960, a man called John Whitmore asked me if he could drive my Lotus in a race. Actually he was Sir John Whitmore, a baronet, but he didn't use the title at the time. He became a good friend, and has remained so ever since. He has now become one of the world experts in personal coaching and leadership training. We agreed that, to start with, he could drive my car in an event at Silverstone. In point of fact the engine blew up under him in practice, but nevertheless the principle was established that he would drive it. Cosworth Engineering rebuilt the engine and did a complete overhaul for about £200, which is amusing when you think they charge about £200,000 today for a proper racing engine! Once it was back on the road John Whitmore agreed to drive it again. He had previously owned a similar car himself, but he had crashed it at Monza – I think he was lucky to survive. In those days he owned quite a large estate around his family seat at Orsett in Essex and also some land in Devonshire. He moved in quite fashionable company. I remember going to a party at his house and Steve McQueen was there – a marvellous driver, too, of course – and other stars of stage and screen.

In between John's outings I went on driving the car myself when I had the chance. In the end it usually worked out that the only time I had to do this properly was during my summer holidays. For the most part that included the German Grand Prix, which – apart from that one time in West Berlin – was almost always at the Nurburgring. Before the main Grand Prix they had a supporting race, which was for GT cars. In those days that included all kinds of saloon cars, from Ferraris and Porsches down to Lotus Elites. I raced in that car three years running. One year I was about to win my class when the rain fell at the wrong moment, and I was using what were definitely dry weather tyres. Most of the other cars in the class were Alfa Romeo Giulietta TIs, with Pirelli Cinturato tyres, which, although they are actually road tyres, are pretty good in the rain. They all passed me. That was 1961, and I still remember it as the year I almost won something!

When John Whitmore was driving my car he was quite successful. He won a big race at Spa with it, for example, for which I still have the cup. When I was driving the Lotus I managed to get round the old fourteen-mile Nurburgring in eleven minutes, which was pretty good. A few months later, also driving my car, John got round the same circuit in ten minutes and twenty-five seconds. And that was the difference between us. He was about five per cent quicker, which was quite annoying. I'm quite sure that if I had had more time to do it I could have got somewhere with racing, but the thing was that in those days you could end up getting killed through no fault of your own because the safety situation was not up to scratch. It was still so early in his career that Jackie Stewart hadn't started to do anything about improving matters, although when he did start his one-man safety crusade he got absolutely terrible insults from all around the motoring fraternity. Now, of course, every car carries more safety devices than could ever have been imagined back in those days.

I think the saddest thing about racing back in the sixties was that you'd get to know people, they'd become very good friends, and then they'd get killed. Jim Clark is a good example, but there were other friends as well, Bruce McLaren, Jochen Rindt, Wolfgang Von Trips. I was a great fan of Von Trips, who was a lovely guy. He was a real German aristocrat and his family castle was used immediately after the war to billet an American regiment. It was a black regiment, and so he spoke English with an African-American accent. It seemed rather at odds to have someone who had such aristocratic bearing saying, "Yeah, man! Wow!" and that kind of thing. Losing friends like this was sad enough, but I suppose that if I had raced more frequently then I would have known even more drivers much better, and probably lost more friends.

I was desperately sad about Jim Clark's death. It's said that most people in the world can remember exactly where they were in 1963 when President Kennedy was assassinated. I am one of those who cannot. But I know exactly where I was when Jim Clark died because we were working that night in the jazz club in Aarhus in Denmark. Maybe the most tragic death of all, and completely avoidable, was that of Graham Hill, who did not take the advice of the air traffic controllers in France and insisted on flying his plane back to his home airfield at Elstree, despite appalling weather. And he crashed into a tree in freezing fog at Arkley, just before his destination, killing himself and five other people. He was a larger than life character, and I suppose this was typical of his insistence to go his own way.

His son Damon was totally the opposite, and I remember the first time I saw Damon after the crash, I said to him, "I loved your father, but he could be rather pig-headed and obstinate."

And he said, "Yes."

I said, "You won't be like that, will you?"

And he said emphatically, "No, I won't."

In the years that followed, I watched Damon slug it out with Michael Schumacher, and turn into a very good driver indeed.

After a few seasons the Elite was past its sell-by date as regards competition. By then there were better saloon or GT racers available, so I sold it. My next car was a Lotus Elan, which was interesting because Colin Chapman did not expect it to be a competitive racing car. The Elite had been designed with competition in mind, but the Elan was always conceived as a sports car. Almost as soon as it was launched people started using Elans for racing, but not being built for it, they had a tendency to break up. Luckily mine never broke up in that sense, because Ernie Prior, my mechanic, looked after it very well. But there were silly things that went wrong. I remember the Bowden cable that linked the throttle pedal to the carburettor snapped in the middle of a race. It wasn't thick enough. Colin Chapman's attitude was, "I said it wasn't fit for racing," and as far as he was concerned, that was the end of it. So after that I sold the Elan and bought a Lotus Europa – a closed two-seater. I did a bit of racing in that, but ultimately I gave it up. It was too expensive and I didn't have the time. So that was that.

I didn't lose my connection with racing, though. For example, in the sixties and seventies the band played from time to time in the tower by the start line at Brands Hatch. We'd normally play as the meeting came to an end, and, at least in part, it was a ruse by the organisers to ensure that not everyone who had been at the race tried to get out of the same car park, through the same single gate, at the same time. Often some of the drivers, like Jim Clark, for example, came and sat up in the control room next to us, and enjoyed it. I also played a part in a film for Castrol Oils, called *Brands Hatch Beat*, in which we played a couple of tunes to back up commercial footage of the 1964 European Grand Prix. We've continued to play for British Racing Driver Club functions ever since, and in 2013 we performed at Silverstone.

Given my interest in cars, it's fortunate that I also happen to love driving. Over the years I've had some quite interesting cars. I've had two twelve-cylinder Jaguars. One was a two-door coupe, and then I had a Daimler double-six which used the same engine. It was a much better built car because the Daimler assembly line did things properly, but Jaguars weren't always up to the same standards. The doors didn't fit on every Jaguar saloon, but they fitted very snugly on the Daimler. One car I had – it wasn't very good in the end, but enjoyable at first – was an Alfa Romeo Giulia. It was a 1.6 litre four-door saloon, which I got new in 1962. It was a very good car to drive on the road. Everything about it was extremely precise, a bit like a Mini. But unfortunately the Italians had bought the steel for the bodywork from Russia. Within three years it was just a heap of rusty steel with a gearbox and wheels. I bought it because it had a great review from John Bolster in *Autosport* saying what a good car it was, in terms of design. It was a shame about the build quality.

Although Ottilie and I occasionally drove to gigs in one of my sports cars, I normally travelled in one of the station wagons with the band. I remember when we first had the Peugeots we got an urgent recall message from the dealer: "Beware, the gearbox might fall apart at any moment!" That warning came a bit late because we'd already done more than thirty thousand miles in each of them! When Vic Pitt joined the band he usually drove one of them (in which I travelled) and Pat drove the other.

One day I was reading an article in the *Sunday Times* magazine about how the big car dealers were selling vehicles to diplomatic customers who didn't have to register them anywhere, because they were not technically resident in the country where they worked. I thought that was interesting because we were increasingly out of the UK for much of each year with the band. We were able to demonstrate that we were out of the country more than we were in it. So, under the rules as they were at the time, this entitled me to get a car on foreign plates and drive it back to Britain, as long as I had insurance. Having just seen *Bullitt*, I bought a Dodge Charger.

It was a new car, roughly the same as the ones that the gangsters use in the car chase scenes in the movie *Bullitt*. It was a beautiful car, and I have a picture with the band all standing around it, taken at the airport in Calais, where we used to land from the Channel Air Bridge flights from Southend. It had a seven-litre V8 engine, delivering 375 horsepower. It could carry five people, it drove magnificently and had excellent acceleration. Its automatic gearbox only had three forward speeds, but it was very well-designed and avoided most of the problems from which automatic gearboxes of the time suffered. Even so, by modern standards, it used a lot of petrol. I think it did about twelve miles to the gallon. Nevertheless I drove it everywhere, and I remember that when I initially filled it up it was the first time I had ever spent over five pounds on one tank of petrol! It went with me to East Germany, to Denmark, and all over Britain. It was initially on Belgian trade plates because I had it delivered direct from the United States to Antwerp docks. Then, on the same principle, I bought a Dodge Maxi-wagon for the band. It's a six-litre V8, which would fit in about ten people, or fewer people and all our stuff. And that was capable of going very fast, too. In due course I cleared it with Customs and Excise that we were entitled to drive this and the other Dodge on "Q" plates. These are British plates designed for cars that are being imported into the country for short periods of less than six months. I got a letter confirming that the Chris Barber Band could bring our cars in under this system.

One day we were driving down the motorway in Britain and we were pulled over by the police. I told them if they were in any doubt about the legality of our plates they should ring Customs and Excise. They did, and I rather think they got such a talking to that they backed down immediately. Certainly they were very apologetic and let us carry on. For the time and for their size, those American cars were very cheap to buy. But they weren't all that cheap to run, and in the end they had to be sold. The other reason was that the rules changed, and we now had to provide a permanent forwarding address on the continent, which of course we did not have. We replaced them once again with European cars. One unforeseen downside of those American wagons was that with their very efficient air conditioning, Vic actually got temporary paralysis in his face from the ice-cold draught.

I still enjoy driving to every gig. It's all part of the fun of being on the road with the band. I tend to think that if I got to the stage when I could no longer drive, it might be time to give up.

Despite my racing driving career coming to an end in the 1960s, I continued to follow racing, and made many friends among those who shared the interest. Chief among them was George Harrison. Although I've often met Pink Floyd's drummer Nick Mason, who has an exceptional collection of cars, and who drives them regularly, he's not a particularly talkative person. By contrast George was a lovely man and everyone liked him. He was a great motor racing enthusiast and went in for some interesting cars himself, including a well-known silver Aston Martin DB5. Among the racing fraternity themselves, apart from Colin Chapman, my other best friend was Ken Tyrrell who was a very sensible and interesting man. He also loved jazz, and over the years he always said the thing he liked best from our repertoire was 'Panama'. I think he liked the way that it went through each instrument in turn, just as we did at the 1992 concert in Bern that came out on CD in 2012 under the title *Clearing the Air*, with a seventeen-minute version of the piece! When Ken died after a long battle with cancer we were asked to go and play 'Panama' in his memory at the memorial service in Guildford Cathedral, held in November 2001. Kiri Te Kanawa sang, the RAF band played, and then we did 'Panama', and finished up by leading everybody out with 'When The Saints Go Marching In'.

One of the advantages of making so many friends in the Grand Prix world was that I came to know Bernie Ecclestone well. There is what you might call an Arthur Daley side to him, but everything he has done has worked really well. Through knowing him, I can always get passes to go behind the scenes, allowing me unlimited access at races. Principally this means getting into the paddock and meeting the people you know. This is much more enjoyable than spending hours sitting up in a grandstand when there are long periods where not a lot happens. It was on one of those occasions in the paddock that one of my favourite photographs was taken, with me, Ken Tyrrell and George Harrison.

Outside racing, I did go and see George from time to time at his house near Henley. Surprisingly, he hated electronic instruments, and liked everything to be acoustic. Among other things he had a wall covered in banjos in his house. On one occasion he was trying to track down the 1930 version of 'Barnacle Bill The Sailor' recorded by Bix Beiderbecke which has Joe Venuti singing the words "Barnacle Bill, the shithead". It's quite famous in jazz circles, and not long before I went to see George we had brought it out on the Timeless label as part of a collection of CDs based on my 78s. So I took a copy over for him.

The next time I went to see him I happened to ask if he'd liked the CD. "Oh yes," he said. "It's in the McLaren." Which is motor sport name-dropping of a very high order! He'd got the CD in his F1 McLaren, a car so valuable that he didn't often drive it, but which was sitting in his garage with the disc in the CD player. He also had a road-going development of a formula-three car known as "The Rocket" – and that wasn't driven often either.

My interest in vintage cars revived in later years and I had a couple of La Salle cars. One of them was a seven-seater saloon from 1930. The La Salle was launched by General Motors as a car to fill the gap between its Buick range and its up-market Cadillacs. To me, it always seemed to have something European about it, resembling a Hispano-Suiza. My saloon was bought new by a Connecticut garage proprietor, who used it to drive his best customers around. Because of the shortage of gasoline during World War Two, he laid it up, and it did not see the light of day until 1989. I bought it the following year and it was pretty comprehensively restored by a Rolls-Royce specialist garage in Sussex. I kept it in roadworthy condition until 2011 when I finally conceded I did not really have the time to use it.

I sold the other La Salle at the same time. It was a 1929 series 328 rumble seat coupé, and with its big V8 engine it was a powerful – if sizeable – two-seater. The car had previously spent most of its life in the Northern state of Minnesota. I found it in Florida, close to where my wife Renate, the children and I spent our holidays in the late 1980s.

8 All the Cats Join in

As well as working with my own band over the years, I've had some interesting collaborations with other musicians from various fields of music. Some of them relate directly to work we have done with American musicians, such as Dr John. For a start there was singer and pianist Eddie Bo. I was in New Orleans around 1992 and I wanted to make some recordings if I had the chance. And I think it was the British enthusiast Tom Stagg who alerted me to the fact that Eddie was around, and that maybe he was somebody with whom I could make a record.

I thought, "Let's get together and see what he wants to do."

Eddie had some interesting ideas, and he wanted an unusual line-up, including having both a tuba and a bass guitar. There was a sax player who was a friend of his, Red Morgan, from one of the great New Orleans jazz families, and Chuck Moore on bass guitar, with Walter Payton playing sousaphone. The drummer was Russell Batiste who had just joined The Meters, and there was a guitar player called Wayne Bennett, who was a very highly regarded musician. I said I'd come along with my trombone and fit in here and there.

So the band met up at Allen Toussaint's Sea-Saint Studios, a building that was completely destroyed in 2005 by Hurricane Katrina. When we got there I found that Eddie Bo's recording technique was to do a number and then keep doing it over and over again until he'd gone through all the permutations. This went on for quite a long time. I know that just getting one of his numbers exactly right occupies the whole side of one of my backup cassettes tapes of the session. It was interesting music, and a very compelling mix of New Orleans blues, old-fashioned jazz, and quite modern Crescent City funk. I can't fault any of the musicians on it, and Russell Batiste in particular was absolutely excellent.

Getting everything right, in Eddie's rather long-winded way of doing things, meant that the recording spilled over into a second day, and Chuck Moore couldn't do it. So Walter Payton took over and played his main instrument, string bass. I was quite apprehensive because the syncopations in this style of funk are not what string bass players normally play, but Walter played them magnificently. It's a good recording.

Eddie, whose full name was Edwin Joseph Bocage, was a fine pianist and singer right up until his death in 2009. He was very much in the New Orleans keyboard tradition of Professor Longhair, James Booker and Dr John. But Mac (Dr John) is more intense, and plays very full chords. He plays piano like an arranger as much as like a pianist, but both his feel and his sense of time are similar. I remember one year in the mid-1980s I was in New Orleans for the Jazz and Heritage Festival, and I went out to the Fairgrounds on the Sunday, the last day, when the main stage was hosting local bands. It began with the Neville Brothers, then Fats Domino, and finished with Dr John. All Dr John's band were from New Orleans, except me.

It was a great experience playing this style of New Orleans funk and blues music, especially in front of a home crowd. It has progressed through the years as a continuously developing tradition, and has really evolved as time has gone on. I think the main difference between playing on stage with Dr John and working with Eddie Bo was that in a recording studio you have to be much more accurate. That was particularly true of one track, which was the slowest version I have ever heard of 'You Are So Beautiful'. It really works at that tempo, but you have to be thinking really hard about the time being subdivided much more than normal, and yet keeping the essential looseness and freedom in the music.

As well as many of the jazz and blues artists with whom we've toured and recorded, there have been several figures with whom I have collaborated from the worlds of rock and pop, one being Eric Clapton.

I knew Eric as a real blues enthusiast way back in the days of the Marquee, and indeed when he walked out of the Yardbirds they were signed to our management office, and Harold Pendleton had to go round to Eric's flat to retrieve a guitar because it belonged to the group. I've listened to him over the years, and noticed that whenever he worked with a brass section it was all just backing riffs, not instruments actually interacting with the blues, which the trombone in particular is capable of doing.

The first time I tried this kind of interaction with Eric, I was playing at a charity concert that Mike Rutherford (of Genesis) ran, and Eric brought me up on stage to do 'Stormy Monday'. As he finished singing the first phrase I played something similar on the trombone to the fill he did on the guitar. And it surprised him because I don't think that happens very much in his world. I made contact with him again when the late Andrew Sheehan, my partner on the Blues Legacy record project (which issued many of our performances with Muddy, Sonny and Brownie and so on), was able to give Eric a lot of video clips of him playing. They were to be used in Martin Scorsese's film biography of Eric. When he got the clips, Eric said to Andrew, "If there's anything I can do for you or Chris, let me know." And so in due course I suggested we record together.

I was thinking of asking members of my band, but Eric immediately suggested Chris Stainton, Dave Bronze and Henry Spinetti, all of whom he works with regularly. So we met at Eric's home in the middle of a period he was there with the family. We got together in his little studio and played without any elaborate separation for the drums, just jamming together as if it was a small concert. I love Eric's playing because he's the only blues musician I've heard apart from B. B. King who can play an opening phrase on the guitar that catches you immediately. An audience can have tears in their eyes before he's even sung a note because of the strength of his playing.

One thing that amused me when Eric recorded with Wynton Marsalis in 2011 was that one of the pieces they played was 'Ice Cream'. When we first recorded it for Karl Emil Knudsen in 1954, we didn't know the words to the song. In fact we didn't know there were words to it, as we had learned it from the wonderful American Music record with George Lewis and Big Jim Robinson, which is just instrumental.

When we were making our record in Denmark, Karl said, "Why don't you sing it?" We told him we didn't know the words. He said, "Make some up!" So Pat and the rest of us made some words up for it, based on some vague idea of what the original song might have been. So we recorded them, and the record became something of a hit all over Europe. Over time I discovered the proper lyrics, which are quite neat and well turned out. But I was amused that when Eric made his record with Wynton, they used Pat Halcox's lyrics!

I first met Andy Fairweather-Low when he was doing a gig with Eric on rhythm guitar, although I knew his voice from his 1960s recordings with Amen Corner and his 1970s hits such as 'Wide Eyed And Legless'. When I got to know him properly, I found out he was a fan of our kind of music, so I asked him to come along and be a guest with the band. We did several concerts together in the month leading up to Christmas 2005. He did some of Lonnie's numbers such as 'It Takes A Worried Man' which he did very well, but he also loves singing spirituals, so he did tunes like 'Precious Lord, Take My Hand' with the full band.

I mentioned earlier that I've occasionally sat in with Van Morrison's band when he is on tour in the UK, but Van has also repaid the compliment and worked with us. In 1998 I made a skiffle CD with him and Lonnie, and, as we had a Fairfield Hall concert coming up that December, I asked Van to join us for a skiffle session and to sing with the band. Dickie Bishop from our old skiffle group also played on the concert, and then Van came on and sang 'How Long' really well. After singing with the skiffle group, Van stayed on and sang Ken Colyer's composition 'Goin' Home' with the full band. Those two numbers appeared on CD in 2010.

Van joined us again in concert when the BBC put on an event at the newly restored Golders Green Hippodrome to celebrate my 70th birthday in 2000. Lonnie sang some skiffle numbers and then Van joined the band on stage. Fortunately it was not until the following year that the ceiling of the Hippodrome collapsed onto the stage and auditorium, leading to the final closure of this historic theatre.

Van's work with us on these events took place shortly before the Big Chris Barber Band became my permanent group. Once it was established I did continue to play in the classic New Orleans six-piece format, not only with a small group from our large band, but on other concerts as well, including some reunions of former members. In 2005 I received an invite to go to Canada and play with a very similar small New Orleans-style group. I didn't know very much about it at the time, but I was encouraged to go by a fan of ours who lived in Canada. The group I was to play with was run by a fellow called Jeff Healey, and because I don't follow the rock and blues scene all that closely, I hadn't really noticed that he had been doing very well with a rock band featuring just guitar, bass and drums, and recording with the likes of George Harrison and Mark Knopfler. Jeff played guitar and sang, and ran his own Toronto nightclub where they played. But Jeff also ran a band called the Jazz Wizards, because his other undying love was 1920s jazz by Louis Armstrong, and the vocals of Bing Crosby. So in that group he mainly played the trumpet and sang. Jeff had a passion for record collecting and he owned over thirty thousand 78 rpm discs of classic jazz and blues. Sadly, just a couple of years after I went over to record with him, he died; he'd been blind from childhood, and suffered from a rare form of cancer that attacks the eyesight which had tragically spread to invade his whole system. He was a lovely man, and while I was in Canada playing with his band we made a record. During the recording I pushed myself forward slightly to have my own blues 'Goin' Up The River' included, but I'm glad we did it because whenever I hear it, I have a way of remembering Jeff Healey.

Jeff recorded with Mark Knopfler and – as it turns out – so did we. I first heard Mark when Dire Straits had their first hits. I liked the band very much, and went along to see them a few times. His song 'Sultans of Swing' showed a certain awareness of jazz and its history. On one occasion, through a mutual friend, I went to hear them at Wembley and that night, after the show, I went backstage and had a brief chat with him. I remember him asking, "Chris, with your band, do you make it all up as you go along, or do you play the same chorus every time you do a tune?"

I explained that we improvised, whereas I discovered that he normally learns things very carefully. A chorus to him is a piece of music, and rather than just playing for sixteen bars he likes to get a bit of form into it. Many of the best country and western guitarists similarly arrive at a well-worked-out solo and, once they're happy with it, they stick to it. Mark's very distinctive "voice" on guitar involves finger picking in a style that derives from that. He's a lovely musician and some time after we first met he felt that he had done the Dire Straits bit, and performed with it so many times, that he didn't want to go on doing the routine in the way that, say, the Stones have done for their entire career. So for a little while he was featured in a somewhat folky band called the Notting Hillbillies, with whom he did a week at Ronnie Scott's. I joined in on the whole week with them and enjoyed it very much. One of the other, older, guitarists who played and sang on that week was, I gathered, a great Ken Colyer fan.

I like Mark's own music very much and I like his ideas – particularly his making a song based on Thomas Pynchon's novel about the explorers Mason and Dixon on his album *Sailing to Philadelphia*. Given the musical context, and the importance of the Mason-Dixon line, it was a brilliant idea and typical of the way his mind works. In 2000 we recorded some tracks with Mark as part of a session for a BBC Radio 2 series I had at the time. He came in with a whole set of tunes agreed, but at one point there was a break in the proceedings and he just sat down and started playing this little ragtime piece which he called 'Dallas Rag'. We joined in, and on the spur of the moment we said, "Okay, let's do it!" So we recorded it. This was a completely spontaneous, unplanned part of the session, and therefore quite a contrast to what he'd told me earlier about how he likes to work.

One thing Mark has done over the years is to play duets with many other musicians, one of whom is Chet Atkins. When I was in the States a lot in the 1980s, holidaying in Florida, I remember seeing country and western shows on the television quite often, and I realised that the standard country band had a lot in common with a jazz group: a piano, bass and drums rhythm section, and maybe a cornet and a reed instrument or a violin in the front line. On one particular occasion I was watching a show and there was Chet Atkins as the guest. At one point the fiddle player and guitarist in his band played the Reinhardt/Grappelli version of 'Tiger Rag'. This proved that they are very broad-minded musicians. I think that is why I was keen to play ''Til The Next Time I'm In Town' with Mark on our BBC session. It was a number he'd done with Chet Atkins, and which we'd later played together with the Notting Hillbillies. It was issued on the 2010 CD *Memories of My Trip*, and I like the section at the end where the front-line players each get a little solo and a namecheck, and the music fits together in a very melodic and comfortable way.

Speaking of Radio 2, I've had a number of very pleasant evenings over the years spent playing with Jools Holland's band, sitting in with the section and joining in. He almost always plays Jelly Roll Morton's 'Winin' Boy' because in most sets he usually includes a couple of numbers from that side of his musical taste. When he does this with his own band it's just him at the piano, singing, and two or three guys from the band backing him in more or less traditional style. We recorded a version of it with Jools, alongside the six-piece line-up from my Big Chris Barber Band in 2010. He's a great enthusiast for New Orleans music – not just Morton but later piano players such as Dr John and Professor Longhair. You can hear Jools's Dr John affinities on a version we made with members of my band of 'Sunny Side of the Street', where he does rather Rebennack-like chords on parts of the tune. They're quite different from the songwriter Jimmy McHugh's harmonies, and yet it still sounds like the original song.

Recollections of sitting in with Jool's big band, or more accurately his "Rhythm And Blues Orchestra", brings me back to my own band, and the decision to enlarge it to the Big Chris Barber Band.

9 Long Time Travellin'

We had occasionally played with a saxophone in the band way back in the early days, starting with Bertie King's guest appearance on 'I'd Love It', and other pieces from our 1954 Royal Festival Hall concert. Then there were all the collaborations we did later with Joe Harriott. Once Ian Wheeler joined we regularly had the sound of his alto across much of our repertoire, but, in terms of finding a distinctive sound, and, in particular, playing some of the more complex Ellington material, we never quite worked out how to do it. I think that was still the case even when we had the eight-piece band, first with Sammy Rimington, and then continuing after Ian Wheeler returned.

I didn't really crack the Ellingtonian sound until I met Bob Hunt in 1990. He could translate the arrangements, to the point where we can now take a piece of Ellingtonia which originally had four or even five saxes, three or four trumpets and two or three trombones, and our seven-man front line can recreate the essence of it. If you can get that quintessentially Ellingtonian sound right, then you have something that's worth doing.

That's not to say we had not tried to learn as much as we could about the Ellington band, its repertoire and members, over the preceding years. I've mentioned some of the jazz and blues musicians who toured with us, but I haven't so far talked about Russell Procope, who came over to work with my band in the 1970s. We'd first met him when we were in New York and he was playing with Wilbur De Paris and his New New Orleans Jazz. Initially Garvin Bushell replaced Wilbur's original clarinetist Omer Simeon, who died during our first visit to America, and we heard Garvin quite a few times with the group. He went off to Africa in the early 1960s and Russell Procope took his place, playing alto and clarinet, but also baritone saxophone. On that instrument he sounded exactly like Harry Carney whom he had been sitting next to for years in the Ellington band, which was still his main job.

I asked Russell if he'd like to come to England. He said he would and that he thought Ellington could do without him for a week or two. I reckoned we probably needed a piano player to come as well, and I was somewhat stumped as to who to ask, until someone suggested that we bring in the organist Wild Bill Davis who had also worked with Duke and several other Ellingtonians including Johnny Hodges and Lawrence Brown. He agreed, and so over they came in 1976, with Wild Bill mainly playing piano. As it turned out, Pete York had just joined us on drums, virtually the same week they arrived.

Russell had a very particular sound on the alto, which I can only describe as a "northern" style – typified by the players who come from Ohio, such as Cecil Scott. It was a lovely sound and he played really well, but, despite offering to hire a baritone sax for him, he flatly refused to play it. He kept saying, "Next time I come, I will." But there never was a next time. We did, however, record an album with Russell and Bill, called *Echoes of Ellington*, and it is a good memento of their playing with us, on pieces such as 'In A Mellotone', 'Perdido' and 'Squatty Roo'. The arrangements for that album and the tour were by Alan Cohen, a British Ellington expert, who had recorded a complete version of 'Black, Brown and Beige'. Alan's arrangements were ideal for us to use with our visiting soloists, but they did not solve the longer-term problem of how the regular band could get closer to an authentic Ellingtonian sound.

Someone said during that tour that Wild Bill Davis should call himself "Mild Bill" because he was such a sweet gentle person. In all the time he was with us he wasn't wild at all. In all the life of the band we've had very few keyboard players work with us. In the early days Johnny Parker recorded with Ottilie and our rhythm section. John Lewis, as I've mentioned, toured with us, and then on 'Cat Call' we had Brian Auger playing the right-hand part on the organ, and Paul McCartney playing the left. But Wild Bill was one of the very select few who played piano with us every night on a long tour.

A couple of years before that, we'd welcomed another famous Ellingtonian, the trumpeter, singer and violinist Ray Nance, to Europe, as a guest of the band. He had somewhat ruined his health by consistent drinking over the years, but his playing was lovely, in particular his cornet on which he had his own, completely individual, sound. Funnily enough, I think of it now as very old-fashioned jazz, in terms of how he played, but it was very good to have him with us. His fiddle playing was rather wilder. I remember we got him a new bow, shortly before we played a gig in Stuttgart. One of our friends there, who worked for our record company, but also for the Stuttgart Chamber Orchestra, brought along a group of her colleagues, including several violinists, to see our concert. The day of the show Ray had taken a drink or two, and when he played on his violin features, usually either 'Summertime' or 'Lady Be Good' – and I think on that occasion he did both of them – he dug in really hard. By the end of it, there were more strands of horsehair hanging down from the frog of the bow than there were left on the bow itself! We could see all the fiddle players in the audience looking rather horrified. When Ray had too much to drink he was rather out of it all, but for the most part he was a very lively person, and he was a delight, musically.

Touring with Ellingtonians certainly taught us a lot about how Duke's soloists worked in his band and their approach to his compositions, but not so much about arriving at a greater depth in the way we played the music ourselves. In 2012 we released the recording of a concert that my eight-piece Jazz and Blues Band did at the Kursaal in Bern in 1992. This includes a version of 'Mood Indigo', for our four-piece front line of the time. That arrangement is one of the first that Bob Hunt did for us. We had often played the piece before that, but we were doing it all wrong. I think the only thing we retained from our original arrangement was the idea of changing into D flat for the last chorus. Ellington didn't do that, so Bob didn't originally include it. But the rest of his chart has lots of little Ellingtonian touches. Holding long notes a bit longer, or everyone playing one note behind a soloist. They're all aspects of a particular sound.

I met Bob a couple of years or so before that Bern concert, and was introduced to him as an arranger, rather than as a fellow trombonist, although he was already running his own big band to play Ellington material. I wanted a version of Luis Russell's 'Saratoga Shout', which I'd had as a 78 on the Parlophone "Race" series – I recall it had a black and gold label when it came out – so I asked him to arrange it for the band. It didn't really happen, but nevertheless that got us talking and he subsequently did a couple of things for us. This was about 1991 or 1992.

Then in 1994 we came to the inevitable 40th anniversary of the band, which involved what turned out to be the final set of reunions with Monty, Lonnie, Ron and Jim. The eight-piece band played a set, then we featured Lonnie's skiffle group and finally the 1954 line-up appeared. Starting in September we travelled all over Denmark, then there was work in Germany and Holland, and in December that year we toured the UK from Walthamstow to Falkirk. The show continued to travel into the first part of 1995.

It was at the time of that tour that I started thinking about doing something different. Consequently, I talked to Bob about having a fuller collaboration with us, and I asked him if he could find the people we'd need. He said, "Yes, there are three of us, saxophonist Nik Payton, trumpeter Mike 'Magic' Henry and me on trombone." He wrote some things for that expanded line-up, we rehearsed them and it sounded great. So I went to our agent Wim Wigt, and asked him to see if anybody would want to book the Chris Barber Band with Bob Hunt's Ellingtonians. (Bob told me that he had been authorised by Mercer Ellington to call his own band Bob Hunt's Duke Ellington Orchestra.)

Wim drew in some interest from a few places and, as the 1990s came to an end, we booked the bigger band to do the odd couple of days here and there. The others drove out and joined us for those occasional concerts, and they went very well. In fact, there was something about the sound that the band made with the bigger front line that was better. That's not to denigrate the sound we already had with Pat Halcox, Ian Wheeler, John Crocker and myself, but I'd always wanted to play more of the 1920s black big band repertoire, and this was clearly the way to do it. We did more concerts as the new millennium began, and we made a record as the "Chris Barber Jazz and Blues Band with Bob Hunt's Ellingtonians", which came out in 2001. We called the album *Misty Morning*, after the record of the tune that I'd made fifty years before, with Dickie Hawdon and Ben Cohen in the front line of my semi-pro band. By the time we came to record, John Defferary had replaced Ian Wheeler in the front line of my eight-piece band, and Paul Sealey was on guitar and banjo alongside John Slaughter. Colin Miller was on drums.

At the beginning of 2001, I thought to myself that I'd like to take Bob and the others on full time. As a result, I spoke to Wim, which basically became a discussion about what he could sell the package for, and to whom. I said I would have to get more money per concert because I had three more mouths to feed, and I'd need an extra vehicle to transport them in. He said he'd pay for one of them, which gave us some extra money, but not enough, and to start with the extra funds came out of my share of the band's money.

As soon as word got around, Vic Gibbons, who was doing our publicity in the UK at the time, started getting letters, or copies of articles in the various jazz information sheets and papers, saying, "What's Chris doing, ruining his band?" But within six months the same people were saying, "Oh I've heard it now, it's wonderful!" It had been just the same when John Slaughter joined the band. I've done this kind of major change several times, and when you do so, you have to be sure in your own mind that it's going to work, and ignore how people think they are going to react. I think I'm only bloody-minded about things that really matter to me. And I couldn't see any possible argument against doing it.

When the bigger band became my permanent group there was some discussion as to what to call it. Then someone pointed out that Carla Bley had the "Big Carla Bley Band" so that was it, we became the Big Chris Barber Band. I said we couldn't use the old name because it wasn't the same format as the old band. If you think about how Hollywood stars make a fuss about the exact form of their name, the point size, the apostrophes, even the typeface, it's quite modest that I just insist on the "Big" as part of the band name. I don't even mind making a joke of it, but it gets the message across.

We still begin our concerts with 'Bourbon Street Parade', just as I have done since the 1950s, but now there are also some staples of the new band's repertoire. For example, the Ellingtonian pieces include 'Black and Tan Fantasy', 'Merry Go Round', 'Jubilee Stomp' and 'Hot and Bothered', as well as later material such as 'Take the A Train'. We still regularly play an arrangement of 'Petite Fleur', alongside gospel pieces such as 'Lead Me On', and the blues that Sonny and Brownie used to do, 'Cornbread Peas and Black Molasses'.

When people ask me which of the many phases of my career I like best, or to which I'd point a new listener to the band, it's very difficult, because everything we've done during the years has seemed to me to be the most important thing in the world at that particular time. I think I'd probably have to say the band I have now, playing something like 'Black and Tan Fantasy', is as good as anything we've ever done.

In the first decade or so of the new band, in addition to our own shows and tours, the Big Chris Barber Band did a lot of "Three B" concerts, with Kenny Ball and Acker Bilk. These continued until Kenny's death in 2013, but they have carried on since with Kenny's son Keith leading the Ball band. At these concerts I prefer to go on stage first, because I like to work on a blank canvas. There's an interval after us, and then a long set with a quick changeover between the other bands.

On stage I do tend to talk a lot because it's just part of my character. But it doesn't come anywhere near the monologues that Ronnie Scott used to do at his club every night. That was really more of a comedy act, although we'd all heard the jokes before. Mind you, that was looking forward to how the world is now, where people go to shows to hear stand-up comics and recite the jokes along with them.

Over the last few years the Big Chris Barber Band has settled into a regular personnel. Perhaps the biggest change for me was when Pat Halcox decided to retire from the band in 2008, after fifty-four years of playing together. Apart from a short break when he was unwell in 1991 and the New Orleans trumpeter Wendell Brunious briefly joined us as a temporary replacement, Pat was with me through all the various changes in the band, taking in all the new ideas and developments in his stride. He retired because he had developed Parkinson's, and this made it impossible for him to continue touring and playing the number of concerts we do. In fact I think he had been showing signs of the disease for some ten years beforehand, increasingly finding some actions difficult. Sadly he died in February 2013. Pat is very much missed. He had a great understanding of the music and a great feel for it.

Maybe it was a blessing in disguise that he did not join us immediately in 1953, and we had that period with Ken Colyer. That's because, when Pat came back, he really wanted to play, and what's more we'd proved to his parents that he could make decent money doing it. They'd been worried because they weren't a rich family, his father was a dental technician and his mother kept a china shop, so that is why they had set such store by the money they'd put aside to pay for his training. There's no doubt that he would have been a good research chemist. I remember many years later when we were having a discussion in the band about the link between cancer and smoking. I'd read somewhere that there's a very strong link between barbecue smoke and cancer. I said, "I think it's called benzoapyrene." Pat said, "Yes, and I'll draw you a molecule!" That knowledge of long carbon chain molecules was just sitting there inside him, along with everything else he had learned. Most of all, though, he knew about jazz, and he knew instinctively what to play in my various bands over the years.

Pete Rudeforth joined us the very day that Pat left. He's a very versatile musician whose gigs between our tours are as likely to be classical as jazz! At one point, the same would have been true of Mike "Magic" Henry, a trumpeter who is a very experienced player in all forms of music. He was in the Jeunesse Musicales World Youth Orchestra, and toured with them to Canada to play at the Montreal Olympics while he was still a student at the Guildhall. He's a very fine classical and jazz player. Bob Hunt worked hard with him to make the approach of the key Ellington soloists in the big band arrangements as authentic as possible. In particular he can emulate the Bubber Miley "jungle" sound for the arrangements from the early Ellingtonian period with uncanny accuracy.

For a while in the Big Band we had Trevor Whiting on reeds. He left for a period, and then rejoined temporarily when his replacement Mike Snelling decided he didn't want to carry on with our touring schedule. We had to get someone who was equally as versatile a reed player, and for a while we had the excellent Zoltan Sagi. Then Bob told me about a young girl he'd heard who had been voted a rising star in the British Jazz Awards and who had just qualified at the Royal Northern College of Music. He thought she'd be able to play all the parts very well. Her name was Amy Roberts. I checked her out, and then invited her to come along and try out with the band. She learned the music very quickly and very accurately. One thing I have noticed is that someone who has been through a contemporary full-time course at music college (compared to my own time at the Guildhall) quickly learns how to get music down very fast, and get it right immediately. Amy's a brilliant musician and actually an even better flute player than she is a saxophonist or clarinetist. You might ask yourself after a hot alto solo, a powerful trumpet solo and a strong trombone solo, what a flute can do, because it's too quiet. But actually it's not. Amy has volume, plus clarity and precision.

Bert Brandsma is Dutch and a very versatile musician, who plays – among other things – bass saxophone. He hasn't brought it to England yet, but with us he plays clarinet, alto and tenor saxophone. When he's not playing with us he has his own band, the Dixieland Crackerjacks, which is a sort of corporate Dixie showband. His wife, who is also a member of the Crackerjacks but who does not play with us, is a trombonist and has a degree in jazz. Then we have Richard Exall, who's a very, very good player indeed. He spent three years in America playing with an all-Cuban band, and so he knows Cuban music really well. Rather like traditional jazz, you have to know how to start and finish numbers and all the right things to do in an ensemble. He's also really got inside the Johnny Hodges style, which means he can play a Hodges section lead part, and without actually directly imitating Hodges it just sounds right, which is difficult to do. He's also a very good baritone player, and he's been in the band since 2004.

Dave Green played bass in the Big Band once Vic decided to retire in 2007, but Dave has always had plenty of people wanting him to play for them, and after a while he withdrew from touring with us to focus on returning to his life as a busy freelancer in London. Since 2010 Jackie Flavelle has been back with us, having rejoined after being with the band for the best part of ten years before Vic Pitt. Joe Farler is on banjo and guitar – a good solid player, very studious. He comes from a traditional jazz family and his uncle runs a band in Bristol. Joe was christened Joseph Morton Farler, so he links us both to "Joe" King Oliver and Jelly Roll Morton! For a time Joe played guitar in Wales as a member of a string band with our sound technician Rebecca Evans. They also had a bass and a Continental violinist and the band was called "Django Chutney". Becky is currently organising an all-girls big band in Wales, when she is not on the road with us.

Gregor Beck on drums is from Germany, and to me he seems to have elements of Gene Krupa in his playing – certainly, shall we say, more Krupa than Buddy Rich. He's a very jazzy player.

Just as it was with the eight-piece band, we have no music on the stage at all. Everybody has to have learned the arrangements for everything we do, so, unless somebody comes in just for a night or two to help out, who's either new to the band or hasn't been with us for some time, there's no sheet music. Trevor Whiting recently came back for a couple of jobs when Amy had a prior commitment, and he had to read some new material, but otherwise we focus on playing and not reading music on stage. Some of the music is very demanding. The arrangement of 'Hot and Bothered' is a tough one, especially for the saxes, who play with just drum and bass accompaniment. Bob also produced a very nice version of 'Rockin' In Rhythm' for us. And the rules of how you make a piece swing are the same, whether it's a 1926 King Oliver arrangement or something in a later Ellingtonian style.

From the 1940s to the present, I've looked for players who can sound convincing and who know these rules about swing, whatever period of music we are playing. I'm lucky now to have a good group of people who understand what is needed and are happy to do it. At the time of writing, it's coming up to the sixty-fifth anniversary of my first records, and sixty years of continuously leading my own band. As you will know from everything in this book so far, I've not been afraid of change, and of moving forward. The received wisdom is once you arrive at a successful format, you stick to it, or else! We've done the opposite for sixty years – if we like it, we do it. And that's still how I feel, going forward into the band's sixty-first year.

Chris Barber on CD: A Selective Record List

At the time of going to press, this cross section of Chris Barber's recorded work was currently available, including almost every period of the band's evolution. The arrangement of the list is broadly chronological, and where there are spans of several years, the majority of tracks fall within the timescale of the CD's position in the list. The personnel listings are collective.

Abbreviations: arr = arranger; as = alto saxophone; b = bass; bars = baritone saxophone; bj = banjo; cond = conductor; c = cornet; cl = clarinet; d = drums; fl = flute; g = guitar; hca = harmonica; kb = keyboards; mand = mandolin; org = organ; p = piano; snare d = snare drum; sousa = sousaphone; ss = soprano saxophone; t = trumpet; tb = trombone; ts = tenor saxophone; tu = tuba; v = vocal; wbd = washboard

Various Artists
The Great Revival – Traditional Jazz 1949–58. Vol. 4
Lake LACD137

Chris Barber's Washboard Wonders: Ben Cohen, c; Alex Revell, cl; Ferdie Favager, bj; Chris Barber, b; Brian Lawes, d; 1951.

Whoop It Up; Everybody Loves My Baby.

Chris Barber and His New Orleans Jazz Band: Keith Jary, t; Ben Cohen, c; Chris Barber, tb, v; Alex Revell, cl; Brian Baker, p; Ferdie Favager, bj; Brylo Ford, b; Brian Lawes, d; 1951.

Snake Rag; Oh, Didn't He Ramble.

Various Artists
The Great Revival – Traditional Jazz 1949–57. Vol. 5
Lake LACD158

Chris Barber and His New Orleans Jazz Band: Dickie Hawdon, t; Ben Cohen, c; Chris Barber, tb, v; Alex Revell, cl; Brian Baker, p; Ferdie Favager, bj; Mickey Ashman, b; Brian Lawes, d; 1951.

Stomp Off, Let's Go; Camp Meeting Blues; When Erastus Plays His Old Kazoo; Misty Morning.

Ken Colyer's Jazzmen
New Orleans To London & Back To The Delta
Lake LACD209

Ken Colyer, t; Chris Barber, tb; Monty Sunshine, cl; Lonnie Donegan, bj; Jim Bray, b; Ron Bowden, d; 1953.

Isle Of Capri; Harlem Rag; Too Busy; Goin' Home; La Harpe Street Blues; Cataract Rag; Stockyard Strut; Early Hours.

Ken Colyer's Jazzmen and Skiffle Group
The Lost 1954 Royal Festival Hall Tapes
Upbeat URCD 198

Ken Colyer, t; Chris Barber, tb; Monty Sunshine, cl; Bruce Turner, as; Lonnie Donegan, bj; Jim Bray, b; Ron Bowden, d; 1954.

Put On Your Old Grey Bonnet; Lord Lord Lord; Harlem Rag; Original Tuxedo Rag; Michigan Water Blues; At A Georgia Camp Meeting; Black and Tan Fantasy; Bourbon Street Parade; Easter Parade; We Sure Do Need Him Now; Joplin's Sensation; Temple Blues; Bobby Shaftoe.

Ken Colyer, Lonnie Donegan, g, v; Chris Barber, b; Bill Colyer, wbd; Johnny Parker, p; 1954.

This Train; This Cotton Song; Casey Jones; Good Morning Blues.

Chris Barber's Jazz Band
Jazz Sacred & Secular – Vintage Chris Barber
Lake LACD222

Pat Halcox, t; Ben Cohen, c; Chris Barber, tb; Monty Sunshine, cl; Lonnie Donegan, bj; Jim Bray, Mickey Ashman, b; Ron Bowden, d; 1954–56.

Double Check Stomp; Take My Hand Precious Lord; Black & Tan Fantasy; White Christmas; God Leads His Dear Children Along; Sing On; Shout 'Em Aunt Tillie; On A Christmas Day; Lord, You've Surely Been Good To Me; Going To Town; Camp Meeting Blues; Brownskin Mama; Blue Sunshine; Original Tuxedo Rag; Ice Cream; Saratoga Swing; Tiger Rag; Down By The Riverside; South; Whistling Rufus; Everybody Loves My Baby; Double Check Stomp (version 2); Ice Cream (version 2); Take My Hand Precious Lord (version 2).

Chris Barber's Jazz Band
The Complete Decca Sessions, 1954–55
Lake LACD142

Pat Halcox, t, v; Chris Barber, tb; Bertie King, as; Monty Sunshine, cl; Lonnie Donegan, bj, v; Jim Bray, b; Ron Bowden, d; Beryl Bryden, wbd; Ottilie Patterson, v; 1954–55.

The Studio Sessions: Bobby Shaftoe; Chimes Blues; The Martinique; New Orleans Blues; Merry Down Rag; Stevedore Stomp; Nobody Knows You When You're Down & Out; Weeping Willow Blues; Rock Island Line; John Henry; Nobody's Child; Wabash Cannonball. *The Live Sessions*: Lord, Lord, Lord; Merry Down Blues; Skokiaan; I'd Love It; Storyville Blues; It's Tight Like That; Bury My Body; Diggin' My Potatoes; Ice Cream; Oh Didn't He Ramble; The Girls Go Crazy; I Never Knew Just What A Girl

Could Do; St Louis Blues; I Hate A Man Like You; Salutation March; Reckless Blues; The World Is Waiting For The Sunrise.

Chris Barber's Jazz Band with Lonnie Donegan's Skiffle Group & Ottilie Patterson
Chris Barber 1955
Lake LACD235

Pat Halcox, t; Chris Barber, tb, b; Monty Sunshine, cl; Lonnie Donegan, bj, v; Dickie Bishop, g, v; Pete Korrison, mand; Jim Bray, Mickey Ashman, b; Ron Bowden, d; Ottilie Patterson, Bob Watson, v; 1955.

> You Don't Understand; Tishomingo Blues; Wild Cat Blues; Everybody Loves My Baby; Papa De Da Da; High Society; Trouble In Mind; Jailhouse Blues; Doin' The Crazy Walk; Baby; Magnolia's Wedding Day; Dixie Cinderella; Here Comes My Blackbird; Can't We Get Together; Sweet Savannah Sue; Porgy; Diga Diga Do; Harmonica Blues; Worried Man Blues; Blue In Wood Green; My Bucket's Got A Hole In It; Lord, Lord, Lord; Blues Is Knocking On My Door; Momma Don't Allow.

Ottilie Patterson with Chris Barber's Jazz Band
That Patterson Girl
Lake LACD244

Pat Halcox, t; Chris Barber, tb, b; Monty Sunshine, cl; Lonnie Donegan, bj; Dickie Bishop, bj, g, v; Eddie Smith, bj; Jim Bray, Mickey Ashman, Dick Smith, b; Ron Bowden, Graham Burbidge, d; Ottilie Patterson, v; 1955–57.

> Poor Man's Blues; Make Me A Pallet On The Floor; Trouble In Mind; Careless Love; I Wish I Could Shimmy Like My Sister Kate; Ugly Child; I Can't Give You Anything But Love; New St Louis Blues; Beale St Blues; 'Taint No Sin; Jailhouse Blues; Shipwreck Blues; Trombone Cholly; When Things Go Wrong; Kay Cee Rider; Don't Fish In My Sea; Salty Dog; Mean Mistreater; As Long As I'm Moving; Backwater Blues; Heavenly Sunshine; Lonesome Road; Weeping Willow Blues.

Chris Barber's Jazz Band & Skiffle Group
Chris Barber 1956
Lake LACD246

Pat Halcox, t; Chris Barber, tb, b; Monty Sunshine, cl; Lonnie Donegan, g, v; Dickie Bishop, bj, g, v; Johnny Duncan, g, v; Eddie Smith, bj; Mickey Ashman, Dick Smith, b; Ron Bowden, d; Ottilie Patterson, v; 1956.

> *Studio Sessions*: Whistling Rufus; Big House Blues; April Showers; One Sweet Letter From You; Hushabye; We Shall Walk Through The Valley; Thriller Rag; Texas Moaner; Wabash Blues; Bugle Call Rag; Petite Fleur; Sweet Georgia Brown; A Smooth One. *Live sessions*: Bourbon Street Parade; New Blues; Willie The Weeper; Mean Mistreater; Yama Yama Man; Ol' Man Mose; Mood Indigo; Bearcat Crawl; Lowland Blues; Panama; Bourbon Street/ When The Saints. *Lonnie Donegan's Skiffle Group*: Railroad Bill; Ballad Of Jesse James; Old Riley; Lost John; Stewball; Stackalee. *Chris Barber's Skiffle Group*: Doin' My Time; Where Could I Go; Can't You Line 'Em; Gypsy Davy.

Chris Barber's Jazz Band with special guest Sister Rosetta Tharpe
1957 – Historical Concerts
Lake LACD130

Pat Halcox, t; Chris Barber, tb; Monty Sunshine, cl; Eddie Smith, bj; Dick Smith, b; Graham Burbidge, d; Sister Rosetta Tharpe, Ottilie Patterson, v; 1957.

 Fidgety Feet; Georgia Cakewalk; Washington & Lee Swing; Chinatown; Yes Lord; The Old Rugged Cross; Lord, Lord, Lord; Joshua Fit The Battle Of Jericho; Everytime I Feel The Spirit; Up Above My Head; Peace In The Valley; Down By The Riverside; Old Time Religion; When The Saints Go Marching In.

Chris Barber's Jazz Band
Chris Barber 1957–58
Lake LACD268

Pat Halcox, t; Chris Barber, tb; Monty Sunshine, cl; Eddie Smith, bj; Dick Smith, b; Ron Bowden, Graham Burbidge, d; Ottilie Patterson, v; 1957–58.

 Kay Cee Rider; I Love My Baby; When The Saints Go Marching In; Olga; The Old Rugged Cross; Bye & Bye; Pound Of Blues; When You And I Were Young Maggie Dear; Just A Closer Walk With Thee; Bourbon Street Parade; Savoy Blues; Lonesome Road; The Sheik Of Araby; Won't You Come Home Bill Bailey; You Took Advantage Of Me; Sweet Sue; Moonshine Man; You Rascal You; Trombone Cholly; Lawdy Lawdy Blues; Bugle Boy March; Pretty Baby; Majorca; Indiana; New Orleans Hula; St Phillip Street Breakdown; Georgia Grind; Rockin' In Rhythm; My Old Kentucky Home; Rent Party Blues; Careless Love; Strange Things Happen Every Day; Mama Don't Allow.

Chris Barber's Jazz Band with Sonny Terry & Brownie McGhee
Sonny, Brownie & Chris
Lake LACD278

Pat Halcox, t; Chris Barber, tb, b; Monty Sunshine, cl; Eddie Smith, bj; Dick Smith, b; Graham Burbidge, d; Sonny Terry, hca, v; Brownie McGhee, g, v; 1957–58.

 Washington & Lee Swing; Georgia Cakewalk; I'm Gonna Wash That Man Right Outa Of My Hair; Big House Blues; Sing On; Midnight Special; Climbing On Top Of The Hill; Custard Pie; Betty & Dupree; This Little Light Of Mine; Southern Train; Cornbread, Peas and Black Molasses; John Henry; Key To The Highway; If I Could Only Hear My Mother Pray Again; No Worries On My Mind; Glory; Do Lord; If I Ever Cease To Love; Blue Bells Goodbye; When You And I Were Young Maggie; Just A Closer Walk With Thee; Runnin' Wild.

Chris Barber's Jazz Band
Chris Barber 1959–60
Lake LACD324

Pat Halcox, Ed Allen, t; Chris Barber, tb; Monty Sunshine, cl, ss; Cecil Scott, cl, ts; Don Frye, p; Eddie Smith, bj; Dick Smith, Leonard Gaskin, b; Graham Burbidge, d; Floyd Casey, wbd; Ottilie Patterson, v; 1959–60.

Hiawatha Rag; Si Tu Vois Ma Mère; Darling Nellie Gray; Give Me Your Telephone Number; I'm Gonna Wash That Man Right Out Of My Hair; Swanee River (version 1); Squeeze Me; Creole Song; Golden Striker; Lift The Lid; Don't Go 'Way Nobody; Tell It To The Marines; Li'l Liza Jane; Soudan; X Marks The Spot; Cecil's Groove; The Sheik Of Araby; Swanee River (version 2); How Long Blues; Well Alright, OK, You Win; Lonesome (Si Tu Vois Ma Mère); New Orleans Hula; Burgundy Street Blues; Bagatelle; Solitariness; Do Lord; There'll Be A Hot Time In The Old Town Tonight; 'Taint Nobody's Business; On The Sunny Side Of The Street; Oh, Baby!; Making Whoopee; Phil's Late; When You Wore A Tulip; Camp Meeting Blues; South; Doctor Jazz; Chimes Blues; Saratoga Swing; The Martinique.

Ottilie Patterson with Chris Barber's Jazz Band
Blues Book And Beyond
Lake LACD296

Pat Halcox, t; Chris Barber, tb, b; Monty Sunshine, cl; Keith Scott, p; Alexis Korner, g; Eddie Smith, bj, g; Dick Smith, b; Graham Burbidge, Ron Bowden, d; Ottilie Patterson, p, v; 1957–60.

> Bad Spell Blues; Kidman Blues; Four Point Blues; Backwater Blues; Kansas City Blues; It's All Over; Mama, He Treats Your Daughter Mean; Tell Me Why; Can't Afford To Do It; Blues Before Sunrise; Me And My Chauffeur; Trixie's Blues; Lordy Lord It Hurts So Bad; Only The Blues; Squeeze Me; The Little Town In The Old County Down; The Real Old Mountain Dew; The Mountains Of Mourne; Let Him Go, Let Him Tarry; There'll Be A Hot Time In The Old Town Tonight; Sobbin' Hearted Blues; Steamboat Bill; Burgundy Street Blues.

Chris Barber's Jazz Band
Elite Syncopations
Lake LACD294

Pat Halcox, Ken Colyer, t; Chris Barber, tb; Monty Sunshine, Ian Wheeler, Kohn Defferary, cl; John Crocker, cl, as; Eddie Smith, Lonnie Donegan, Stu Morrison, Paul Sealey, bj; John Slaughter, g; Dick Smith, Mickey Ashman, Jim Bray, Vic Pitt, Jackie Flavelle, b; Graham Burbidge, Ron Bowden, Colin Miller, d; 1953–2001.

> Swipsey Cakewalk; Bohemia Rag; Elite Syncopations; Cole Smoak; The Peach; St George's Rag; The Favourite; Reindeer Ragtime Two Step; The Entertainer; Georgia Cakewalk; Hiawatha – A Summer Idyll; Merrydown Rag; Whistling Rufus; Harlem Rag; Maple Leaf Rag; Cataract Rag; Harlem Rag.

Chris Barber's Jazz Band
Classic Concerts Revisited
Lake LACD323

Pat Halcox, t; Chris Barber, tb, v; Monty Sunshine, Ian Wheeler, cl; Joe Harriott, as; Eddie Smith, bj; Dick Smith, b; Graham Burbidge, d; Ottilie Patterson, v; 1959–61.

> Climax Rag; Easy, East Baby; Gotta Travel On; What's I'm Gotcha; Maryland; Petite Fleur; Hushabye; C Jam Blues; Chimes Blues; Market Street Stomp; Soudan; Beautiful Dreamer; Margie; Blue Turning Grey Over You; Goin' To Town; Rent Party Blues;

High Society/The Saints; Just A Little While To Stay Here; Too Many Drivers; Lord, Lord, Lord; Creole Love Call; 'S Wonderful; Squeeze Me; Revival; Fidgety Feet.

Chris Barber's Jazz Band
208 Rhythm Club – Radio Luxembourg Sessions
Vocalion CDNJT 5315

Pat Halcox, t; Chris Barber, tb, v; Ian Wheeler, cl; Joe Harriott, as; Eddie Smith, bj; Dick Smith, b; Graham Burbidge, d; Ottilie Patterson, v; 1961.

Give Me Your Telephone Number; Sweet Lorraine; I'm Crazy 'Bout My Baby; Basin St Blues; Trad Tavern; Stevedore Stomp; Up A Lazy River; T'Ain't What You Do; Til We Meet Again; New Orleans Parade (Just A Little While To Stay Here, takes 1 and 2); Room Rent Blues.

Chris Barber's Jazz Band
Chris Barber 1961–62
Lake LACD325

Pat Halcox, t; Chris Barber, tb, v; Ian Wheeler, cl, ss, as; Eddie Smith, bj; Dick Smith, b; Graham Burbidge, d; Ottilie Patterson, v; 1961–62.

We Shall Walk Through The Streets Of The City; Chiquita; Basin Street Blues; Up A Lazy River; 'Taint What You Do; King Kong (version 1); Gonna Build A Mountain; If You Can't Be Good Be Careful; Stevedore Stomp; I Can't Give You Any Thing But Love; Moose March; Cookie; Sweet Lorraine; It's Only A Paper Moon; New Stack O'Lee Blues; I'm Crazy 'Bout My Baby; Blueberry Hill; New Orleans Parade; Revival (version 1); Trad Tavern; Come On Baby; I Hate Myself (For Being Mean To You); Til We Meet Again; Revival (version 2); King Kong (version 2); It Looks Like A Big Time Tonight; Cottage Crawl; Ory's Creole Trombone; Mood Indigo; Original Charleston Strut; Ca C'Est L'Amour; Down By The Riverside; When The Saints Go Marching In; Lord, Lord, Lord; Chiquita (version 2); The Mountains Of Mourne; Trad Tavern (version 2); Mama, He Treats Your Daughter Mean; Ice Cream; Mood Indigo (version 2); Whistling Rufus; Some Of These Days; The Longest Day; Doin' The Raccoon.

Chris Barber's Jazz Band
Chris Barber at the BBC – Wireless Days
Upbeat URCD146

Pat Halcox, t; Chris Barber, tb; Ian Wheeler, cl, as; Eddie Smith, bj; Dick Smith, b; Graham Burbidge, d; Ottilie Patterson, v; 1961–62.

Just A Little While To Stay Here; Bobby Shaftoe; Jeep's Blues; Georgia Swing; Do What Ory Say; Give Me Your Telephone Number; I Can't Afford To Do It; Isle of Capri; Ol' Man Mose; Stevedore Stomp; Tuxedo Rag; Ory's Creole Trombone; Maple Leaf Rag; St Louis Blues; Black and Tan Fantasy; I Can't Give You Anything But Love; It Looks Like A Big Time Tonight.

Chris Barber's Jazz Band
Ball, Barber and Bilk: At The Jazz Band Ball
Upbeat URCD 166

Pat Halcox, t; Chris Barber, tb; Ian Wheeler, cl, as; Eddie Smith, bj; Dick Smith, b; Graham Burbidge, d; Ottilie Patterson, v; 1962.

At The Jazz Band Ball; Panama Rag; Mood Indigo; Ory's Creole Trombone; T'Ain't Nobody's Business If I Do; Pretty Baby; Stevedore Stomp.

Chris Barber's Jazz Band
There Were Some Changes Made (1961–65)
Lake LACD305

Pat Halcox, t; Chris Barber, tb; Ian Wheeler, cl, as; Eddie Smith, Stu Morrison, bj; John Slaughter, g; Dick Smith, b; Graham Burbidge, d; 1961–65.

Weary Blues; Come On Coot & Do That Thing; Wrap Your Troubles In Dreams; All Of Me; Black & Tan Fantasy; Jazz Lips; Original Charleston Strut; El La Bas; Some Of These Days; Crying For The Carolines; Blue Blood Blues; Yellow Dog Blues; I Never Shall Forget; Petite Fleur; Shout Em Aunt Tillie; Georgia Swing; There'll Be Some Changes Made; Bye And Bye; Jeeps Blues; Sideways.

Chris Barber and Louis Jordan
Black Lion BLCD 760156

Pat Halcox, t; Chris Barber, tb; Louis Jordan, as, v; Ian Wheeler, cl, as; Eddie Smith, Stu Morrison, Steve Hammond, bj; John Slaughter, Johnny McCallum, g; Dick Smith, Jackie Flavelle, b; Graham Burbidge, d; 1962–74.

Fifty Cents; A Man Ain't A Man; No Chance Blues; I'm Gonna Move To The Outskirts Of Town; Don't Worry 'Bout The Mule; Choo Choo Ch'Boogie; I Wish I Could Shimmy Like My Sister Kate; Is You Is Or Is You Ain't My Baby; Indiana; Messe Blues; Jazz Lips; Black and Tan Fantasy; I'm Slapping Seventh Avenue With The Sole Of My Shoe; Whatcha Gonna Do?

Chris Barber's Jazz Band
The Best of Chris Barber's Jazz Band
EMI Gold 7243 5 40181 2 1

Pat Halcox, Jimmy Deuchar, t; Chris Barber, tb; Monty Sunshine, Ian Wheeler, cl; Ronnie Scott, ts; Peter Bardens, Johnny Parker, p; Brian Auger, org; Lonnie Donegan, Eddie Smith, Stu Morrison, bj; John Slaughter, g; Jim Bray, Dick Smith, b; Ron Bowden, Graham Burbidge, d; Ottilie Patterson, v; 1954–64.

Lawd You've Been So Good To Me; Take My Hand Precious Lord; God Leads His Dear Children Along; Sing On; Double Check Stomp; Shout 'Em Aunt Tillie; Goin' To Town; Black & Tan Fantasy; Wini Wini; You Just Can't Win; Cryin' For The Carolines; Young Fashioned Ways; I Never Shall Forget; Tell Me Where Is Fancy Bred; Ah Me What Eyes Hath Love Put In My Head; Blow Blow Thou Winter Wind; When In Disgrace With Fortune; Hello Dolly; The Ballad of the Liver Bird; Brands Hatch; Morning Train; Hamp's Blues.

Chris Barber
Chris Barber & The Clarinet Kings
Lake LACD314

Pat Halcox, Sidney De Paris, t; Chris Barber, Tony Hurst, tb; Edmond Hall, Joe Darensbourg, Albert Nicholas, cl; Ian Wheeler, cl, as; John Crocker, as; Richard Simmons, p; Eddie Smith, Stu Morrison, bj; John Slaughter, g; Dick Smith, Jackie Flavelle, Terry Knight, b; Graham Burbidge, Dave Evans, d; 1960–74.

Chris Barber's American Jazz Band: Down Home Rag; Tishomingo Blues; Oh Baby; Baby Won't You Please Come Home?; You Tell Me Your Dream; Li'l Liza Jane; See See Rider; Sweethearts On Parade. *Chris Barber's Jazz Band with Edmond Hall*: Jamaica March; 8.20 Blues; High Society; Clarinet Marmalade; Making Whoopee; Colla Voce; Dardanella; There'll Be Some Changes Made; Dardanella; Oh Baby; Royal Garden Blues; St Louis Blues. *Chris Barber's Jazz Band with Albert Nicholas*: C-Jam Blues; Black And Blue; Rose Room; Blue Turning Grey Over You; Indiana; Basin Street Blues; Royal Garden Blues. *Chris Barber with Joe Darensbourg*: Ballin' The Jack; All Of Me; Joe's Blues; Rose Room.

Chris Barber's Jazz Band
Chris Barber at the BBC 1963 with Special Guest Joe Harriott
Upbeat URCD 158

Pat Halcox, t; Chris Barber, tb; Ian Wheeler, cl, as; Joe Harriott, as; Ian Armit, p; Eddie Smith, bj; Dick Smith, b; Graham Burbidge, d; Ottilie Patterson, Bobby Breen, v; 1963.

I Shall Never Forget; Swanee River; Route 66; Help Me; Birth of the Blues; Down Home Rag; Jazz Lips; Oh Baby; Tenderly; Hello Little Girl; Jamaica March; Sweet Georgia Brown; Revival; Don't Go No Further; I Know Somebody/I've Got My Mojo Working; St Louis Blues.

Chris Barber's Jazz Band with Alex Bradford and Kenneth Washington
Hot Gospel
Lake LACD 39

Pat Halcox, t; Chris Barber, tb; Ian Wheeler, cl, as; Eddie Smith, Stu Morrison, bj; John Slaughter, g; Dick Smith, Mickey Ashman, b; Graham Burbidge, d; Alex Bradford, v, p; Madeleine Bell, Robert Pinkston, Kenneth Washington, v; 1963–67.

Highway To Heaven; God Leads His Dear Children; Can't Trust Nobody; Jesus Is The Lover Of My Soul; We Sure Do Need Him Now; They've Got To Wait On Me; Just A Closer Walk With Thee; They Kicked Him Out of Heaven; Lord, Lord, Lord; Too Late To Worry; I Never Shall Forget; Over In The Gloryland; Holding On To My Saviour's Hand; God Searched The World; Leaning On The Lord; Jesus Is A Rock; Old Time Religion.

Chris Barber's Jazz and Blues Band
The Very Best of Chris Barber
Bell BLR 89022

Pat Halcox, t; Chris Barber, tb; Ian Wheeler, cl, as; John Crocker, cl, as, ts; Stu Morrison, Johnny McCallum, bj; Steve Hammond, bj, g; Mick Lieber, Rory Gallagher, John Slaughter, g; Paul Buckmaster, cello, p; Tony Ashton, p, v; Kim Gardner, Jackie Flavelle, b; Graham Burbidge, Colin Allen, Roy Dyke, d; 1969–75.

> Lady Be Good; Alligator Hop; Come Friday; Royal Garden Blues; Cortina Run; Wild Cat Blues; Wabash Blues; London Blues; South Rampart Street Parade; The Falling Song; Tiger Rag; Ice Cream; Who's Blues; Undecided; Easter Parade; Sleepy Love; Good Queen Bess; Shoeman The Human; Snag It; Oh Baby; Down By The Riverside; Sweet Sue; Drat That Fratle Rat; Stevedore Stomp.

Chris Barber's Jazz & Blues Band
Chris Barber In Switzerland 1974/75
Lake LACD208D

Pat Halcox, t; Chris Barber, tb; John Crocker, cl, as; Johnny McCallum, bj, g; John Slaughter, g; Jackie Flavelle, b; Graham Burbidge, d; 1974–75.

> My Maryland; Harlem Bound; Whatcha Gonna Do?; Take The 'A' Train; Georgia On My Mind; It's Tight Like That; We Sure Do Need Him Now; Csikos; Just A-Sittin' And A-Rockin'; Stevedore Stomp; New York Blues; Mercy, Mercy, Mercy; Me & Bobby McGhee; Jeeps Blues/Stokin'; Texas Moaner Blues; I Can't Give You Anything But Love; I'm Slapping Seventh Avenue On The Sole Of My Shoe; Somewhere Over The Rainbow; Canal Street Blues; New Orleans Wiggle; Sensation Rag; I'm Walking To New Orleans; Avalon/Crocker's 32; High Society.

Chris Barber's Jazz & Blues Band
Echoes of Ellington
Timeless TTD 555556

Pat Halcox, t; Chris Barber, tb; John Crocker, Russell Procope, cl, as; Wild Bill Davis, p; Johnny McCallum, bj, g; John Slaughter, g; Jackie Flavelle, b; Pete York, d; 1976.

> Stevedore Stomp; Jeep's Blues; I'm Slapping Seventh Avenue With The Sole Of My Shoe; In A Mellotone; Prelude To A Kiss; Second Line; Perdido; Mood Indigo; Shout 'Em Aunt Tilly; Squatty Roo; Blues For Duke; Take The 'A' Train; Warm Valley; Caravan; Sophisticated Lady; It Don't Mean A Thing; Just Squeeze Me; The Mooche; The Jeep Is Jumpin'.

Various Artists
BBC Jazz from the 70s and 80s in Stereophonic Sound. Vol. 2
Upbeat 153

Chris Barber's Jazz & Blues Band: Pat Halcox, t; Chris Barber, tb; Sammy Rimington, cl, fl; John Crocker, cl, as; Johnny McCallum, bj, g; Roger Hill, John Slaughter, g; Vic Pitt, b; Pete York, d; 1977–78.

> I Want To Be Happy; Indiana; When The Street Band Played That Ragtime Melody; Rent Party Blues.

Chris Barber's Jazz & Blues Band
Come Friday
Bell 84011

Pat Halcox, t; Chris Barber, tb; Ian Wheeler, cl, as; John Crocker, cl, as, ts; Johnny McCallum, bj, g; Roger Hill, g; Vic Pitt, b; Norman Emberson, d; 1979. [recorded direct to disc]

Alligator Hop; St Louis Blues; Wild Cat Blues; Come Friday; Sweet Sue; Stevedore Stomp.

Chris Barber & Dr John
Take Me Back To New Orleans
Black Lion BLCD760163

Pat Halcox, Teddy Fullick, t; Chris Barber, Roy Maskell, tb; Ian Wheeler, cl, as; John Crocker, cl, as, ts; Dick Cook, cl, as; Dr John, v, p; Johnny McCallum, bj, g; Roger Hill, g; Vic Pitt, b; John Beecham, tu; Freddie Kohlman, Norman Emberson, d; 1980.

Chris Barber's Jazz & Blues Band: Take Me Back To New Orleans; Ti-pi-tina; Perdido Street Blues; New Orleans, Louisiana; New Orleans; Meet Me On The Levee; Harlem Rag; Ride On; The Big Bass Drum.

Chris Barber's Brass Band: Just A Little While To Stay Here / What A Friend We Have In Jesus / When The Saints Go Marching In; Buddy Bolden Blues / South Rampart Street Parade / Burgundy Street Blues / Canal Street Blues; Bourbon Street Parade / Do You Know What It Means To Miss New Orleans / Professor Longhair's Tip / Brass Band Blues; Basin Street Blues / Take Me Back To New Orleans.

Chris Barber's Jazz & Blues Band
Barbican Blues
Lake LACD273

Pat Halcox, t; Chris Barber, tb; Ian Wheeler, cl, as; John Crocker, cl, as, ts; Johnny McCallum, bj, g; Roger Hill, g; Vic Pitt, b; Norman Emberson, d; 1982.

Bourbon Street Parade; Mary Had A Little Lamb; Perdido Street Blues; Ory's Creole Trombone; Spanish Castles; Barbican Blues; Bugle Boy March; Good Queen Bess; The Weight/Caledonia Mission; Wildcat Blues; Rose Room; Basin Street Blues; Ice Cream.

Chris Barber's Jazz & Blues Band with Ken Colyer
New Orleans Parade
Lake LACD293

Pat Halcox, t; Ken Colyer, t, v; Chris Barber, tb; Ian Wheeler, cl, as; John Crocker, cl, ts; Johnny McCallum, bj, g, snare d; Roger Hill, g; Vic Pitt, b, sousa; Norman Emberson, d; 1984.

Chris Barber's Brass Band: New Orleans Parade; Just A Closer Walk With Thee/The Saints. *Chris Barber's Jazz & Blues Band with Ken Colyer*:

The Sheik Of Araby; Tipitipitin; Breeze; Sing On; Going Home; Weary Blues; Panama; All On A Mardi Gras Day.

Chris Barber's Jazz & Blues Band
Who's Blues
Bell 84009

Pat Halcox, t; Chris Barber, tb; Ian Wheeler, cl, as; John Crocker, cl, ts; Johnny McCallum, bj, g; Roger Hill, g; Vic Pitt, b; Norman Emberson, d; 1984.

The Weight; Who's Blues; Lady Be Good; Creole Love Call; Undecided; Each Day; United Blues; At The Jazz Band Ball; Snag It.

Chris Barber's Jazz & Blues Band
Take Me Back To New Orleans
Bell BLR 89310

Pat Halcox, t; Chris Barber, tb; Ian Wheeler, cl, as; John Crocker, cl, ts; Johnny McCallum, bj, g, snare d; John Slaughter, g; Vic Pitt, b, sousa; Norman Emberson, d; Grosses Rundfunkorchester Berlin, Robert Hanell, cond; Richard Hill, arr; 1986.

A New Orleans Overture; Bourbon Street Parade, Lead Me On; Goin' Up The River; South Rampart Street Parade; Music From The Land Of Dreams; Mood Indigo; Harlem Rag; Wild Cat Blues; Concerto For Jazz Trombone And Orchestra: (1) Ragtime (Andante); (2) Blues (Largo); (3) Stomp (Presto); Reprise Stomp; Take Me Back To New Orleans; Under The Bamboo Tree; Immigration Blues; Down By The Riverside; Ice Cream; Ice Cream (Reprise).

Chris Barber's Jazz & Blues Band
Down On The Bayou
Timeless TTD 612

Pat Halcox, t; Chris Barber, tb; Ian Wheeler, cl, as; John Crocker, cl, ts; Dr John, v, p; Nick Coler, p; Johnny McCallum, bj, g; Tony Atkins, g, v; John Slaughter, g; Vic Pitt, b; Norman Emberson, Alan "Sticky" Wicket, Ian Richardson, d; 1985–89.

Dedication; Down On The Bayou; They Took My Money; Music From The Land Of Dreams; Going Up The River; Baby Of Mine; Waiting For A Train; Corinne Across The Sea; Beg Steal or Borrow; Whose Blues; Battersea Rain Dance / Crocker's Eleven; Nobody Knows You; Black Widow; New York Town; Big Bass Drum; Skippin' and Jumpin'; Pick and Shovel; Oh, Didn't He Ramble.

Chris Barber's Jazz & Blues Band
In His Element
Timeless TTD 572

Pat Halcox, t; Chris Barber, tb; Ian Wheeler, cl, as; John Crocker, cl, ts; Johnny McCallum, bj, g; John Slaughter, g; Vic Pitt, b; Norman Emberson, d; Grosses Rundfunkorchester Berlin, Robert Hanell, cond; Richard Hill, arr; 1988.

The Sheik of Araby; Battersea Rain Dance / Crocker's Eleven; Working Man Blues; Royal Garden Blues, Stardust; Sweet Sue; Going Up The River; Oh, Didn't He Ramble; A New Orleans Overture / Jazz Elements; Creole Moods, Basieland; Blues Colours, New Orleans Celebration; Alligator Hop; Basin Street Blues; Ice Cream.

Chris Barber's Jazz & Blues Band
Clearing The Air In Bern '92
Lake LACD312

Pat Halcox, t; Chris Barber, tb; Ian Wheeler, cl, as; John Crocker, cl, as, ts; Johnny McCallum, bj, g; John Slaughter, g; Vic Pitt, b; Russell Gilbrook, d; 1992.

> Bourbon Street Parade; Chasing Tails/Sister Kate; Careless Love; Royal Garden Blues; On The Sunny Side Of The Street; Panama; When You Wore A Tulip; Mood Indigo; Snake Rag; Goin' Up The River; Ain't Misbehavin'; Second Line Saints; Tiger Rag.

Chris Barber's Jazz & Blues Band
Going To Town In Carlisle '94
Lake LACD319

Pat Halcox, t; Chris Barber, tb; Monty Sunshine, cl; Ian Wheeler, cl, as, hca; John Crocker, cl, as, ts; Johnny McCallum, bj, g; John Slaughter, g; Lonnie Donegan, bj; Vic Pitt, Jim Bray, b, sousa; Russell Gilbrook, Ron Bowden, d; 1994.

> *Chris Barber's 1954 Reunion Band*: The Isle Of Capri; Chimes Blues; Hiawatha Rag; We Sure Do Need Him Now; It's Tight Like That; The Old Rugged Cross; St Philip Street Breakdown; Hushabye. *Lonnie Donegan & The Skiffle Group*: Can't You Line 'Em; Over In The New Buryin' Ground; Worried Man Blues; The Grand Coulee Dam. *Chris Barber's 1954 Reunion Band*: Down By The Riverside. *Chris Barber's Brass Band*: Ice Cream. *Chris Barber's Jazz & Blues Band*: Bourbon Street Parade; All The Girls Go Crazy; Ellingtonia – Double Check Stomp/Stevedore Stomp/Goin' To Town; Working Man's Blues; St Louis Blues; Going Up The River; Petite Fleur/Sweet Georgia Brown/ Slap'n'Slide; Tiger Rag/Mile End Stomp.

Chris Barber Band & Bob Hunt's Ellingtonians
Misty Morning
Timeless CDTTD641

Pat Halcox, Mike Henry, t; Chris Barber, Bob Hunt, tb; John Defferary, cl, ts; John Crocker, cl, as, ts; Nik Payton, cl, as, bars; Paul Sealey, bj, g; John Slaughter, g; Vic Pitt, b; Colin Miller, d; 2000.

> Misty Morning; Harlem Rag; Isle of Capri; Take the 'A' Train; Mood Indigo; It Don't Mean A Thing; Creole Love Call; The Jeep Is Jumping; Snag It; C Jam Blues; When The Saints Go Marching In.

The Big Chris Barber Band
Jubilee Stomp
Timeless CDTTD 654

Pat Halcox, Mike Henry, Ken Colyer, t; Chris Barber, Bob Hunt, tb; Monty Sunshine, cl; John Defferary, cl, ts; John Crocker, cl, as, ts; Tony Carter, cl, as, bars; Trevor Whiting, cl, as, ts; Paul Sealey, bj, g; Len Page, Lonnie Donegan, bj; John Slaughter, g; Vic Pitt, Jim Bray, b; Ron Bowden, Colin Miller, d; 1953–2002.

> *Ken Colyer's Jazzmen:* Blue Blood Blues; Slow Drag Blues; Merrydown Rag; Chimes Blues; Carolina Moon. *The Big Chris Barber Band*: Misty Morning/Jungle Nights in

Harlem; The Spell of the Blues; Freeze And Melt; All Blues; Battersea Rain Dance; Devaluation Blues; Jubilee Stomp; Black Tan Fantasy. *Chris Barber's Jazz Band:* The Martinique; Lead Me On.

The Big Chris Barber Band
Barber at Blenheim
World Chris Barber Collection CBJB 4004

Pat Halcox, Mike Henry, t; Chris Barber, Bob Hunt, tb; Mike Snelling, Tony Carter, Richard Exall, cl, as, ts, bars; Joe Farler, bj, g; Dave Green, b; John Sutton, d; 2007.

> Bourbon Street Parade; Rent Party Blues; Merry-Go-Round; Jubilee Stomp; Lead Me On; The Martinique; Petite Fleur; C Jam Blues; Cornbread, Peas and Black Molasses; Watcha Gonna Do; Hot'n'bothered; Basin Street Blues; When The Saints Go Marching In.

Chris Barber
Memories Of My Trip
Proper PRPCD073

Pat Halcox, Mike Henry, Keith Smith, t; Chris Barber, Trummy Young, Eddie Durham, tb; Monty Sunshine, Edmond Hall, Joe Darensbourg, Albert Nicholas, John Defferary, James Evans, cl; Ian Wheeler, Christopher Plock, cl, as; John Crocker, Sammy Rimington, as; David Horniblow, cl, ts; Jonny Boston, ts; Keith Emerson, org; Sammy Price, Richard Simmons, Pinetop Perkins, Keith Scott, Jools Holland, Brian Graville, Dr John, p; Chris Stainton, kb; Eddie Smith, Stu Morrison, Johnny McCallum, bj; John Slaughter, Alexis Korner, Mark Knopfler, Bob Margolin, Rory Gallagher, Paul Sealey, Marlow Henderson, Joe Farler, Jeff Healey, Anton Fenech, g; Brownie McGhee, Andy Fairweather Low, Eric Clapton, Muddy Waters, g, v; Dick Smith, Jackie Flavelle, Vic Pitt, Terry Knight, Dave Bronze, Calvin Jones, Colin Bray, Reggie McBride, Gary Simons, b; Graham Burbidge, Dave Evans, Colin Miller, Henry Spinetti, Willie "Big Eye" Smith, Alan "Sticky" Wicket, Gary Scriven, Ollie Brown, John Whitfield, d; Jimmy Cotton, Sonny Terry, hca, v; Ottilie Patterson, Alex Bradford, Paul Jones, Van Morrison, v; 1958–2010.

> Memories Of My Trip; When Things Go Wrong With You; Do Lord, Do Remember Me; Weeping Willow; Kansas City; Love Me Or Leave Me; Can't Be Satisfied; Diggin' My Potatoes; Goin' Up The River; How Long Blues; Goin' Home; Didn't He Ramble; Lonesome Road; I'll Be Rested; Precious Lord, Take My Hand; Couldn't Keep It To Myself; Another Sad One; St Louis Blues; High Society; Rock Candy; Georgia On My Mind; Rose Room; C Jam Blues; Tea Party Blues; Jack Teagarden Blues; Tailgate Boogie; Sunny Side Of The Street; Winin' Boy Blues; Blues Stay Away From Me; Dallas Rag; The Next Time I'm In Town.

The Big Chris Barber Band
European Tour 2011: New Faces
World Chris Barber Collection CBJB 4005

Peter Rudeforth, Mike Henry, t; Chris Barber, Bob Hunt, tb; Amy Roberts, David Horniblow, Richard Exall, cl, as, ts, bars; Joe Farler, bj, g; Jackie Flavelle, b; Gregor Beck, d; 2011.

Bourbon Street Parade; Rent Party Blues; Jungle Nights In Harlem; The Spell Of The Blues; Jubilee Stomp; Precious Lord, Lead Me On; Wabash Blues; Wild Cat Blues; Merry-Go-Round; Black And Tan Fantasy / The Mooche; C Jam Blues; Cornbread, Peas and Black Molasses; Hot'n'bothered; Petite Fleur; When The Saints Go Marching In; Ice Cream.

Index